THE SEA IS KNEE-DEEP – VOLUME 1

Paulina Zelitsky and Paul Weinzweig

ISBN 9780991853830

Dedication

To my dear father for his unconditional love, support, and guidance. He always cautioned me with the Russian proverb: "To you, the sea is only knee-deep."

Paulina

About the Authors

Paulina Zelitsky is a Canadian Professional Engineer in the security, transportation, and energy sectors. She obtained her initial M. Eng. degree in Coastal Marine Engineering from National Marine University in Odessa, Ukraine, and in Permafrost Engineering at the University of Alberta, Canada.

Paulina started her career as a port designer for Soviet, Cuban, and later in the 70s for private Canadian engineering companies across Canada. After Paulina's naturalization and certification as a Canadian Professional Engineer, she jump-started her new career in Arctic Engineering in the energy sector, initially with the Northern Canada Power Commission in Edmonton and later with Petro-Canada as a Systems Engineer and with Ports Canada as a Program Manager. From 1984, Paulina served as a Safety and Risk Analysis Engineer at EMR COGLA in Ottawa and the National Energy Board (NEB), where she participated in the development of Canadian Onshore Pipeline Regulations and Canadian Diving Regulations.

Paul Weinzweig grew up in Toronto, Canada, where he earned a Ph.D. in Sociology from the University of Toronto and went on to do volunteer research work in West Africa at a community mental health project. He has taught in the social sciences at several Canadian universities and helped to pioneer and present televised distance education. Paul served as Associate Director of the Ontario Confederation of University Faculty Associations where he managed negotiations between university teachers and the new provincial distance education authority (TV Ontario) that laid the ground rules for the participation of university teachers in the new electronic educational media. Paul has researched many areas, including private school education, the role of international non-governmental organizations in peace and disarmament, the plight of Canada's indigenous peoples migrating from rural to urban areas, and cultural programming for Toronto's Harborfront development.

In 1987, during the advent of Perestroika, Paul was invited to the Soviet Union, where his book on creativity and self-realization was published in Russian. The book became a best-seller, and he was encouraged to make a television series for Soviet Central Television based on the book's themes. The 14-part TV series ("To the Promised Land..."), blending Russian performing arts with talks on social and psychological change, became part of a fund-raising effort by Paul and his wife, Paulina, to support the renowned but struggling Natalya Sats Musical Theater.

Other books by Paulina Zelitsky and Paul Weinzweig are available at Amazon:

- ***The Sea is Only Knee-Deep – Volume 2***
- ***Dog Days in Cuba: A Quest for Treasure Book 1***
- ***The Dreamer Whose Dream Came True***
- **Moscow Book of Promises**
- ***Technology and Humanism***
- ***A Fare to Remember: Taxi Stories, School Confessions, and Family Reflections***
- ***Odessaphile***
- ***Adios Angelina***
- ***A Practical Antidote for The Ills of Capitalism***

Preface

"It is said that before entering the sea
A river trembles with fear.
She looks back at the path she has travelled,
from the peaks of the mountains, the long winding road crossing forests and villages.
And in front of her, she sees an ocean so vast that to enter it seems nothing more than to disappear forever.
But there is no other way.
The river cannot go back.
Nobody can go back.
To go back is impossible in existence.
The river needs to take the risk of entering the ocean because only then will fear disappear because that's where the river will know it's not about disappearing into the ocean, but of becoming the ocean."

~Khalil Gibran

The Sea is Only Knee Deep[1] is a true story of Paulina, a Jewish/Ukrainian girl from the city of Odessa (currently renamed Odesa) in Ukraine, written as a memoir about her personal experiences in Ukraine and Cuba during the second (1970) Cuban Missile Crisis, about which the public was unaware. For the benefit of detente, the American administration pretended that the Cienfuegos crisis was solved in secret diplomacy. This was not true: the Cienfuegos Soviet submarine base operated for 22 years until Russia closed it in 1992.

Paulina's memoir was inspired by the resurrection of new Russian global ambitions leading to the next Cuban Crisis. This renewed Russian undertaking, once again in Cuba, comprises the Russian navy submarine base for a modern surface and submarine fleet equipped with nuclear-tipped cruise missiles, the SKIF launchers for nuclear-tipped cruise missiles installed on the ocean floor in Cuban offshore, the military airport for Russian military aircraft, and the new Russian Intelligence Control Center GLONASS/SIGINT already in operation in Cuba.

These Russian installations represent a key strategic advantage in the struggle for global military supremacy. Once again, Cuba is at the forefront of veiled Russian military expansionism, consolidating its strategic hemispheric power base in the Gulf of Mexico for the third time (1962, 1970, 2020). The winner of this game will dictate terms not just for Ukraine and other ex-Soviet republics but also for Cuba and Venezuela and will assure the position of preeminence during the forthcoming Intermediate-Range Nuclear Forces Treaty negotiations in the current nuclear arms race. A Russian win would mean a return to Russian and Soviet colonial ambitions in the great game of world supremacy.

Paulina's story describes the third Holodomor (forced famine) in Ukraine in 1946-1947, when her mother died, and her father, a sea captain, brought her up. An optimistic and energetic kid despite her early introduction to the treachery and deception of the cruel, paranoid, and anti-Semitic Soviet system, she learned how to overcome discrimination, oppression, and bigotry to graduate with an M.Eng. degree in coastal and offshore engineering while avoiding collaboration with the political system she despised. In 1968, she was reassigned temporarily to a small group of Soviet naval designers who were developing a top-secret Soviet submarine base in Cuba.

The main purpose of this base was to provide secure terminals for the fleet of Soviet nuclear submarines armed with ballistic and cruise missiles with nuclear warheads. The Cienfuegos Soviet navy base for submarines with nuclear ammunition, the military airport for Soviet bombers, and the Soviet Spy SIGINT center in Cuba breached the 1962 Agreement between Khrushchev and Kennedy, following the Cuban Missile Crisis of 1962, whereby the Soviets would take their missiles permanently out of Cuba, and the US would remove its missiles from Turkey and refrain from attacking Cuba. Paulina's dramatic experiences culminated in the indignity of attempted rape by her boss and pressure from the KGB to inform on her colleagues.

Paulina opened 'The hole in the iron curtain' in Gander, Newfoundland, Canada, in 1971 when she defected with her two small children by running on the tarmac of Gander's airport, chased by an armed Soviet security guard. Her personal experiences corroborated the dangers and misery of life under the oppression of a tyrannical, dictatorial system.

VOLUME 1

TABLE OF CONTENTS

1. The Sea is Only Knee Deep

"A well-thought-out story doesn't need to resemble real life. Life itself tries with all its might to resemble a well-crafted story."

-Isaac Babel

Paulina with her sons, Havana, 1970

In the autumn of 1968, I found myself in a situation that was both improbable and perilous. Having only recently graduated in marine engineering and married to my classmate, also a recently graduated Cuban naval architect, I was assigned to work with a Soviet marine terminals design team in Cuba. As if it would not be enough on my plate trying to learn and fulfill my first engineering mandate, in addition to taking care of my husband and our two small children, one of them still only a baby, I was reassigned temporarily to a small group of Soviet naval designers who were developing a top-secret Soviet submarine base in Cuba.

The main purpose of this base was to provide secure terminals for the fleet of Soviet nuclear submarines armed with ballistic and cruise missiles with nuclear warheads. Located in Cienfuegos in the southwest of the island, this Soviet submarine base was built in Cuba in secret at a time of great tension during the Cold War between America and the USSR. This Soviet submarine base operated from Cuba in secret for over 20 years in contravention of international agreements. Neither the Soviet nor Cuban governments ever admitted to its existence, just as they have never admitted to the existence of Lourdes – the world's largest Soviet spy SIGINT center in Cuba, which operated for 36 years. By 1971, I wanted to escape from both Cuba and the Soviet Union for reasons that will become clear.

My predicament was dangerous, and the possibility of escaping was much more so. '*Cuba NYET, Yankee DA*' was not really about the Yankees. I knew next to nothing about the United States. In my mind, Yankee was not so much a country as an idea symbolizing freedom and human rights. Nor was it about Cuba.

The Cuban system was less oppressive than the Soviet, except that the whole country appeared to have fallen into a hypnotic spell under its charismatic leader, Fidel Castro. His relentless grip on power reminded me of our Soviet leaders who had inflicted terrible suffering upon the people of my country. Of course, the contrasts were marked: Cuba was only an island, and, compared to our drab leaders, Fidel was a handsome Caribbean version of 'the great dictator', hot for power and numb to the suffering of his people. Yet, he was exceptionally crafty and deceptive about his true ambitions. Still, my life in Cuba was an improvement compared to Soviet society, with its dismal complacency and lifestyles frozen in fear. Cuban revolutionaries looked so exotic, romantic, and attractive that I married one. Born several decades after the Russian Revolution, I was a Soviet citizen for whom Cuba offered a fresh libertarian breeze, compared to the fossil of stale Soviet autocracy.

This still young Cuban Revolution and cheerful Latin personality awoke my rebellious nature, feeding the fire of my already independent character that had developed under the influence of my father. My father brought me up on his own since I was two years old in the City of Odessa (Odesa in contemporary Ukraine) on the Black Sea after my mother died during the third Holodomor (the name for the third Soviet forced famine in Ukraine). Whenever I was in trouble, Papa was always by my side with sound advice and reassurance. Now, in Cuba, I was alone in my difficulty and had no one to help me.

It all started with an abrupt turn of events and an expedient but careless and arrogant breach of security by the Soviets in Cuba. Unwillingly, I became witness to an exceptionally dangerous, devious, and cynical game for control of global power. Just a few years earlier, the 1962 Cuban Missile Crisis had brought the world to the edge of nuclear holocaust, more so than ever before or since. Now, in front of my naive eyes, Cuba was once again a nuclear powder keg, and the world media, in retrospect, seemed ignorant of this deadly fact.

However, there were precipitating personal circumstances that created urgency and drama for my family and me. The Soviet State Security (KGB) had attempted to conscript me into their Cuban services (for reasons I will mention later in the story). Born into a society crushed in the grip of fear, a society in which millions of our citizens were persecuted worse than slaves for possible or imagined disobedience, I was afraid to turn down their offer openly.

There were good reasons to be fearful of complicity with the dreaded Soviet security because their reputation was notorious for pursuing those whom they called traitors to the death. The role of the KGB's informant and the KGB's 'honey trap' in Havana during the concealed second Cuban missile crisis beginning in 1969 was not acceptable to me, for my romantic aspirations for professional accomplishments and self-respect conflicted with the grim reality. I sensed that the unconsummated KGB affair, together with my natural rebellious attitude, could prove lethal.

The apprehension spurred my plans to escape. I was not fully aware of the punishment details for defying the KGB or for escaping. But I knew they would be serious. Under Soviet law, defection was legally equivalent to treason, and the laws against treason and revealing state secrets carried the most severe punishments, not just for the individual but also for family and friends.[2] I was deeply concerned about repercussions for my family, my children, my Cuban husband, and my parents in Odessa. As in all dictatorships, the abyss between the individual and the state was filled only by the bonds of family love and loyalty. My children were our biggest and deepest stimulus in life, our only pride and hope. I was taking a grave risk personally, but my family could pay a high price for it. Still, I believed that my aspirations for our freedom were real and that we would succeed despite all hardships. Destiny is not always in our hands, but when we choose to take fate by the throat (Beethoven's oath), then the keys are courage, determination, and persistence.

In early March of 1971, my husband Eduardo arranged for a week's stay for our two children and me at the inexpensive Hotel St. John's, allocated for use only by Cubans. In those years, all hotels in Cuba were designated either for foreigners or for the use of Cubans (foreigners were not admitted into hotels for Cubans, except in emergency cases). We were deemed an emergency case as a result of having missed our Havana-Prague-Moscow flight by CSA (Czech) Airlines.[3]

Eduardo successfully convinced the Hotel St. John's manager to allow us to stay while we awaited our next scheduled flight. During the twelve years since the Revolution, no new hotels in Cuba had been built, and the number of available units in Havana was scarce. The advantage of Hotel St. John's was that it was cheap. Despite its prestigious location in the best part of the city, located in the Vedado district of Havana, it was very modest. Our room was poorly equipped with two old single metal beds, no television, no air conditioner, poor service, and terrible food in the hotel's restaurant.

I could hardly afford any of it anyway since I had little Cuban currency left after exchanging most of my money for non-convertible Soviet rubles, which I needed for travel expenses in the Soviet Union. However, after missing our flight, we were left in limbo. Unable to pay for an additional week of stay in an expensive and decent hotel for foreigners, such as the National or Capri, but even more important, these were the hotels where the Soviets would expect to find me if they were searching for me.

I felt depressed about missing our flight because a special permit issued to me by the Soviet consulate to fly the Havana-Prague-Moscow route with the Czechoslovakian airline was now wasted. The Havana-Moscow-Czech air service had been suddenly discontinued. We had missed this airline's last available direct flight from Havana, and I was now facing a more serious risk, having no alternative but to purchase the direct flight from Havana to

Moscow by Aeroflot.

MVD[4] (The Soviet Ministry of Internal Affairs) prohibited all Soviet citizens, including Soviet diplomats, from traveling on foreign airlines while Aeroflot flights were available. I had succeeded with difficulty in obtaining a very rare permit to catch the Czechoslovakian plane flying from Havana to Moscow via Prague, but I wasted this opportunity by missing my flight. After the Soviet invasion of Czechoslovakia, many flights of the Czech national airline were canceled in favor of Aeroflot, which provided better security supervision over the passengers. At the airline desk, the attendants told us that we should have considered ourselves very fortunate to be able to purchase tickets for the next Aeroflot flight a week later. I felt disappointed because the success of my childish 'escape plan' depended on avoiding flying by Aeroflot.

However, I also felt relieved because emotionally, my plan to escape was terribly hard for me and Eduardo (my husband and father of our two small boys). We would be separated after that flight, possibly forever. He came, probably intentionally, too late to pick us up for the airport on the original date of departure, and this is how we missed the flight with the Czechoslovakian airline. Under the circumstances and despite the added danger, I felt compelled to purchase three new tickets by Aeroflot to Moscow; otherwise, my stubborn resolution to fly only by the Czech airline could look pointless and suspicious and might be reported to security. There was a good reason for my worries: the change of airlines could cost me my life since each Aeroflot flight was boarded by a team of armed KGB operatives to supervise the passengers.

Constantly imagining how to realize the escape, I was unable to sleep at night, tormented by the fear of being caught. If we were caught, it would mean the end of my life. I was only 25 years old and had two small children. I struggled with my imagination, trying to devise alternative scenarios: plan B and plan C. Getting caught might kill me because my health was not sufficiently strong to allow me to survive the brutalities, hunger, and extreme cold of working in the Gulag in the Soviet northern forced labor camps.[5] Never before had I met or heard of anybody who defected abroad successfully. The rumors we heard were of the failures and the punishments for the culprits.

I witnessed one such attempt a couple of years earlier, and it was so dramatic that it would be better if I could not remember it. Eduardo and I studied engineering at the Odessa National Marine University. We were on board a Soviet cargo ship returning from Havana to Odessa in Ukraine, USSR, to fulfill our yearly summer marine internship.

We were a large group of mainly Cuban and Soviet students from various marine educational establishments: from the Soviet Navy, Naval Academy, and from OIIMF (State Marine University of Odessa), where Eduardo and I studied. We all shared small cabins on the lower deck. I slept in the only cabin for females with seven other girls, and Eduardo shared his cabin with seven navy cadets. We would spend our time together during our meals and rest hours on the deck. To be honest, we were very happy and had a splendid time.

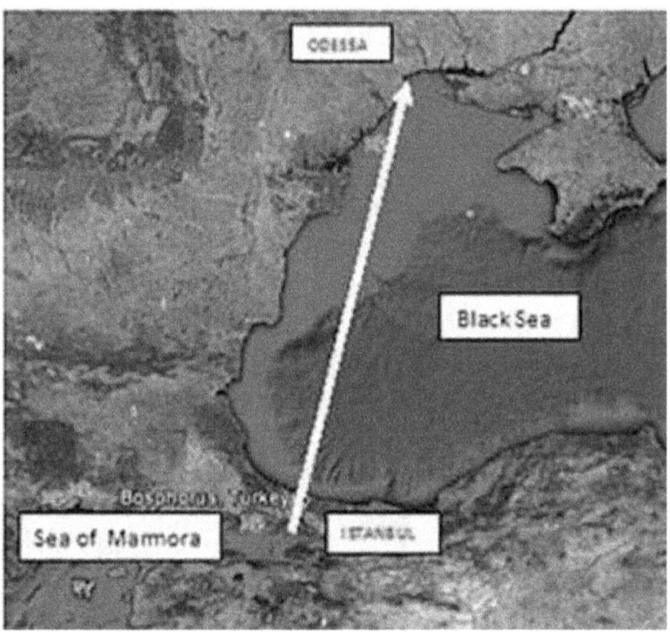

Our ship route from the Sea of Marmara through the Bosphorus to Odessa on the Black Sea

Until one early morning after breakfast, while watching the coastal features of Istanbul from the deck, we noticed the panicking Soviet mariners running toward the stern on the lower deck. An incident occurred after we crossed the Sea of Marmara and were passing Istanbul on the Bosphorus Strait on our route to Odessa. Our ship was passing slowly along this narrow natural strait. There is a very low-speed limit requirement for all ships when they navigate through the Bosphorus. Suddenly, we heard the splash of something heavy fall into the water. Immediately after this, we heard the shouting and running of KGB security officers assigned to guard us.

There was a serious commotion. Eduardo and I tried our best to penetrate the sea with our eyes to understand what had fallen into the water, but the sea was rough, and we could not yet detect anything. We were ordered to move away from the lower deck area because the security officers were now clearing the deck. They told everybody to return to their cabins. Almost everyone did, except Eduardo and me, because we were standing beside the upper deck ladder. This position and our curiosity persuaded us instead to climb quickly to the upper deck to view more clearly the surrounding sea. The Soviet ship's crew was also there for the same purpose, and somebody explained to Eduardo that a man had fallen overboard. We witnessed how five or six security officers gathered on the lower starboard deck and shouted to the man whom I could now see. He was swimming strongly towards the shore, but the sea was rough, and his progress was slow. The security officers began firing their guns at him. Now, Eduardo and I felt scared that they would kill him, but the rough sea appeared to help him thus far to escape the bullets.

A Soviet mariner beside us explained that the boy who jumped the ship was a Cuban military cadet who had climbed unnoticed during the night into a lifeboat raised above the deck, where he spent all night waiting for the ship to approach Istanbul and enter the narrow Bosphorus Strait. Nobody had noticed him there. When the ship entered the Bosphorus, he stood up and jumped overboard.

I was terrified that the bullets would hit the swimmer and asked the mariner to tell me his opinion. He didn't think so because the rough sea made the swimmer an unstable target. Now, we could see how local Turkish fishermen from the coast, having heard the shooting, started their motorboat and rushed towards the swimmer in an attempt to rescue him. Our ship was slowly moving ahead, leaving the swimmer behind. The security officers continued firing their guns at the swimmer, apparently without success, because we could hear them swearing angrily. Secretly, I felt relieved because the distance between the swimmer and the ship was increasing. No other ships were following us through the Bosphorus Strait, except the motorboat of local fishermen who were coming closer to the swimmer, and it was obvious that they would rescue him.

Suddenly, we heard the security operatives order our captain to stop the ship and reverse gears. The captain was annoyed because it is forbidden to stop and reverse while the ship is proceeding through the Bosporus. But he obeyed their order, which was not difficult since the ship's engine was in its lowest gear already. He stopped the engine and reversed the gear, but this time, he was speeding up the ship in reverse. In horror, we watched our ship catch up with the swimmer, slow its speed, and run directly over him. I felt paralyzed by the savagery before me. The swimmer just disappeared. There was only the boat with Turkish fishermen who were stunned as well by this barbaric and hideous assassination of the swimmer. They shouted hysterically in anger for a while, then turned their motorboats back to the shore. This means there was nobody left alive in the water whom they could help.

I could not believe my own eyes. Who could be capable of shredding this boy alive with such calculated calm? What monstrosity! Eduardo dragged me inside, took me to my cabin, and asked me not to say anything to others about the episode we witnessed. The girls from my cabin did not know what happened and began asking me questions. I knew better than to admit that we had witnessed the unspeakable execution of a young defector. After all, Eduardo and I had disobeyed the orders of security to clear the decks. If I told them anything, it would mean that Eduardo and I broke the rules, so I kept my mouth shut. Later, in the afternoon, we were called by our superiors for a general meeting at which we were told by security that nothing had happened, that no further rumors about this incident would be tolerated, and that this warning was final. We kept quiet about the incident and never shared it with anyone because we were frightened and did not know all the details. But an image of our ship running over the swimmer and the ship's propellers shredding alive this young boy haunted me for the rest of my life.

I wondered what could have happened to this boy if the security agents had recovered him alive. Thinking about that, I remembered another terrifying tale about Soviet prisoners told to me in secret by Dimitry, a friend and one of my neighbors in Odessa. I did not even believe him at the time.

Dmitry lived on my street in Odessa, but he was eight years older than me, and such a significant age difference was the reason we did not mingle much when growing up. He appeared to be much more mature than I, a muscular, athletic senior student with a broad, good-natured face, balding head, and stocky, always dressed in all black or navy blue. He was enrolled in the 5th level of the Mechanical faculty at our Marine University after serving with the Navy. He was a Communist Party member of Russian ethnicity, and I kept away from him because, to my mind, it was a boring combination. He courted me during my first year at university and tried to convince me to date him. I did not particularly like him, but kept special respect for his status since I was still called by other older boys on my street a *pisher* (bed-wetter puppy in Odessa slang) for being too young at the age of seventeen.

Once, while chatting with me on a bench in our neighborhood park on an improvised date, he shared with me his worries and asked me to keep them secret. He said that he was thinking of dropping his university studies because his superiors had been given clues that he would be sent to work as an engineer-mechanic on submarines of the nuclear-powered class after his graduation. This was the reason why he was sent to spend the last summer practice on the board of an early nuclear-powered submarine, Project K-19. The result for him was a really scary experience. He said that it was nothing like the traditional diesel-powered subs on which he previously completed his Navy service as a mechanic before the Navy recommended his enrollment at the University. He was afraid of experimental nuclear technology, which he claimed was affecting the health of all their mechanics. The traditional navy joke on this sub was that the mechanics in nuclear submarines are intentionally exposed to radiation to economize on submarine energy expenditures: the nuclear crew did not require any lighting inside the submarine because they would illuminate the surroundings with their radioactivity. In the process, they will lose their hair and teeth and have no need for sex or food and, therefore, no longings for the coast. He was afraid that the only solution to avoid radiation sickness would be if he did not graduate.

I knew he had no choice if he stayed with the Navy. He had already spent the summer on another top-secret nuclear sub. When he shared his worries about radiation leaks with his long-time local friend, he was told that everybody who refuses the service would be accused of treason. He heard about this type of punishment in forced labor camps for army and navy officers during his practice service on one of the Arctic bases above the Arctic Circle. He shared with me a horrific story about two such labor camps on the Island of Kildin in the Bering Sea above the Arctic Circle, north of Murmansk,[6] related to him by a close friend who pertained to the family from a native Norwegian tribe of Kildin. "It is so cold on Kildin that the permafrost never thaws. Above Kildin, there is only Arctic ice. One labor camp was for Soviet Navy generals and senior officers; the other was for women. Each was surrounded by barbed wire around wooden sleeping barracks. The men were building the bunkers and defense infrastructure for a secret nuclear military base.[7] Female prisoners were marched every morning in Arctic conditions to build a cobblestone road in the permafrost, about one kilometer long; that would provide access for a future anti-aircraft missile system military base to be built in secrecy in the interior of this island, called Verchniy Kildin. The road was named The Golden Kilometer of Rokossovsky in memory of a renowned Soviet general.

The women prisoners were dying out very fast in these inhuman conditions. Every month, new replacements were brought in, and those who survived after they had finished their mission were forced to board empty barges, which abandoned them without any shelter or supplies on the uninhabited Kulgaev Island, in a closed zone in the Barents Sea. Without provisions and shelter, they quickly died from cold exposure and starvation, the strongest eating the weak, one by one. Nobody knows exactly how many prisoners died there, but Kulgaev formed part of the Solovki Archipelago Gulag network, where 1 million prisoners were exterminated.

A Golden kilometer of Rokossovsky cobblestone road on Kildin Island

I was shocked by Dimitry's report. Dmitry was more concerned about the suffering of the male prisoners, who were Soviet generals and naval officers, while I was more impacted by the story about the women prisoners. Was this how they treated women-prisoners? I was so upset by this story. I could not believe Dmitry because, in my mind, not even a beast would commit women to such abuse and torture. Also, I did not understand why the choice to build an Arctic road had fallen on women. After all, women certainly are much more fragile than men; they would produce less and die faster. When I asked him this question, he answered: "Probably women are more expendable than men." Such an assumption made me feel terribly angry with him, and my best protection was to think that he had invented the whole story only to impress me and degrade women with traditional Russian male chauvinism.

I reacted with a mixture of agitation, confusion, mistrust, and anger. Feeling frightened and repulsed, I told Dmitry that I was expected home earlier. I ran home, fleeing from him as if he was a devil. His story traumatized me deeply. I could not accept that my country treated women prisoners with such savage cruelty. Eventually, feeling helpless and frazzled, I broke my promise to Dmitry to keep the secret and shared the Kildin Island horror story in the Barents Sea with my father. I asked Papa to promise me to keep the secret, which, in my mind, would allow me to break my vow to Dmitry.

To my surprise, my father did not accuse Dmitry of lying. He simply said that he did not know if it was the truth. He added that from now on, he forbids me to chat with Dmitry ever again for my safety. He said that he was not certain why Dmitry told stories like this to me; maybe Dmitry was a provocateur. My father did not have to forbid me from talking to Dmitry. I did everything to turn down his dating advances in the future. When he insisted again, I was forced to tell him the cruel truth: I was not attracted to him. This did the trick! He never again came close to me.

Later, in my university final year, I again heard complaints from other graduating students in the same Mechanical faculty that they were scared to death to be assigned after graduation as mechanics on submarines because those first nuclear-powered submarines were considered to be considered be ‘underwater cemeteries’. These were nuclear-powered (November Class) submarines of Project 627 and (Hotel-1 Class) submarines of Project 658, both nicknamed ‘Black Widows’.

Today, I can appreciate the fact that my repulsive reaction to the story of Kildin was produced by the shock of Cognitive Dissonance syndrome, from which we Soviet people suffered then, and the large majority of Russians still suffer today. Psychology describes it as the pressure to resolve the internal discomfort caused by holding conflicting, painful ideas. If I considered that Dmitry's Kildin story was true, it could mean that I, too, was an unwilling party to such a monstrous system of tyranny and slavery. This is why the most popular metaphor in the Soviet Union was then, and in modern Russia, it still is today, "The less you know, the better you sleep."

Over time, I forgot Dmitry, but was unable to forget his story about Kildin Island and how female prisoners were digging a road in permafrost conditions in temperatures as low as -30° Celsius and were simply left to die from hunger or were eaten by others on Kolgaev Island, only because they already knew too much. It was very dangerous in the Soviet Union to know about such savage, hidden slavery, but the cruelty with which those poor women were murdered traumatized my young mind to such a degree that I refused to believe it took place at all. Only many years later was I able to find the information confirming the story of Dmitry.[8]

Back in the unrelieved heat of our small room at the Hotel St. John's in Havana, these images and anxieties continued to unnerve me. If they do catch me while we are trying to escape, I would prefer to be shot than become one of those women prisoners on Kildin Island. It was terrifying to contemplate that scenario, and I decided to forbid myself from thinking of it. Otherwise, their images tortured me and tormented my nights. My Czechoslovakian friend in Cuba, who was working in Havana as a medical assessor to the Cuban government, told me once that after the recent Soviet invasion of Czechoslovakia, the Czech security services received special training by the Soviets to shoot anybody under suspicion without questioning. However, most probably, the Czech agents would not watch us too closely because we were Soviet citizens, the role models for communism. And even if they start suspecting me, I would be able to confuse them. To my mind, compared to the KGB, the Czech agents lacked half a century of experience in oppression. Since we missed the flight by the Czechoslovakian airline and were forced to purchase the Aeroflot flight, the danger had become much greater of being shot in our backs by KGB agents, whose job is precisely to ensure that none of the Soviet passengers escape. I had to be a realist.

It was necessary to spend a lot of time thinking and planning how to ensure the protection of my parents and Eduardo from punishment by the security services after my defection. The new, more liberal Soviet law (Art. 54 of the Ukrainian Criminal Code in 1960) stipulated up to five years of labor camp punishment for family members who shared the same household with the defector for at least three years before defection (down from the previously applied punishment of up to fifteen years with confiscation of property). I had resided in Cuba apart from my parents for more than three years. My parents lived in Odessa, USSR, and I lived in Havana, Cuba. Still, it was clear that my parents would be fired from their jobs, which was no longer critical since they were already at the pension age.

However, the Soviet people were accustomed to not trusting the protection of the law because the authorities could do as they pleased at any time. Thank goodness, my husband, Eduardo, was not a Soviet citizen. He was a Cuban, and the Cuban government was lenient in this matter compared to the Soviet authorities because everybody in Cuba had some relatives who escaped abroad, even Fidel Castro himself. Cuban families were never directly punished by their government for their family members who escaped.

Also, I convinced Eduardo to take additional precautions. We registered a formal divorce in a Cuban registrar's office (hard to believe, but the whole divorce procedure took less than 30 minutes), and we stopped living together before my departure. This way, he could aspire to retain his privileges at work because he could prove that he had divorced me before my defection, arguing that he knew nothing of my real intentions. He would simply explain that I was departing for the Soviet Union, and he had formally endorsed the return of his children with their mother and grandparents back to Odessa. Accompanying our children and me to the airport could be regarded as a simple formal obligation of a parent. Anyway, Cubans were much more forgiving, more family-oriented, and less stringent than the Soviets. They did not even have a law by which the relatives of defectors should be imprisoned.

It was apparent that the dangerous consequences were mine alone. The children were too young to be responsible for anything. In the worst case, if we are caught, they would be brought up either by their father back in Cuba or by my parents in Odessa. It was clear to me that I had no alternative: I was the only one responsible for my actions, and unless I escaped, I would never have a hope of gaining control over my life.

I did not fit any longer into the life of a slave, nor did I want slavery for my children. Being traumatized in my early childhood (this story will be related later) by the treachery and perversion of a cruel and sinister scheme engineered by Soviet security, I was determined not to get involved with the KGB (in any role) and to escape before they could force me to co-operate with them. My determination was so strong that it felt almost like an intuition: *Everything could end well,*" I was telling myself, *if I find smarter ways to mislead the security agents and confuse them, they will be unable to stop us.*

I was hoping to escape in Gander, a northern Canadian airport in the Atlantic Province of Newfoundland, where both the Czechoslovakian and Soviet airlines had about a 40-minute refueling stop before continuing their flights from Havana, Cuba, to the European continent. But I had not the slightest idea of conditions in Gander which might provide or might prevent an opportunity to escape. Never before had I taken this flight. My two previous flights were routed via Africa and the Middle East. It would be the first time for me to experience a refueling stop in Gander.

It helps to be young when learning a new language. I picked up my conversational Spanish from Eduardo, his family, and our friends. I conquered the written Spanish by pure determination, just by reading books in Spanish and later writing my work in Spanish with the help of a Russian-Spanish dictionary. My love of reading in Spanish helped me to learn Spanish very fast without taking any formal language instruction. I could translate from Spanish to Russian with remarkable speed because, learning Spanish by ear, like a small child, I did not have to worry about faulty pronunciation.

But my English was a serious problem. There were no books in English sold in Cuban stores. The Cuban government did not encourage English but made Russian the obligatory second language in all Cuban schools. To force young people effectively to forget English, they removed all English-language literature from the bookstores and flooded them with Russian publications. The method I developed for learning English was by copying the meaning of words from the English dictionary in our Transport Ministry library onto small cards, which I always carried in my pockets. I would look at these cards and try to memorize the words at any moment when it appeared safe to do so - when nobody was watching me. But I could not learn the correct pronunciation of English words because I was afraid to let anybody know that I was learning English, nor did we have any TV programming, audio recordings, or radio sources in English. Therefore, the words that I memorized, I pronounced in ways that others often failed to recognize when, later, I had a chance to practice my English. This malpractice caused my English interlocutors deep puzzlement.

Still, I was determined to force myself to feel and act confidently; otherwise, I would fail. The only mood I could afford was the Odessa motto, which my parents, teachers, and neighbors used when they joked about my excess of optimism and my preferences for difficult tasks. They would say, "'Tebe more po koleno y gori po plechu'[9] (To you, any sea is only knee-deep, and the mountains are shoulder high)." This is how 'More po koleno' (the sea is only knee-deep) became our family adage. We often used it as a code. It was my only power and my sole possession.

I am not sure that if the planned escape was for me alone, I would have the motivational power to overcome so much danger and uncertainty. However, what a mother would do for her children often exceeds rational abilities. At the time of my escape, I was a 25-year-old Soviet technical assessor in Cuba. Our older son Edik, whose curly blond angelic looks concealed the character of a small tropical hurricane, had recently celebrated his fifth birthday. His younger brother Ernestico, an irresistibly sweet and always happy toddler, was almost three years old.

Meanwhile, my safest strategy was to temporarily disappear into an inconspicuous Cuban hotel rather than return to my mother-in-law and her apartment in Havana, which normally I would do. And this is what Eduardo would prefer me to do. The reasons for my decision to hide in a cheap hotel for Cubans were twofold: first, the Soviets would not look for me there because foreigners were not normally admitted into hotels for Cubans only. Also, I did not want my Cuban family or my friends to have contact with me before my escape since they could be held accountable for my escape, and this might create a dangerous blemish on their revolutionary record. Secondly, I was hoping to confuse the intelligence services about my plans since the KGB had already instructed my father to provide them with the details of my arrival in Odessa.

I was naïve and ignorant about their procedures and hoped that if I did not arrive in Moscow on a scheduled date, they might (I would like them to) get a false idea that I changed my mind and instead took my holidays somewhere in Cuba at a beach resort. I didn't want Soviet security spoiling my forthcoming attempt to escape in Gander from the Aeroflot flight since Aeroflot is especially well equipped for catching defectors.

I asked Eduardo and his mother to be discreet regarding my whereabouts and tell no one about my flight scheduled for next week to Moscow. I also asked them not to communicate with the children and me during this week (for their own safety), but please answer my father, when and if he calls, that I have missed the flight, got very mad at Eduardo because of it, and took off without sharing with Eduardo and his mother my plans.

We needed to mislead Soviet security, who might be eavesdropping on the phone calls of my father. I was hoping that such a description of my behavior would tip off my father while providing an excuse as to why Eduardo and my father don't know about my plans. If Soviet security organs learned where I was staying, it would have to be by their own effort; I would not help them.

All the while, I was trying to convince myself that I was not such a serious target for the KGB, only a young mother, innocent and inexperienced, hiding behind a mask of feminine charms. Perhaps, my naiveté will help confuse them. These were the musings of a hopeful mind. Still, I refused to be their informer and was not yet compromised by the KGB, but I needed to escape before being forced into it.

And finally, I asked Eduardo not to tell my father about my plans in case he calls; instead, he should drop, as naturally as possible into the conversation, our family Odessan motto, which I assured him that Papa would understand, "For her, '*more po koleno*' (the sea is only knee-deep, meaning an extreme undertaking)." My father always repeated this phrase to me when he made a point that he knew of my reckless plans, in which I would engage, regardless of the danger. The phrase now served as a cipher between us. Recently, my father secretly wrote me a letter with this phrase and a few other similar ciphers, warning me of the KGB awaiting my return in Odessa. Being afraid that I might not be able to see him again, I wanted him to know that, thanks to his loving guidance, I had the courage and strength to walk across the sea, to overcome impossible obstacles. He would understand what I meant.

2. Cuba's Grand Hotel

Hotel National, Havana, Cuba

In the 1932 Hollywood film classic *Grand Hotel,* one of the characters famously comments: "Grand Hotel. People come and go. Nothing ever happens." Havana's Hotel National was Cuba's Grand Hotel. In the 30 years before the Revolution, its fame came from world-renowned celebrities; its infamy from American mafia gangsters. During my residency, the hotel was a center of international intrigue that unfolded before my eyes. Whether or not anything ever happened, there was a matter of conjecture, subject to vigilant observation.

The Hotel National is a beautiful and luxurious colonial hotel in Havana, provided with its private park and pool located on a hill in the center of the city overlooking the sea and the *Malecon* (the main seaside promenade of Havana). I often took the children to its large garden after returning from work and on weekends. There we met many of the foreign guests who would come to the hotel garden to enjoy the shade and salubrious sea breezes, a respite from Cuba's tropical heat. Many of the hotel guests felt safe bragging about themselves to a young and attractive Soviet mother with two small children when they encountered us in the hotel's park.

Since the revolutionaries came to power in 1959 and until 1974, the Cuban government shut down all international tourism to assure the purity of the Cuban people, whose spirits, Cuban officials believed, might become contaminated by foreign tourists' corrupt and subversive ideas. All large, luxury, famous hotels in the same area, especially the National, where we lived for several years, were reserved exclusively for the prestigious foreign official crowd: diplomats, foreign-friendly advisers, and senior foreign technical personnel. The National was also used by quite a weird assortment consisting of the so-called 'foreign friends of Cuba', including all kinds of less important foreign emissaries, foreign non-disclosed products suppliers, utopians, adventurers, liberal intellectuals (strong believers in their own dreams), foreign mercenaries, troublemakers, and criminals, as well as rebels, with or without a cause, who were undergoing guerrilla and terrorism training in special camps.[10]

Besides organizing, equipping, and training

the Cuban intelligence personnel in the City of Minsk (Belarus, USSR), the KGB (Soviet State Security Agency) designed and supervised the courses for future international guerrillas and terrorists operated by the DGI (General Intelligence Directorate)[11] of MININT (Cuban Ministry of the Interior). Foreign recruits brought to Cuba from around the world were trained in guerrilla warfare, terrorism, insurrection tactics, explosives, subversion, and propaganda dissemination. These training courses lasted three to six months, depending on their level of complexity.

During their training, the bulk of young volunteers from around the world (an international crowd of students, artists, adventurers, and bohemians brought to Cuba indirectly via European capitals) were living in secluded guerrilla camps, away from the public eye. However, some of the more important ones were awarded special hospitality treatment in our hotel. Some of our hotel visitors, relaxing on the benches in the park of the hotel, could be seen reading the propagandistic Cuban literature. This literature was brought to the hotel in boxes, free for future distribution in their countries. One of the guests gave me a small pocketbook *Mini-Manual of the Urban Guerrilla* by Carlos Marighella, with specific subversive terrorist instructions.[12] It was an anarchist-terrorist manual about how to overthrow the government in power. I returned the book to him the next day, explaining that the possession of a book like this in the Soviet Union would be a serious criminal offense, and if arrested, I would have to reveal the perpetrator who gave me this book. At that point, I lost touch with this enthusiastic fellow.

Another visitor was a redheaded, nervous-looking, young American man who politely asked me once if he could sit at my table in the hotel restaurant. He then proceeded to scare the hell out of me, not only with his ugly physical appearance but also with his impressive recounting of how he hijacked an American passenger airplane from the USA to Cuba. (62 American airplanes were hijacked to Cuba during the three years I resided in the hotel).[13] From that moment on, I did my very best to limit our meals in the hotel restaurant, even when we were hungry, in an attempt to avoid such company. I was certain that DGI was monitoring some of these eccentric, unstable, and shady characters, despite their 'friends of Cuba' status.

Therefore, I was very careful to keep my mouth shut about politics during our residential years at the Hotel National. My Soviet status assured me of a politically impeccable image. Largely due to that, hotel guests felt free to impress me with their stories about why they were brought to Cuba on full Cuban scholarships. They described their three months of training in subversion and propaganda distribution, or their six months of training in a guerrilla war and terrorism in secluded camps in Pinar del Rio and on the Isle of Pines. Thousands of youth from the Middle East, Asia, Latin America, and Africa, including radicalized African Americans, were undergoing a brief guerrilla training by DGI and KGB to import the Cuban Revolution to their native countries or third countries if they were directed to do so.[14] Contrary to popular faith in the revolutionary spirit, many of them told me that they were not interested in revolution but were more attracted to the opportunity for free travel and adventure paid for by the Cuban government.

My childhood vaccinations against Soviet deception created skepticism about any state propaganda: this crowd was, in my opinion, the parasitic victim of the Cuban government's cunning extravagance. At work, the Soviet embassy and my superiors prohibited all Soviet staff from mixing with such a crowd, fearing that some of them might be carriers of capitalist germs. Still, in general, the behavior of foreign friends of Cuba fits well with the superficialities of Latin guerrilla culture. I mean that the participants did not treat the whole affair of training mercenaries in Cuba seriously. Their Cuban sojourn had an air of a game for spoiled middle-class kids who were driven by ambition to become important and famous at any expense (echoing the Irish poet Brendan Behan's remark that "there is no such thing as bad publicity - except your own obituary"). Among foreign liberal intellectuals who also frequented our hotel, there were a variety of types: some were hard utopians, others were well-intended Don Quixotes, while still others appeared to me as simply vain and needed an admiring audience, which they lacked at home. They expected to cleanse themselves from their society's 'capitalist excesses' and seek 'their personal redemption in Fidel'.[15]

Everyone had their motivation, but there was something they had in common: they were willingly misinformed about what was really going on in Cuba. Cuba was their escape, their dream. They refused to acknowledge the realities and saw only what they wanted to see. I became convinced they did not want to know the truth; they preferred to behold the beauty and romance of their fantasies and utopian dreams. Other well-meaning liberal individuals had psychological reasons: they were ridden by guilt about being born in rich countries and being privileged, while the majority of the poor in the underdeveloped world had no chance against the corruption and brutality of power structures. Unfortunately, these missionaries were misled and shamelessly used.

Fidel Castro was a diabolical dramatist and ingenious author and actor who benefited from attracting intellectuals, liberals, and rebels from around the world with his charismatic biblical image of David (Cuba) against Goliath (United States of America). This theatrical talent, performed on a world stage, had little to do with the actual gains of his Cuban Revolutionary Army, which, in reality, were not significant. Fidel's foreign admirers refused to notice that those youthful, handsome, cool, romantic, bearded guerrillas - like heroic characters from a Greek myth – had become master hypocrites: arrogant, cynical, ambitious, bureaucratic chameleons with unlimited power to do whatever they pleased.[16]

The world failed to notice that the show was a fake soap opera called *Revolution* - very good for the media, especially for TV. This TV soap opera should be titled *The Poor Also Cry*, a twist on the celebrated Mexican TV serial *The Rich Also Cry,* which was so immensely popular. Whenever it aired in the Soviet Union during Perestroika, it mesmerized workers, shuttered stores, and offices, and temporarily paralyzed the already shabby economy. The impoverished Soviet public was beginning to dream of becoming rich, and many Soviets felt intensely curious about the affluent life and loved to anticipate the feeling of wealth.

Hearing the stories of other hotel guests, I could not help but think of the poor Cubans who are paying the true costs for the American Weathermen[17] and International Solidarity Brigades[18], or Puerto Rican Macheterros[19], or Basque Separatist Group ETA[20], or Irish Republican Army (IRA), or Chilean MIR (*Movimiento de La Izquierda Revolucionaria*), or LASO (Latin American Solidarity Organization), or FSLN (*Frente Sandinista de Liberacion Nacional*) of Nicaragua, or FARK (*Fuerzas Armadas Revolucionaria*) of Colombia, or PLO (Palestine Liberation Movement) and Popular Front for the Liberation of Palestine from the Middle East.

These costs involved not only travel and training but also large financing of future warfare in third countries all around the world. I felt annoyed when I heard these stories because I knew that ordinary Cubans were not allowed to enter these good hotels; they were not even allowed to visit their foreign colleagues in those hotels, their restaurants, bars, swimming pools, or any other hotel premises. Armed guards at the entrance checked the documents of everybody and prohibited entrance to ordinary Cubans, regardless of whether the Cubans had money to pay for the services. For example, I could not invite my Cuban colleagues and friends to meet with our children and me at my hotel. I felt distressed at such humiliation and discrimination against my Cuban friends. It was a painfully shameful and unfair deal for Cubans whose meager food rations would not even provide the basic essential nutrition for their children. Not the US embargo, but pretenses to world revolution bankrupted the Cuban state.

Ordinary Cubans have always been hungry, but now they were forced to finance Caribbean tourism for spoiled foreign delinquents and bored middle-class youth from the Venceremos Brigade who searched for adventures in addition to their traditional lifestyle of drugs and sex. The Venceremos Brigade was an international mask for future guerrillas brought to Cuba on the pretext of cutting sugar cane - a skill not as easily learned as a revolution. Only Chilean boys (there were many) who said they came on false travel documents provided by DGI seemed to be more serious and curious, interested in learning about Cuban realities. They also appeared to be well-educated, civilized, and attractive young people.

I was particularly impressed by the quality and charm of some of their frequent visitors, like Beatriz Allende Bussi (called Tati). A medical doctor, young and beautiful, Tati was the daughter of the future Chilean President Salvador Allende. She was trained in Havana in the management of guerrilla war and subversion tactics under the cover of medical upgrade courses. She was passionate and genuine but immature and, in contrast to her father, romantically fanatical. Violence appealed to her as a means of achieving social change. During 1968 and 1969, Tati was preparing the clandestine guerrilla network Marcela in Bolivia to start the second guerrilla war after the death of Che Guevara. These guerrilla efforts failed in 1970. In September of the same year, her pacifist father won the Presidential election in Chile without resorting to violent means that he abhorred.

Beatriz returned to Havana a few days after the election, now in the capacity of an informal ambassador of her father. However, neither the Cuban nor the Soviet governments were in agreement with the peaceful and legal methods for social change of Salvador Allende.[21] To sway him to their side, they resorted to numerous manipulations. Cuban DGI assigned Luis Fernandez Oña (alias Demid) as a political attaché to Chile to seduce and marry Tati (Beatriz Allende) by assuring her father's conversion to their armed Latin American struggle and to keep effective checks and controls on him. Luis Fernandez was apparently in love with his first wife, but under orders from his Cuban boss, Manuel Piñeiro, head of DGI, he divorced her and married

Beatriz, who was already pregnant with their first daughter. Chile at this time was suffering a terrible economic crisis, but when Salvador Allende solicited assistance or credit, he was turned down by both the Soviet Union and Cuba. Despite disagreement with his daughter, who was also his Chief of Staff, as well as a serious economic upheaval in his country, Allende continued stubbornly to adhere to the path of peace, refusing Soviet and Cuban pressures to join the militant revolutionary movement in Latin America. Ironically, he was deposed in a CIA-backed military coup in September 1973.[22]

I felt even more sorry for Tati when, later, I learned from my friends in Cuba that after she had gone into exile in Cuba with her husband, he returned to his first wife after telling Tati that he had never loved her and had only married on orders from the Cuban DGI. In 1977, despondent about his betrayal, she wrote a long letter to Fidel Castro and then shot herself dead. She left a daughter, age five, and a son, age four. This is the way the world is orphaned by revolutionary zeal and missionary violence. It is unlikely that Fidel lost any sleep as a result of her letter.

Cuban leaders were overly generous with the leftist Western crowd because they did not have to pay the bills to promote international terrorism. The bills were paid liberally by subsidies from the Soviet Union. Cuban leaders and senior Cuban *apparatchiks* (a Russian colloquial term for a professional functionary of the Communist Party and a loyal subordinate) and their families did not suffer from scarcity, to put it softly. They had home delivery of most of the imported goods they wanted, and when they wanted. I witnessed such direct delivery of requested goods and food to their homes by military trucks. They would simply pick up the telephone, call their special storehouses, charge their accounts, and wait for the delivery of goods. Accounts were seldom settled.

The products and services were provided in those years by the Soviet Union and other socialist countries and by some corrupt foreign businesspeople from everywhere in the world. The notion that the economic blockade by the United States created economic hardship for Cuba is less than credible: no other countries in the world are prevented from doing business with Cuba, and many American companies are doing business with Cuba through third countries or directly if classified as agricultural or health products. The reason for blaming Cuba's economic disasters on the US blockade is purely a political convenience. I personally met many foreign businesspeople from around the world who were aggressively competing in Cuba. Only those who were swift to corrupt the Cuban *apparatchiks* succeeded.

Over the years, I also met in Cuba with some Western foreign businesspeople who bragged that they were not in business at all before they came to Cuba. They also boasted of exceptionally good luck: Cuba invited them to become third-party Cuban traders and financed their purchases for Cuba with Soviet subsidies. Cuba permitted these third-party traders to make large margins on transactions (legal or illegal) without having to invest or risk their own money. To continue with this *kaif* (easy life), these newborn middlemen needed only sufficient savvy for keeping their Cuban benefactors happy "on the table and below the table" (bribing their Cuban partners and superiors). Nobody cared about how much was left on the margins for the middleman as long as everybody was happy. After all, the Cuban purchases were paid for by the Soviet Union! The families of Cuban leaders could have a wonderful time in luxury hotels. They never had to pay for goods and services because nobody would ever dare present them with the bill. Only as a foreign resident living in the country was it possible to appreciate how prophetic and universal George Orwell's allegorical novel, *Animal Farm,* is.

Somebody like me, coming from the Soviet Union, knew very well that such privilege (freeloading) comes only with absolute power. The so-called revolutionaries never intended to pay for goods; all they had to do was to appropriate them. This is why all Communist countries, after ravaging the resources of their own nations, are bound to go bankrupt. The utopian 'pure revolutionary' comrades who disagreed with these premises were eliminated: they were killed, imprisoned, or punished until they submitted in obedience to the highest power. After 50 years of 'victorious communist power' in the USSR, I knew all too well that those who dared to question the legitimacy of such privileges would be declared 'the agents of imperialism conducting anti-Soviet propaganda' and would be removed. The punishment of those who dared to question was applied not only to the guilty culprits but also to members of their families.

The name of this law was The Rehabilitation of the Family. Like many of our Soviet laws, it cruelly mocked the essence. The essence was that all members of the family became collectively responsible for all punishable deeds committed by one of their relatives. Depending on the gravity of the crime, the members of a Soviet family were sentenced to a minimum of two to five years in prison labor camps; but it was customary to significantly enlarge their sentences in the labor camps, with the result that only a few would survive the ordeal. This law was repealed after 1960, but even then, after 43 years of terror, it was so deeply ingrained in the social makeup of *Homo Sovieticus*[23] or *Sovok*[24] that it simply continued its presence not only in the minds of Soviet people but also in all official forms and documents we had to fill out. The sentencing practices continued because most laws were applied at the will and whim of those in power.

Additionally, this law was in force under Article 58 of the Soviet Criminal Code (especially dangerous crimes), and after 1960, it shifted to Article 70 (anti-Soviet propaganda) and Article 190-1 (distribution of false information damaging to the Soviet system) of the Soviet Criminal Code.

Political prisoners were never called political

because they were charged under the Criminal Law; therefore, they were not recognized as political when it was not convenient to do so. Instead, they were persecuted much more harshly for their political character than any real criminal. This is how the Soviet government and later the Cuban government would be able to answer inquiries about their political prisoners: there simply were not any in their country.

The oppression in Cuba looked like a 'Latin Fiesta' compared with the oppression in the Soviet Union of the period. The main reason for such contrast was that everybody in Cuba, including Fidel, had family relatives just 90 miles away in the USA, and the Revolution was still very young and fragile. The other reason was that the majority of the Cuban population was entirely taken by surprise when their Supreme Leader suddenly declared in 1961 that he had a change of heart: the previous purely national political aims would be transformed into new international communist goals.

The Cuban Revolution, in Soviet opinion, was also vulnerable because of its geopolitical position. If tough Soviet-style oppression would take place in Cuba, similar to that applied in other communist satellite republics, the reaction from America could reverse this Revolution. But nobody should have underestimated the talents of the Cuban supreme leader in media drama exploitation. The Jesuit upbringing of Fidel Castro, similar to the Jesuit education of Stalin, taught very useful lessons about the need to secure full control and nothing less than total power. This is why Cubans call their political system *Fidelismo*. They are not fools. They say that the whole country is Fidel's private estate, where he manipulates the public response to his fiery exhortations by instilling fear. The media campaigns and propaganda became the most effective instruments used by the Cuban leadership in deceiving international sympathies. Hollywood could take a few drama lessons from Fidel Castro. *Viva Animal Farm*! *Viva Castrolandia*!

3. Spy vs. Spy[25]

After the Bolsheviks had come to power in my country, they ensured that they would never be threatened with a new revolution by other political movements. With the help of aggressive propaganda, terror, and genocide of a productive part of the population, it did not take them very long to convert the Soviets into passive and obedient citizens whom we mockingly called '*Sovki*' (plural of Sovok, meaning dustpan).

I was raised on the streets of Odessa in the postwar Soviet Union, where all of us survived by learning to adapt to and hide from the tyrannical state. We would not easily succumb to romantic illusions, revolutionary or otherwise. Besides, I learned from my older compatriots in Cuba that Soviet embassies were known traditionally for their long hands. It was clear to me that I had to be careful with the Soviet embassy employees because all of them, without exception, even in a friendly nation like Cuba, were linked to the KGB

(Committee for State Security) or GRU (Soviet Military Security). It was also clear to any Soviet citizen that Cuba was not really a foreign territory but a strategic ground for Soviet intelligence and military operations. Soviet intelligence (KGB) was deeply involved in creating this miraculous geopolitical advantage for the Soviet military in America's backyard from the start of the Cuban Revolution. They designed and trained DGI (Cuban Intelligence Services) on the Soviet model and invested extraordinary efforts in controlling it.

During traditional alcohol-fueled Soviet celebrations held privately for technical staff in our embassy in Havana, we were occasionally and confidentially enlightened with information about how much the Soviet Union was really in control of events in Cuba and how our leaders engineered this power during the modern history of Soviet-Cuban cooperation. It all began with the old Soviet KGB agents: Fabio Grobart[26] and Osvaldo Sanchez.[27] They assured the unquestioning commitment to Moscow of Cuban revolutionaries as early as the spring of 1953, a few years before Castro's guerrillas formed in the mountains of Sierra Maestra. This meant that the collaboration and exchange of information between the Soviet KGB and the Cuban DGI were at the highest level.

It was well known that Raúl Castro Ruz was an old friend of a young Spanish-speaking KGB officer, Nikolai Sergeevich Leonov, who was stationed at the Soviet Embassy in Mexico City in the mid-1950s at the same time as Fidel

Castro. Here, Fidel spent his Mexican exile after release from prison, where he served two years for attacking Cuban army barracks. Leonov was already a handler (intelligence manager) for and a friend of Raúl Castro, with whom he had traveled by cargo ship to Mexico.

Advised by his brother Raúl, Fidel Castro suddenly appeared in 1955 in the Soviet embassy in the City of Mexico[28] and appealed personally to Nikolai Leonov for financial assistance and arms to support the guerrilla campaign against Cuban President Batista. Though the request for arms was turned down, Leonov was immediately impressed by Fidel Castro's potential as a charismatic guerrilla leader. He began regular meetings with Fidel and offered him enthusiastic moral support. Leonov regarded Castro's politics as immature and incoherent but noted his determination to retain complete personal control over his Twenty-Sixth of July Movement and his willingness to give his future regime some sort of socialist coloring. The Soviet government, after analyzing Fidel's background and behavior, concluded that he was not yet ready to become a 'reliable player' because they largely considered him an anarchist or a gangster capable of staying loyal only to himself. This is why Moscow mainly relied on the traditional Communist Party in Cuba (PSP)[29], which has been legally operating there since 1925.

Leonov made an outstanding career in the KGB due to his Cuban success and became the Deputy Director of the First Chief Directorate

(Foreign Espionage) of the KGB (the most important KGB Division), responsible for all KGB operations throughout North and Central America - a speedy climb from his humble beginnings as a simple KGB agent.[30] As the most important Soviet specialist in Cuban affairs, Leonov was generously treated by Raúl Castro, who bestowed upon Leonov a large estate, a beautiful house with lakes and rivers in a privileged, protected location, a natural preserve, near Havana. Russian Television (RTV) made a documentary about Nikolai Leonov and his relationship with Raúl Castro. Nikolai Leonov[31] claims in this Russian documentary repeatedly broadcast by Russian Television since 2007 that his success was based on his personal and fortunate discovery of the brothers Castro.[32]

However, the relationship between Fidel Castro and Moscow was not always easy. Cuba, on its own, was incapable of producing even enough food for its citizens - amazingly absurd for such a fertile and mineral-rich soil and gentle tropical climate. As a result, Cuba depended on subsidies from its big and rich neighbors (Americans or Soviets). Cuba's tremendous agricultural potential was undermined before the Revolution by large foreign landowners who produced cash crops for export, and state-controlled farms were restricted to sugarcane production for export to the USSR after the Revolution. The Cuban people, for generations, had lost touch with their fertile soil as well as with the discipline and skill necessary to grow nutritional food. The

Soviets misinterpreted as sheer laziness this long-term, politically instigated Cuban alienation from the earth. A current Soviet joke was: "What does a Cuban need to do when he is hungry? He needs to lie down under the banana tree, open his mouth wide, and wait for the fruit to drop."

Fidel Castro proved to be truly a loose cannon, and his capricious behavior reminded the Soviets more of a spoiled megalomaniacal bully than of a mature leader. Fidel had a strong personal friendship with Nikolay Sergeevich Leonov. Still, the Soviet Ambassador in Cuba, Aleksandr Shitov, KGB resident or intelligence chief - alias Alekseev, was perpetually annoyed with Fidel. Despite receiving huge Soviet subsidies (4-6 billion American dollars annually in addition to military aid), Fidel was unreliable, unstable, and difficult to control.[33]

Fidel Castro came to power through a coalition group known as The 26th of July Movement. Along with it in 1959, where the Student Revolutionary Directorate (*Directorio Revolucionario Estudiantil*) and the Communist Party (*Partido Socialista Popular* or PSP, the only party backed by the Soviet Union). PSP (communists) believed that Batista could be overthrown only by the Cuban workers' popular uprising led by the communists. However, the Cuban workers were not interested in the uprising, and Fidel was not partial to sharing power with anyone, even with the PSP. Fidel Castro, in the opinion of Soviet analysts, was a Marxist but a Fidelist. All power, accreditation, and all control had to be exclusively his. This was not the attitude the Soviets expected from their satellite states.

Soviet analysts were also intrigued about how it became possible for the Castro brothers and their few lieutenants to survive the Moncada barracks attack and to obtain full amnesty after 20 months of their 15-year prison term. Most likely, they suspected, Fidel made a deal with Batista: an exchange of the seats, which belonged to the Orthodox Party in the Cuban parliament, for amnesty from prison. Other rumors attributed the Jesuit teachers of Fidel with successful lobbying on his behalf. Whatever the cause of such a miracle, the result was the elimination of the original Orthodox Party (representing the students of Havana University). That this was the same Orthodox Party that gave him birth as a politician, became a glaring example that Fidel could 'bite the hand that fed him'.

After their release from a Cuban prison in May of 1955, the Castro brothers spent a year in exile in Mexico, where the KGB agent Nikolai Sergeevich Leonov was stationed. As mentioned earlier, the brothers Castro appealed to Nikolai Leonov for arms to support the guerrilla campaign against Batista. The 27-year-old Leonov thought of Castro as a charismatic guerrilla leader but immature and incoherent, unlike his Marxist brother Raúl and chief lieutenant Che Guevara. Still, Leonov felt optimistic since he promised to exert influence on his brother. This motivated Leonov to take personal risks in recommending to the Latin American Department of the KGB to support these promising candidates as allies of the Soviets against America.

In pursuit of armaments, Raúl Castro went to Prague (to avoid the appearance of being a Soviet puppet), where his friend Nikolai Sergeevich Leonov had delivered to him an invitation from Nikita Khrushchev to come to Moscow. As a result of Raúl's visit to the Soviet Union, Alexander Shitov (alias Alekseev) - a KGB intelligence chief in Buenos Aires - came to Havana in October of 1959, following Fidel's seizure of power, to establish a Soviet embassy with full diplomatic recognition. He stayed on in Cuba as a cultural consular officer when, in reality, he continued as a Resident (the head of Soviet intelligence services) to organize the Cuban State Security on the Soviet Model. He helped to establish the Ministry of the Revolutionary Armed Forces (MINFAR) and the Ministry of Foreign Affairs (MINREX). Raúl Castro was placed in charge of both services.

However, his fortunes with the KGB began to change after Fidel purged PSP (the Cuban Communist Party created and trusted by Moscow) without any consultation with Soviet leaders. The PSP, from the start, believed that a tactical alliance with Fidel was necessary for the time being. However, Fidel surprised them by purging PSP of most of its leadership and using the party as a vehicle to obtain total control over the country in keeping with his dream of becoming 'The Bolivar of the Caribbean'.

When Fidel Castro understood that his move

upset Soviet leaders to the point of endangering Soviet oil and arms supplies to Cuba, Fidel Castro sent Ramiro Valdez (head of Cuban G2)[34] to start secret meetings in Mexico City with the KGB. The KGB immediately sent hundreds of security and military intelligence advisors to Cuba from the special KGB forces formed mainly of *'Los Niños'* (The Children). These were the children, mostly of Spanish communists, brought to the USSR after the Spanish Civil War and trained as future intelligence operatives for Latin America in Spetsnaz.[35] They helped to control the general Cuban population by organizing neighborhood spying and "guerrilla training schools" for international volunteers under a free educational program in Cuba.

Spetsnaz gathered intelligence abroad through diplomatic channels and international organizations such as the United Nations, using their contacts and agents. Internal state security was established in the Ministry of the Interior (MININT). It incorporated Cuban G2 internal security (DIER) of Ramiro Valdés and the External Intelligence Directorate (DGI) of Manuel Piñeiro.[36] MININT was made subordinate to Raúl's MINFAR, with Raúl and MINFAR responsible for watching over the military exercises of the MININT. That is why Raúl Castro was the true power behind the throne of his brother.

Raúl and Che have been dedicated Marxist adherents to the Soviet Union since their youth, while Fidel did not have any ideology, except for himself in power at any cost. This megalomania did not frighten Soviet leaders because, by that time, nobody in the Soviet Union believed in any ideology except power.

Overcoming his initial reluctance, Nikita Khrushchev began pouring military and economic assistance to Cuba, which Fidel used largely to finance revolutions around the world. The USSR spent over 100 billion American dollars in financial and military support to Cuba over three decades. The prescient observer would not have to look much further to appreciate a major cause of the bankruptcy of the Soviet Union. In a twist of irony, the observer might say later that Cuba was instrumental in creating the conditions for Soviet Perestroika.

The Cuban victory at the Bay of Pigs over the CIA-sponsored invasion in April of 1961 was guaranteed not only by the buildup of Soviet artillery on the island but also thanks to an early warning about the details of the planned invasion garnered and transmitted by KGB agent Oswaldo Sanchez from his base in the Soviet Embassy in Washington. The Cuban success at the Bay of Pigs provided an opportunity for Khrushchev to formalize an agreement with Fidel Castro for establishing sovereign Soviet ballistic nuclear missile bases in Cuba. They also agreed to the establishment of the Lourdes SIGINT Center at Torrens near Havana.[37] Lourdes was the world's largest Soviet SIGINT (an acronym for electronic signal intelligence data interception of satellites, rocket telemetry, and radar gathering center). Fidel and Cuba offered an opportunity for the

Soviet government to establish a military foothold in the backyard of America. Still, the Soviets mistrusted Cuba; after all, it was only a Caribbean island, and surprises from "the aboriginals" could be expected at any moment.[38] Fidel had alarmed Khrushchev on several occasions by insisting on a pre-emptive nuclear attack against American imperialists who, he insisted, would invade Cuba once again.[39]

Despite Soviet largesse, the ambition of Fidel Castro to become 'the savior of the world', or at least of Latin America and Africa, at the expense of the Soviet Union, became a serious irritant in Cuban-Soviet relations. Castro declared that his own '*via armada*' (armed struggle) is the route to power for all Latin American communist parties. In 1966, he announced in Moscow that it would be Havana and not Moscow that would succeed in liberating the world from imperialism.

In 1968, the Soviet-Cuban crisis became especially serious when all 35 leaders of the Cuban pro-Moscow Communist Party were brought to trial in Havana, accused of conspiracy (of being a 'micro faction'), and sentenced to lengthy prison terms for 'clandestine propaganda'. Moscow had to replace the ambassador in Havana and warn Cuba of economic sanctions that would completely paralyze the Cuban economy. Ambassador Alexander Shitov was replaced by Alexander Soldatov. It now took some special effort by Fidel Castro to regain Soviet subsidies; to that end, he made a public endorsement of the Soviet aggression in Czechoslovakia, despite its unpopularity among the Cuban people.

The ambitious approach of the brothers Castro was not that different from the approach of Leon Trotsky[40] (who was obsessively hated by Stalin). In 1970, Fidel Castro, despite objections from Moscow, set himself up as the Leader of the Third World. This situation in Cuba necessitated a particularly strong KGB presence from the Soviet point of view when I became part of the team of Soviet naval designers in 1968.

Since I knew from my Soviet friends about the very close relations between DGI and KGB, I was particularly careful to exercise the utmost discretion with the hotel guests. I would encourage them to dominate the conversation (after all, everybody likes to be heard) before I satisfied my curiosity and escaped their company, avoiding commentaries. It was clear that Cuban and Soviet intelligence were spying on all the guests. Even if these guests would not gossip about me intentionally, there was still a risk that a private and friendly conversation could have legs. Somebody, sufficiently naive, might babble with friends, and those friends might report me to DGI, who in turn will undoubtedly notify the KGB. I never forgot my stepmother Shura's admonition, quoting the rule of survival in the USSR: "keep the mouth small and ears big". Regardless, my curiosity often made my day. It was a fantastic opportunity to gather choice morsels of information from and about a variety of people.

During this period of my life, my emotions were very complex, coping with the explosive mixture of attraction and repulsion for the associations in this adventurous chapter of life. I was fascinated when witnessing such a reckless and motley international crowd, and yet angry that all this extravagance was at the expense of ordinary, ill-fed Cubans. I was not exposed to any subversive information. I never heard, for example, of '*paredon*' (the Cuban name for the sentence by firing squad of thousands of Cubans branded as counter-revolutionary). Still, my own eyes could not avoid seeing events around me, and these observations were revealing.

While many of my Soviet colleagues felt superior to most Cubans, arrogantly calling them aboriginals, I sympathized with the Cubans, respected their political innocence, and enjoyed these romantic and emotional people over my cynical Russian compatriots for many reasons, not least because of the paranoia and fear generated in the Soviet company. In particular, I began to mistrust them after I was given, by my Cuban friend Nora (our translator), the Spanish language publication of Alexander Solzhenitsyn's *One Day in the Life of Ivan Denisovich,* which was forbidden reading in the Soviet Union since 1966. Nora was arrested a few days later by DGI, but the charges against her were never specified. Of course, in the first instance, I was terribly worried that Nora was punished for giving me this forbidden publication, and I too would be shortly detained and questioned about this book; however, nobody mentioned anything over time, and I decided that Solzhenitsyn was perhaps not the reason for her arrest. Despite all my sympathy for the Cuban people in general, after learning about the close relations between DGI and KGB, I knew that I could never seek refuge in Cuba from the KGB.

Back at the Hotel St. John's, tucked into the crowded side streets of Vedado, I had to apologize to my chambermaid. After purchasing new flights for the boys and me and paying in advance for the unanticipated expense of an extra week's hotel stay, I ran out of money and could not leave her tips. My Cuban chambermaid, who appeared to be a kind and compassionate middle-aged woman, asked me if I had the money to purchase food for the children and myself in the hotel restaurant. When I replied in the negative, she took care of us by stealing a few boiled eggs, milk, and some boiled potatoes from the hotel's kitchen, which she delivered to our room very early every morning. I was so very grateful because I knew that she was risking her employment. Her kindness was not the result of any ulterior motives unless, of course, she was reporting me to Cuban security.

I was especially careful during this week and avoided any personal contact with anyone I cared for - my husband, our families, or any of my friends - because contact with me could seriously jeopardize them during future investigations of my case after my escape. I did not call, speak to, or meet in person anybody except our chambermaid. Still, I managed to find solutions for providing my children with hot meals by taking them without permission to the municipal daycare they had attended the previous month.

Yes, my situation was embarrassing, but I preferred to hide in a cheap Cuban hotel rather than inform the Soviet embassy about my unexpected delay. My father warned me from Odessa in a letter secretly sent to his friend that the KGB in Odessa had requested him to expedite my return home to Odessa and inform them when I do. They said that they planned a meeting with me on my return to Odessa. In my naiveté, I was hoping to confuse everybody regarding my whereabouts and the date of my final arrival. It was childish, of course, to think that I could simply get lost (my secret desire) in the wrinkles of international airports because of this missed flight with the Czechoslovakian airline.

The truth was that I had become fed up with our living in constant fear in this psychiatric asylum and was planning to escape with our small children before it became too late to do so. This could be my last chance of escaping because of my very rare and temporary privilege to travel abroad. I already had an antagonistic relationship with my Soviet supervisor and possibly with the KGB when I refused to report on the behavior of my colleagues and friends. The KGB had ordered my father to notify them of my return home for the holidays, and that was a strong indication of their interest in me, which would have consequences. Being uncertain of their intentions, I was not sure what exactly they wanted from me. However, I could not afford to risk finding out. I could only surmise that their interest in me was the result of a recent denunciation of me by Boris, my direct supervisor, or they might have decided to contract me directly as a spy or informer, similar to some other Soviet and young Cuban women whom the KGB or GRU used as informers, '*swallows*' or '*honey traps*'[41].

And yet, I have been aware of the policy in the KGB of not domestically contracting Jews or half-Jews (officially, it was never recognized, but rumors put their unofficial stamp on this quiet policy, and rumors were the only source of information people trusted). Still, I had heard about the KGB not using this ethnic criterion in working abroad. However, why so much secrecy? If they wanted me for anything, all they needed to do was to request my appearance at the Soviet embassy in Havana, where they could do with me whatever they pleased. So, perhaps, Soviet security was seeking to hire me in secret, away from the eyes and ears of Cuban DGI. Cubans had a weakness for pretty women, so when the KGB needed to access information independent of DGI, they occasionally employed attractive female spies; my Soviet-Spanish personal friend Carmen, or the most famous example being the brave and beautiful Argentine-born East German Tania. Her real name was Tamara Bunke, and she was a secret triple agent (KGB/Stasi/DGI). She was rumored to be a lover of Che Guevara while Che had a Cuban wife with four children. If, on the other hand, the KGB had no intention of taking advantage of my feminine charms, it was possible that they simply intended to punish me. I was afraid to learn their true intention because my instinct for self-preservation was stronger than my curiosity.

All Soviet citizens in the post-war period knew better than to turn down any request of the KGB because it would result in nasty persecution, which would end in punishment. The KGB was omnipotent and disliked any precedents of rejection. Even when their interest is superficial, they need to be consistent with the policy of punishment for insubordination to prevent future similar occurrences. They would orchestrate how to frame you (often by falsifications or provocations) to arrest you on those often-false charges, then sentence you to a forced labor camp. The KGB employed an enormous number of people: it has been estimated at between 3 and 7 million employees. This estimate does not include the 14.4 million employees of the military-industrial complex, where cooperation with the KGB is obligatory, as well as the border guards, volunteer snitches, and informers.[42] Rumors were that those who signed up with the KGB as collaborators or agents later defected abroad, and the KGB would eliminate them as a procedural matter. To keep their troops terrorized, the KGB's internal rules simply demanded to do so without exception.

Rumors in the Soviet community were that

not even a safe house could protect the KGB defector. Their agents abroad will launch a very long search, if necessary. When they find the defector, they will kill him regardless of his insignificance to their organization. Such rumors could also have been spread intentionally to terrorize potential defectors and prevent any future dissent.

This was my rationale for escaping before they had a chance to punish me for refusing to cooperate or before they could force me to get involved in their spy business. I was literally willing to jump into a black hole rather than get trapped by the KGB. I knew absolutely nothing about Canada, the country to which I had chosen to escape. Neither was I sure if the Western system would be any better for somebody like me without relatives or friends abroad, lacking financial support, and with two small children. To me, the most important factor was the Western concept of individual freedom. Soviet propaganda described the horrible torments of oppressed American citizens, especially during the war in Vietnam. But in Cuba, I could see with my own eyes other foreign engineers and technicians from Europe, Latin America, and Canada. They did not look either frightened or poor. On the contrary, they appeared and behaved relaxed, sophisticated, and totally in control of themselves and their destiny. In truth, the poor and frightened ones were my Soviet compatriots and me.

I was not willing to play the spy game at any price. I knew if I did, I would lose. At this stage, my only objective was to get away before they conscripted me. For those who made a deal with the KGB, there was no escape. Once Faust sells his soul, there is no buyback clause. Honestly, to me, it was not a matter of morality but my dignity. Growing up, my role model was the first woman cosmonaut, Valentina Tereshkova. My spirit refused to become an obedient informer, swallow, or honey trap for the KGB.

Cuba also disappointed me. The Cuban people who remained on the island (all those who did not emigrate) lost their political, cultural, and human rights. They were, by now, converted into a docile herd, obedient to the authorities. Fidel Castro continued to exercise those snake-charming skills he learned from Mussolini and Hitler to develop and manipulate nationalistic hysteria to control the enslaved masses. While in the Soviet Union, our leaders - Stalin, Khrushchev, Brezhnev, and other bosses - could afford to enslave and rule us without wasting their precious energy on charming us. In the Odessan spirit, my private joke was that the main difference between the Soviet Union and Cuba was when the people wet their pants. In the Soviet Union, people wet their pants when they were invited for a chat with security. In Cuba, people wet their pants when Fidel Castro was delivering his interminable speeches - some as long as 8 hours - in front of audiences who were afraid to leave for the washroom because they were all watched by Cuban informers who would note those who displayed less enthusiasm in receiving the speech. Later, these people could be accused by informers of abandoning the ideas of Jefe Maximo only because they left to go to the washroom. Ultimately, in both societies, there are always wet pants. I was adamant about rejecting this destiny of fear. We were too young to submit to a life of the 'living dead' with wet pants.

I was also convinced that I wanted to raise our children in complete freedom; otherwise, there was no true value in giving them life. In the history of Cuba, I read that when Spanish conquerors attempted to enslave the natives of the island, the aboriginals refused to have children and preferred collective suicide rather than becoming enslaved. This is why none of the Cuban aboriginals - Guanahatabeyes, Siboneys, and Taínos - survived the Spanish conquest of the island, while other Latin American countries still have large native populations today. Cuban aboriginals could not conceive of a life without freedom. I felt the same as the Cuban aboriginals.

4. Odessa Mama

Primorsky Boulevard and Memorial to Duc de Richelieu

I was two years old when my birth mother died in the bleak Ukrainian aftermath of the Great Patriotic War.[43] So, I was not only born in Odessa but partially orphaned there and raised virtually carefree on the streets of this beautiful city by the Black Sea. Odessa replaced my lost mother. Odessa Mama.

Odessa was a unique Soviet city that combined a natural mix of East and West with its Mediterranean population (Jewish, Russian, Ukrainian, Greek, Italian, French, Turkish, German, Polish, Armenian, Tartar). Historically, the only Porto Franco (freeport) of Russia, Odessa, is relatively young (only 200 years old). Odessa was built in the place of an ancient (about 700 BC) Greek settlement, Olbia, which later became the Italian port Dginestra, and afterward, the Turkish fortress and palace Hadzibey. Before the Revolution, Odessa became home to Haskalah[44] (Jewish reform and enlightenment movement) and contributed to broad Jewish participation in the city's science, commerce, and arts. By the Twentieth Century, Jews constituted the largest ethnic group in the city (32-40% of its multi-ethnic population). However, pogroms,[45] the Revolution, and the occupation by the Romanian-German army during the Second World War decimated its prosperous Jewish middle-class population. As the major port connecting Russia to the Mediterranean, it had a rogue character similar to any major seaport. But it was also a modern cosmopolitan city of the Enlightenment, rich in beauty and cultural life.

Like the rest of Odessans, I cannot be unbiased about its beauty, cultural mosaic, imaginative and imposing baroque architecture, and the salty and pungent iodine smell of the Black Sea. No other Soviet city was so ethnically mixed and culturally liberal. On its streets, besides Russian, you could hear every Mediterranean language and Yiddish in particular. We, the residents of Odessa, even created our own language, a mix of Russian-Ukrainian with Yiddish, Italian, Greek, and French. Spoken with ironic twists, it served as our psychic armor, our only protection against the oppressive Moscow rulers.

My Soviet generation was unfamiliar with and uninterested in religions. We were the second generation of those who were taught that all religions were archaic, ignorant, and outlived concepts designed to separate and antagonize people. All six synagogues of the city, its churches, and mosques were closed by Lenin's decree in 1922[46], except a small synagogue on the outskirts of the city, which was under observation by the KGB. The world-famous Brodskaya Synagogue, built-in 1840 as the first

Russian choral (Reform) synagogue, currently houses the State Archive of the Odessa region.

Those who displayed their religious beliefs were "re-educated" as atheists or pretended to be so under threat of arrest and exile to forced labor camps of the Gulag. The priests who were permitted to function in the few temples and churches intentionally left open were forced to become KGB agents or informers. No one else was allowed to provide religious service. This situation was a reality for all of the Soviet Union, not just for Odessa. We were the brave second generation of Soviets who were never introduced to religion and knew nothing about it. To be honest, we, the new Soviet generation, never suffered nostalgia for religion; instead, we were expected to become fanatical adepts of Stalinist ideology.

Odessa's Industrial Port

Odessa is the largest port in the Black and Azov Seas. Its berth length is more than 8 kilometers. With 1.2 million inhabitants (today), the city stretches along almost 50 kilometers of the bay that bears its name. It is a strange mixture of industrial port and seaside resort.[47]

We lived in a four-story heritage building just one block from the beautiful City Park, which is on *Deribasovskaya Street*, the main street of the city, and only two blocks removed from the principal cultural center of Odessa, the Opera Theater, and its surrounding park. Facing *Voyeniy Spusk* or Military Descent in English - the main avenue from the port, my window ledge became the natural podium for a four-year-old "general" to receive her military honors while exchanging salutes with the marching Navy (often accompanied by a musical band), following the arrival of naval ships to the port.

Our address, ironically, was House #1, Apartment #2 on *Havannaya Street* (*havannaya* in Russian means that this street belongs to the harbor). We were incredibly lucky to live there. From the early age of three or four, as soon as I learned to push our heavy chair to the window to climb onto the outside second-floor window ledge of our four-story building, I would salute in military fashion the Soviet Army troops arriving from the port and the naval parades accompanied by spirited and heroic martial music. It was a lot of fun and excitement.

Despite the strict prohibition of my father, I would climb onto this window ledge when I was alone at home, which was the normal state of affairs since Papa was usually at work or out somewhere. Navy ships arrived regularly at the port, and the sailors would march towards the city along Military Descent Road, passing directly under my window, which did not have a balcony or outside staircase when we lived there. The balconies and staircases were added after the privatization of this building in 2006.

Our second-level corner window faces Military Descent Road.

I never missed an occasion to salute these smartly uniformed sailors marching to the rhythms of their military band leading the parade. My father tried to explain to me that he prohibited my climbing onto the window ledge only because of the danger of losing my balance. If I fell, “There would not even be a wet mark left on the street beneath the window,” he often repeated to me; presumably, because I was so small and our window so relatively high. From my father’s expression, I imagined that I would simply evaporate if I fell, but even this image could not dampen my enthusiasm when I heard the horn of the ship's arrival in port. I would open the window wide, push the chair near the window, and climb onto the ledge with the help of that chair.

Completely overtaken by the excitement, I would forget about the danger and prohibitions and stand tall on the ledge of my window. Then, like a self-appointed Admiral, I would give my military salute to the incoming Navy. The troops loved it, and everyone smiled at me. I felt like I was becoming an integral part of their ranks and was overcome with joy and pride. The marching naval parades on Military Descent Road continued to be an emotional pinnacle of my childhood. My papa learned from the caretaker of the building about my dangerous behavior, but instead of spanking me, he attached a rope across the window frame with a knotted loop in the middle and taught me how to wear it around my waist so I would not fall while perched on the ledge.

Where the city runs along the Black Sea coast, my friends and I enjoyed not only observing the arriving and departing ships from the beautiful promenades above the port, but we also explored the seacoast and the large underground network of the famous Odessa catacombs, an entire multilevel underground city along the coast, carved out of limestone and stretching beneath the whole of Odessa. Over the years, the catacomb network was built by sea pirates, contraband traders, and notorious criminal groups, and was used during wars by Odessa resistance defenders. For example, when the Soviet Army in WW2 retreated from Odessa, at least 10% of the remaining population escaped into the catacombs, where they joined the partisans to launch an active resistance against the aggressor and occupier of the city, the Romanian allies of Nazi Germany. The catacombs connect underground with most of the city's older buildings, and each building would have a secret entrance into this network. Papa said that one of his cousins, a 17-year-old girl, was an underground partisan fighter and lived in the catacombs during the occupation of Odessa by Romanians.

Russian Empress Catherine the Great, who built Odessa as a model city of the Enlightenment, insisted upon Italy's contemporary and outstanding architectural styles. City streets still sparkle with the original sculpture-decorated buildings, green parks, and Greek statues. The streets are shaded by mature and aromatic flowering trees, especially acacias.

Every child in our city was expected to develop musical talent. It was the tradition of the city, particularly after the Great War: the new generation was supposed to compensate for the talents of those who were killed. The famous Stolyarsky School of Music for Talented Children, half a block away from our windows, graduated some of the world's most famous violin players: David and Igor Oistrakh, Nathan Milstein, Mikhail Fikhtengolts, Boris Goldstein, Samuel Furer, Leonid, and Oleg Kogan, Eduard Grach, Elizabeth Gilels, Victor Pikayzen, Semion Snitkovsky, Liana Isakadze, Gidon Kremer and many others. So prolific and far-flung were these talented Odessa musicians that an anecdote described a cultural exchange between the Soviet Union and America: "when a violin player from Odessa is exchanged for a violin player from Odessa".

When I was very young, an accident damaged my hearing. I always thought that I could listen to the beautiful violin classes without leaving our apartment if my hearing was better. Instead, I had to run half a block and stand under the windows of Stolyarsky School together with the always-present crowd to listen to the audition of its students or a class led by famous violinists visiting the school. Italian opera and Russian ballet became my spiritual and cultural obligations despite my hearing impairment or absence of musical training. The famous Odessa Opera Theater was located only two short blocks away from the building with our communal apartment.

My father insisted that I come to the theater every Sunday because he bought two of my friends from our building and me a full subscription every season. Even if I had to watch the same show and the same performers many times, I was still obliged to be there repeatedly because this was a tradition in our city. I could not complain: the theater and the performances were outstanding and featured the very best performers. *Forbes Magazine* included the Odessa Opera House on a list of the most important sights in Eastern Europe.

Parks also surround the opera theater with fountains, Greek sculptures, colonnades, and benches around which we kids were never tired of running and playing. The old walnut trees and tall acacia trees with their white or rose blooms filled the theater park with their heavy fragrance; though, this sweet scent was often overpowered by the smell of the sea, which, we were told, was very good for the development of our brains because of the strong concentration of iodine at the coastline.

Odessa Opera House

After each theater performance, we children would play 'hide and seek' games in the theater gardens. As we grew older, these simple games were transfigured into staged dramas where we would imitate the performances we saw but change the often-tragic endings to suit a child's optimistic sense of justice and fair play. Kids love cheerful endings.

There was not in the past, and there is not at present, another city in Russia or Ukraine more hospitable to its residents than Odessa. It was designed rationally, using a model of Napoli, and built aesthetically to take advantage of its warm climate and its open seacoast. We, residents of Odessa, did not take for granted our good fortune to live in this beautiful city; we adored it and were very proud of our privilege.

Despite the drabness of the Soviet system, we were blessed with a beautifully temperate climate, the city's ancient history and multi-ethnic origins, the fabulous cosmopolitan architecture, and world-famous musical and literary achievements of some of the city's inhabitants.

Opera House roof sculpture detail

These natural and human treasures brought us closer in spirit to those Olympian gods and goddesses whose statues were present everywhere in the city center where I lived. Odessa was and is the largest, busiest, and constantly expanding port of the Black Sea, crowded with ships from every nation. Everyone in the city was connected to the port and the ships; this is why we had a different vision of the world compared to the rest of the Soviet people. Our perspective was global and not confined or parochial. Our families were all engaged, economically and culturally, in those sea voyages. We were the children of the sea, and Odessa was our dear mama who was always waiting for our return home.

5. Manna from Heaven

Berta Naumovna Zelitsky

My mother, born Bertha Naumovna Alter, died a week past my second birthday in 1947 of health complications resulting from malnutrition. Over 1 million residents of Ukraine died in 1947 from the famine imposed by the Soviet government.[48] My father was born Wolff Izrailevich Zelitsky. He was called Vladimir or, by his family, Volodya, the Russified version of his name. Papa was a typical Odessan by character and profession. He was a Marine captain and spent most of his time at sea. The reason for the death of my mother was supposed to be kept secret because Stalin needlessly enforced famine in Ukraine, and he did not want the international wheat clientele to hear rumors about the lack of anything (especially food) in our Soviet paradise. Meanwhile, the Soviet Union was selling grain abroad for hard currency and using the money for political maneuvering and manipulation among its new satellites in Eastern Europe. For many outsiders today, these huge famine casualty numbers appear as an old statistic[49], but to those like me, who lost a mother at the age of two, it was a deeply personal and traumatic event.[50] "One death is a tragedy," observed Stalin, "a million deaths are only a statistic."

Paulina, after her mother's death

As a young child, I was afraid to ask my father about my mother because his eyes would tear up, and deep sadness would frighten me. He appeared unable to deal with his emotions and cut short talking to me about her. I was afraid to see him cry. Everybody, all our friends and neighbors, loved Berta and spoke of her using words like ‘angel’. She was, according to them, a generous person who played her piano beside our open window to cheer up the passersby, even when she was suffering from malnutrition and hunger. They loved her music, which had a particular emotional resonance immediately after the war when much of the city remained destroyed. Pedestrians gathered under her window and applauded, asking for more. Papa used to say that Mama was a very kind and beautiful person, always thinking about how to help others and how to better their lives.

After her death, my papa had a hard time keeping me alive. Years later, he told me that I lost a lot of weight and often refused what little food was available. To keep me with him, he had to stop going to sea. Instead, he appealed for permission to demobilize and work transfer at the newly established Black Sea Institute.[51]

The Institute was located only one and a half blocks away from our communal apartment. To become accepted for permanent employment at the Institute, my father had to undertake night studies in marine transport engineering. He abandoned his chosen career because he was determined to take care of me, his only child.

The Black Sea Institute was located on the left side of Langeronovskaya Street.

He refused an offer from my strong-headed maternal grandmother to marry her other younger daughter, my aunt Eva, whom my father disliked. I did not like Eva either, but I loved my grandmother.

Bubeleh Mania

Papa refused to follow the Jewish tradition to marry a sister of a deceased wife, a tradition he explained based on a need to keep the family together. Instead, my father assumed single-parent obligations by renouncing his cherished career as a marine captain. The degree of my gratitude for his sacrifice and his loving care is beyond words. I believe it was he who instilled in me the strength of character and independence from the earliest age that prepared me for a difficult future.

After it had become clear by 1944 that the Soviet Union would win the war, my parents thought it would be safe and wonderful to have a child. Berta wanted to return to Odessa, despite the absence of housing (most buildings in the city were destroyed) or any family help, because she wanted me to be born in Odessa. She returned there on her own; the rest of our family and my father, who was serving in the Navy, were not allowed to return to Odessa.

The pre-war Odessa apartment of my parents was bombed and destroyed by Romanian and German occupiers. Papa served in the Soviet Navy and Mama in the naval medical services during the war, both in Murmansk in the Soviet Arctic. After my mother had become pregnant, my parents decided that it was time for her to return to Odessa, which she did when the Soviet army liberated the city, and before I was born. The government gave her one room with three large windows in a communal apartment located on the second level of a corner building facing Military Descent Road. This was the principal transportation artery leading from the naval terminal in the Port of Odessa.

My father was in the naval service, stationed in Sevastopol, often at sea and without communications. Whenever my father's ship came to port, he would send letters to Berta. He wrote one letter every day; so, when he arrived in port, he would have as many as 20 letters to mail to her. She was fortunate to be awarded one room in a communal apartment where I was born healthy in July of 1945. For this occasion, my father was granted a leave from the Navy to visit his wife and newborn baby.

The starvation in Ukraine was not so bad during its first year in 1946, but during the second year, drought crippled the harvest, and the population of Ukraine was starving. Berta couldn't work because she had to stay at home with me; this is why she was not awarded a worker's food ration and was forced to purchase food on the black market at very high prices. There was no milk or meat or even vegetables, and bread rations fell to 250-150 grams per day for dependents. My father sent her most of his salary and rations, when possible, but such occasions were rare because the postal service would not accept food parcels or money transfers to Ukraine.

Finally, the government removed all rations from those adult family dependents who couldn't work. My mother had to continue breastfeeding me because otherwise, I would not have survived without her breast milk. Though her health was weakened by malnutrition, she had good breast milk and continued breastfeeding me for the first two years of my life. This is how Berta saved me from starvation.

My father was not allowed a leave from the Navy to visit his wife and me in Odessa for the first six months of 1947. My mother never admitted to him in her letters how serious her physical condition was. When, finally, my father obtained permission for two weeks' leave to visit his wife and daughter, he found Berta already terribly frail. My father took her to the best doctors in Odessa, but she could not be saved, and she died before his return to the Navy. Almost everyone in Ukraine at that time was badly depleted and sick, suffering from diseases and various symptoms of malnutrition, including severe anemia.[52] Doctors were prohibited from recording the true medical reasons on the death certificates of the deceased. In those years, countless citizens died in Ukraine for reasons that were kept secret.[53]

When I asked my father how it became possible that Ukraine did not grow more of their food in kolkhozes (Soviet collective farms), he answered that the Ukrainian kolkhozes produced more and better harvests than anywhere else in the country, for it is well known that Ukraine is the breadbasket of the whole Soviet Union. But the Soviet government decided to send all food to the central areas of the Soviet Union, all other new socialist countries, and Europe. **The truth was that the Ukrainian harvest was sold for hard currency and shipped from Odessa to Bulgaria, Romania, Poland, Czechoslovakia, and France.**

My father saw with his own eyes how the agents of the NKVD (predecessor of KGB) were arresting those few miserable '*binduyzhniki*' (stevedores) in Odessa Port who attempted to steal a few grains from the European-bound ships loaded with wheat. Each of them was punished with at least 10 to 15 years in the Gulag. All the while, their families were starving to death. This is why I was prohibited from telling anybody the true story of my mother's death. Even doctors were ordered to lie about the causes of illness in death certificates. Still, my father thought I was now big enough to know the truth.

For my father, it was a very traumatic experience because he loved Berta very, very much. I also did not make his life any easier because I refused to eat, except for sucking on the piece of bread which my Papa would tie up for me inside his handkerchief when he had to leave me alone at home. He was obliged to report for duty. If he did not, he would have been arrested for desertion and shot, according to military law. Work was the sole source of his bread rations, which he was now sharing with me; otherwise, I would not survive either. It was not so simple. He could not possibly leave me for long with my grandmother *Bubbeh* Mania (mother of Berta) because she insisted that he marry my auntie Eva (Berta's sister), who became a widow during the war and now lived with my '*bubbeh*' (grandmother). He was afraid that if he left me with *Bubbeh* Mania, even temporarily, she would gain my custody and forbid him to see me until he marries Eva. He felt that after losing my mother, he was not prepared to lose me as well, especially to such a '*chaleria*' (evil woman in Yiddish).

My father used strong language to express

his distaste for Eva. However, Papa was a pretty good judge of character because later, Eva falsely denounced her other sister to the KGB. This treacherous act against her own family was rewarded by the state for 'patriotic vigilance'.

When I asked my father why Bubbeh Mania was forcing him to marry Eva, he said that it was because of an ancient Jewish tradition to marry a deceased wife's sister to help raise children and keep the family together, but he disliked my Auntie Eva. She was a '*yenta*' (a gossipy lady in Yiddish, a blabbermouth, talks too much), and he would do anything to avoid marrying her.

When I asked him why he doesn't normally speak to me in Yiddish, he answered that, despite Yiddish being the language of our family, he wants me to talk to others only in Russian. The Soviet government prefers Soviet people use only Russian. Learning Yiddish or Hebrew is not encouraged.

Still, we needed my father's food rations - about 600 grams of bread a day and nothing else during 1947. After his resignation and demobilization from the Navy, he wanted to stay home with me full-time, but then we would lose his rations. Those who did not work for the state were not given any ration. So, he got a job in the Black Sea Institute[54] , only one block from our apartment in Odessa. This way, he could look after me by himself and feed me with his rations. This is how I survived.

Papa said that my big trouble was that I was used to being breastfed until Berta became sick and died. After that, I refused to eat the piece of bread he would bring home every day for me. He had no choice but to leave me at home by myself while he was at work. The kindergartens (a daycare system for young children) did not accept children younger than three years old at that time. The children younger than three years old were to be cared for by their mothers or close family members. **My father's solution was to wrap and tie down a piece of bread in a handkerchief before leaving for his job. This seemed to work well. I stayed home by myself, sucking the bread juices from the handkerchief as if it was a baby bottle**. There was no cow's milk or baby food during that period. My *bubbeh* and our neighbors would drop in on me to feed me with cooked food whenever it was available. This is how my father kept me alive: busy sucking on a handkerchief all day long until he could return home from work.

Three other extended families shared this converted four-bedroom apartment with us. Each family got one room for themselves, regardless of the number of family members. A minimum of 19 at any given moment, all of us shared one small toilet and a single kitchen. Despite such incomprehensible crowdedness, all the residents considered themselves very fortunate because our building was unique. A heritage building of the 19th Century known as Novikov House, it was located in the beating heart of the city center. All rooms in the apartment were (in the eyes of a small child) large, especially ours, which previously served as a '*gostinnaya'* (the living room) for the previous owners.

My earliest memories of childhood are fragmentary. Mostly, I remembered my disgust at the constant compulsion to eat *mannaya kasha*[55] (creamed wheat semolina porridge cooked with lard) force-fed to me by our neighbors - adults conscripted by my papa to ensure that I eat according to the doctor's recommended diet. My father could not find the strength in his heart to force me; our neighbors undertook this task. They compelled me to sit over a dish covered with a hard skin of creamed wheat with yellow fat swimming in the center of it. Just looking at it was sufficient to provoke my vomiting.

This 'food from heaven' became my hell. My answer to this torture was to escape by any means possible, which in turn produced endless complaints from the *mannaya kasha* executioners who invariably ended up eating my cold meals of kasha themselves and permitting me to chew some bread instead. Even better, I was very keen on anything spicy, but please, no fat.

Why was I so difficult? When I was six or seven years old, I asked my father what was wrong with me. Why do I hate the food that everyone else loves? Papa attempted to explain that there was nothing wrong with me when I was a baby, but after my mother died, my character changed. I became as strong-headed as a mule, and this will lead me to an unhappy ending. He said that I was a happy and plump baby while being breastfed by my mother. Still, after her death, I became skinny because I categorically refused the breast milk substitute food recommended by doctors. Pediatricians determined that I, just like my mother, had severe anemia, clearly resulting from poor nutrition.

The doctor said that the best way to help me was to feed me with *mannaya kasha*. Papa would exchange our food rations for *mannaya kasha* grain and milk, but wheat with fat made me vomit, and I hated it. Our family members and neighbors in our communal apartment took this mandate very seriously and launched a "holy kasha war" on me. I would frustrate their efforts every single time with the same procedure: the first fight, then cries, and finish by vomiting. I was dragged to the pediatricians again and again. They could not understand why anyone would refuse *mannaya kasha*, this food from heaven. Something was wrong with me.

Pediatricians concluded that I had anemia, or a low red blood cell count caused by iron deficiency; therefore, all my blood would have to be changed, if not all at once, then little by little. My poor father rapidly volunteered as a donor. Every third day, he took me to the clinic where his blood was transfused into me for the next three years. But it did not change my attitude towards the kasha. I still hated it and vomited when forced to eat. Finally, they all gave up torturing me. They said that I was an invincible '*dummkopf*' (the stupid), and they finally let me be.

What a relief! As soon as they stopped torturing me with *mannaya kasha*, I began to grow normally. I spent most of my free time running with other kids on the coastal slopes, where we were exposed to the pungent and invigorating sea air. Without the '*kvetching*' (fussing) of adults, I became physically fit and was even recognized as a local street fighter in the gang of my age group on our city block. My health improved due to the healing sea breezes and vigorous exercise on the steep coastal slopes. I even grew taller than many other children of my age and developed a healthy appetite (for some simple foods without wheat with fat). In my school, I was considered above average in both learning and physical development.

I began to eat tasty and nutritious foods for which our city was traditionally known. We did have wonderful local ways of preparing food in Odessa: Greek, Jewish, Italian, Turkish - all spicy Middle Eastern food. Whether it was an allergy to wheat or the high gluten content in semolina products, or disgust at the floating pool of yellow fat, it became clear to me as an adult that my violent reaction to *mannaya kasha* was a simple reflex of my organism for self-protection. As soon as they stopped pushing hated food at me, I became healthy. This is how I learned that it was good to listen to your body's instincts and your heart's desires and to keep your convictions. Who is the true '*dummkopf*' (the stupid one) about kasha? Not me!

My papa did not like to speak with me about Berta, my birth mother, because he would become too emotional. In Russian culture, 'the real man does not cry', but his eyes were filled with tears when he spoke of her. Then, one day in July, when I was ten years old, Papa took me to visit the Mother's gravestone in the Second Christian Cemetery.

He had taken me there every year on the anniversary of her passing, but this particular visit became especially emotional for both of us because, for the first time in my life, he told me the whole story of her death, which until that moment was always covered in unspoken mystery. Even our neighbors would never comment on a reason for her untimely passing. Perhaps I was too terrified to ask about this tragic and irreversible event or to insist upon an answer. Maybe the silence of others was my cue to keep quiet as well. Nobody spoke about it, neither my *Bubbeh* (grandmother) Mania nor other relatives and friends. Initially, I treated the disappearance of my mother as if it was a bad dream, but the dream persisted, and nobody bothered to explain clearly to me what it meant.

The Romanian occupiers had destroyed the city's Jewish cemetery during the Second World War, and officials from the Christian Cemetery invited Odessa Jews to bury their dead there until the Jewish cemetery could be rebuilt. We always came with flowers and laid them beside her modest limestone grave marker. During this visit, Papa told me the truth about her death for the first time. Standing with me at the foot of her headstone, and after I had promised him that I would never share this story with anyone else, he confided in me that her death could have been avoided, just like the death of many others who died from this terrible famine of 1946 -1947 enforced in Ukraine by Stalin[56].

My father said that in 1946 and 1947, there were poor harvests in the whole country. Everyone was affected. The people in Ukraine, including Odessa, suffered most of all. Despite producing most of the food for Russia, they were living on extremely miserable food rations. There was no milk at all for the children. Papa said that I survived only because my mother was able to breastfeed me. I was the first and only child, and my parents waited all these years during the war to be able to have me.

Papa refused to follow the Jewish tradition to marry a sister of a deceased wife, a tradition he explained was based on a need to keep the family together. Instead, my father assumed single-parent obligations by renouncing his cherished career as a marine captain. The degree of my gratitude for his sacrifice and his loving care is beyond words. I believe it was he who instilled in me the strength of character and independence from the earliest age that prepared me for a difficult future.

Our communal neighbors became an extended family to me. Our communal apartment, shared by four families, who were not related or connected in any way, was originally a one-family apartment with four large rooms; its single toilet and small kitchen are now to be shared by all families.

As a child, I never had any hard feelings towards our neighbors, even when everyone would get upset about the unfairness of lining up for their turn to use the communal facilities or when my bladder was about to burst when Fimka, the brother of my friend Anushka, refused to free up the tiny toilet room. During the early hours of the morning, everybody would aim to get up sooner to line up in a corridor queuing for the toilet or competing for the kitchen stove to cook breakfast.

Our neighbors called me little orphan, sometimes '*jesoime*' in Yiddish and other times '*sirotka*' in Russian. They always blamed my papa's friends or my innocent stepmother, Shura (abbreviated form of Shurochka), for everything that they considered was wrong with me. But when my papa remarried, Shura became a blessing for my father and me. In this regard, I thought of our neighbors as small-minded and jealous.

Their blaming Shura was outright unfair and incorrect. Shura never supported any of my rebellions. She always encouraged the development of adaptation techniques in me, and obedience was number one on her list. She never spoke Yiddish to me because she believed in assimilation. She said that Yiddish was the language of poor and ignorant peasants from the Pale (Jewish ghetto). She insisted that I make more progress reading in the public library rather than staying at home, exposed to neighbors' *kvetching* (complaining). What Shura tolerated about all of us Odessans, independent of our nationalities, was the stubborn use of the Odessan language jargon, so dear to our hearts, which she herself used. This unique jargon was created from a mix of basic Russian-Ukrainian with massive Yiddish overtones and spiced by all the Mediterranean and European languages.

This jargon was our psychological border, invisibly separating us from the rest of the drab and the dreadful Soviet Union. The use of the Odessan language jargon was not punished, unlike almost every other departure from Soviet cultural protocol. The Odessan language jargon also played the role of diffusing Jewish/Yiddish culture among all the other ethnic groups in Odessa. Indeed, when Odessans traveled elsewhere in the Soviet Union, their accents betrayed a Jewish affiliation regardless of their ethnicity. Finally, this unique blended language jargon became an acceptable means for projecting rebellious Odessan attitudes against the uniform Communist Party culture.

Because Jews constituted as much as 40% of the Odessan population during its previous history, Jewish and Yiddish culture and linguistic influence insinuated themselves into other minority nationalities, invisibly coloring the personalities of virtually everyone in the city, never mind their ethnicity. Others who would come from the north did not understand either our idioms or anecdotes or the temper of our humor. We all belonged to our new race of rugged and secular Odessans. Many of my best childhood friends have often been a mix of Russian and Ukrainian. We never took notice of ethnic differences. Nor did I have any interest in coming home after school to chat with adults in the kitchen. I preferred running and playing on the streets with my friends, reading in public libraries, escaping into movie theaters, and joining art clubs and sports groups.

After my mama had died, I lost weight, cried a lot, and became irritable and rebellious. In those years, there were no toys for children in stores, and papa made for me a handcrafted doll, Mashenka. I loved it so much that I kept it on my shelf until I permanently departed to Cuba. Its face he painted with ink, and its little body was stuffed with the fill from our pillow. Whenever possible, he took me with him anywhere he went.

Even during his trips at sea, a couple of times, his superior felt sorry for me and granted him special permission to take me along. When I became sick with *scarlatina* (scarlet fever), my *bubbeh* went with me to share my hospital bed for 40 days. No second bed for caretakers was allowed. **In general, thanks to the handkerchief with bread, I managed to survive a difficult situation.** I also learned that when feeling lonely, to call on our communal neighbors who would pick me up and bring me to their rooms when they returned from work.

But one day, after my father came home from

work, he could not find me. Immediately, he thought that our neighbors or *Bubbeh* Mania removed me. Before he ran to her place or asked our neighbors about me, he looked into the wardrobe and under our bed. Odessa had no running water at that time, and everyone was storing some water at home for drinking and washing. Ours was stored in a small tub under our bed, hoping that it was not accessible to me. My father's instinct made him pull the tub out, just in case, and he found me inside and under the water and without breath. He panicked, spread me on the floor, and succeeded in bringing me back to life by mouth-to-mouth resuscitation. After I vomited water and started breathing, he put me in my breadbasket, which he used to carry me around, and ran with me to the hospital.

The doctor told him that he was a very lucky man. If he had returned home that night a minute later or, instead of looking under the bed, he had run to the neighbors or *bubbeh*, I would be dead. Once again, we were lucky. The doctor was a generous man, and he helped by giving us a medical certificate requesting "a full kindergarten service" for me, even though I was not yet three years old.

This saved me. From that moment on, my father took me every morning in my breadbasket to the kindergarten and would pick me up at night after work. Meanwhile, the kindergarten looked after me and fed me. But, according to my kindergarten teachers, I began to develop a rebellious character, even at that young age.

I remember kindergarten. I also remember how bored I was alone at home. It was unbearable. I tried to climb onto the window ledge using our chair. But the chair was very heavy, and my father made it difficult for me to move by leaving it far away at the opposite wall. I remember trying to get inside the fireplace, but my father blocked it with bars, and I couldn't move them either. I called through the door of our neighbors' to come to play with me, but they were probably at work, and nobody came.

Finally, I found a water tub under our bed. I wanted to play with the water, but I knew it was forbidden. I could not pull the tub out, so I squeezed myself into the tub under the bed, where I tried to play, but I could not keep my head above the tub because my own body forced the water to rise until there was hardly any air space. I attempted to climb out of the tub, but I couldn't because of the narrow space between the bed and the sides of the tub. After a while, I probably fainted from the cold and lack of air.

But I do remember how, after this incident, my father was running with me every morning to kindergarten. It was still completely dark. In the beginning, he carried me in a basket, but later in the winter, I remember how he pulled me on a sled. It was a lot of fun, especially when the sled hit the melted ice and splashed water over me. I loved it.

I also recall how my father was always singing for me: "*Kalinka, Malinka, divchinka moya, krasna devitsa Polinka, Polinka moya*?"

(a popular Russian love song in which my papa substituted the traditional Russian name of a country girl with my name).

I, too, loved him more than anything on this planet, and I love his song for me. How lucky it was for me that he invented a bread handkerchief for a milk bottle. I always said to my father that I felt very fortunate! I would never, ever want to be separated from him, not by *bubbeh* or auntie Eva or anyone. Nobody will ever separate me from my Papa.

This is how I always felt about my father, whom I adored so much that it created some problems with my kindergarten teachers. I remember vividly how my kindergarten group, around thirty-four-year-olds, were made to sit at low tables with small chairs where we were eating, learning to sing, draw, and recite who is who and what is what. I remember that on the schoolroom wall, there were no pictures except two big portraits of Lenin and Stalin. Our teacher would start every meal with the obligatory greeting in a high voice (as if we were saying grace at the dinner table), and we were obliged to repeat after her in a high voice before every mealtime:

"Spacibo nashemu dedushke Leninu y nashemu otsu Stalinu za nashe schastlivoe detstvo." (Thanks to our grandfather Lenin and our father Stalin for our happy childhood).

All the other children, who were a bit older than I, repeated after the teacher. Not me. Instead, I would start crying. At first, they tried to calm me down, asking why I was crying. I answered that I loved my Papa very much and did not want to change him for Father Stalin. My teacher, in vain, would try to convince me that my father still would be coming to pick me up. He will not disappear if I recite greetings to Father Stalin. But I was stubborn and refused because I was afraid that my father might disappear as my mother did. My poor teachers had to face the fact that I was stupid and stubborn because I was too young for the kindergarten program.

What saved me once again was my father's good looks. He was tall and well-built. His bright eyes reflected his dynamic and ironic nature, but also his general optimism. As an olive-skinned Odessan with Mediterranean looks, he was a handsome standout in the uniform of a sea captain. The Second World War killed over 20 million Soviet men; as a result, males were in high demand. When he and I walked together along the streets of Odessa, women would turn their heads towards him. It was I, of course, who would proudly return their yearning glances. Later, my schoolteachers and the mothers of my friends often said to me, "Your Papa looks so Italian!"

My teachers in kindergarten were single females and were subject to the vulnerability of the heart for handsome, unmarried men. My kindergarten teachers agreed, under papa's charms, to leave me in kindergarten, despite my lack of progress, until I would outgrow my stubborn attitudes and adopt appropriate behavior; that is to say, calling Stalin my father.

They risked losing their jobs to keep me: an underage political '*dummkopf*' who refused to learn due respect to Stalin. Just in case, I was kept at the back of my row as the last child for every activity, including the playground and the bathroom (ouch!). There too, I demonstrated stupidity when I discovered that the boys were doing their toilet differently from the girls. I could not figure out why the difference and molested my teacher with many naïve questions about the need for these differences. (Girls and boys used the same washroom space simultaneously for time-saving convenience).

Neither was my teacher happy with my eating habits, since most of the time, we were served the same '*mannaya kasha'.* My teacher always insisted that until I finished everything on my plate, I could not join the other children in play. She would allow the other kids to go outside to play in the backyard, but would leave me behind, feeling resentful, until I finished all of my kasha, which I never did.

I recall how my *Bubbeh* Mania used a more forceful method: holding me tight to her knee to prevent me from slipping down to the floor; she would grip my nose to prevent me from breathing in through my nostrils, which in turn would force me to open my mouth to catch some air. Instead of air, she would shovel a full spoon with kasha into my mouth as soon as I gulped for air. As a result, I would choke, and she would be angry because, in her mind, it was unbearable to leave food uneaten.

Everyone considered my choking on kasha as evidence of my unreasonable character and my consequent vomiting as a protest against authority. Their idea was that I should be punished for stubbornness; otherwise, I would never learn. To me, it was unbearable to choke on this awful kasha, which I hated not just with my eyes but also with my gut. Still, I was not such a stupid girl because my body was smarter than my Soviet doctors and teachers, smarter than my *bubbeh*. My body made me vomit and saved my life. By refusing kasha, I was eventually permitted to eat the food of adults. And that food I loved. Typical Odessa dishes were spicy and richly flavored.

My father took me everywhere he could. I remember hiding under his desk in those offices where he was working and studying; I even remember myself on the deck of coastal ships. I remember how my father brought me to watch a squad of mariners firing their rifles in salute to commemorate the war victory. I was sitting on his shoulders in great anticipation of a wonderful show. My father and our neighbors said it would be great fun, and I was a very lucky girl to be permitted to witness this ceremony from such a close distance.

Then, suddenly, I felt a terrible, huge bang that exploded in my head. I shouted in fright and pain. All went black, and I thought that something had hit me on my head, but in reality, it was not the case. It was only the trauma from the loud noise of the firing. My father ran with me to the emergency ward of the hospital. The doctor who examined me said that my trauma was not physical but emotional. I was too impressionable, he said, and might never regain my hearing.

He explained that I probably misunderstood the salute firing as an assault. After a few days, my hearing slowly returned but was never as good as before. To this day, I respond badly to very loud noises. Because I failed as a child to appreciate the fun in that commemorative war explosion and reacted with terror instead, everyone in our communal apartment called me '*upriamitsa*' (obstinate). Nevertheless, my partial loss of hearing had one good result: I was admitted early to state daycare.

Thinking about my early childhood, I understand now that my most serious problem was being a nonconformist by nature. This was an objectionable and dangerous characteristic for survival in a country where all citizens were expected to submit without questioning, where individualism was destined for elimination, and where collective obedience was demanded. Natural reactions saved my life many times! All I needed to do was to trust my own heart and find my own way.

6. Denouncing my Father

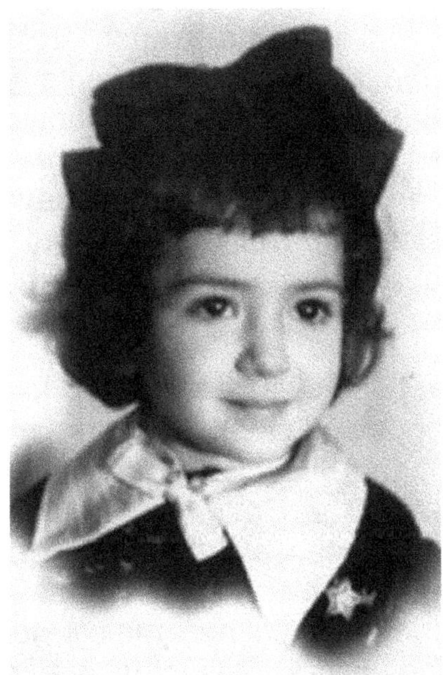

Paulina, six years old, is proud of her Oktebriata star

Soviet schools accepted new students in the first grade only at the age of seven. To keep me in a more demanding, disciplined, and challenging environment, my father arranged with the school director to accept me at the age of six because he argued that I needed to keep up with other children who graduated with me from the daycare center. He had already taught me to read and write, and now he claimed that I would be bored if not accepted to school earlier. I was accepted and began attending Day School for Girls # 36, corresponding to our residence address and located just two blocks away from our home.

Again, I was lucky because it was the best, the oldest, and most famous school in Odessa. Before the Revolution, it was called Richelieu Lycée, named after the French architect who designed the city and became its Governor. None of us knew about the school's previous history, just like we were ignorant of history generally and the eminent pre-revolutionary cultural history of the city. Such information was considered 'anti-revolutionary propaganda' and kept secret from us.

Richelieu Lycée was considered to be one of the best schools in Odessa for primary, middle, and secondary levels (grades 1 to 10). Established by the Governor of Odessa, Duke de Richelieu, it was the only prestigious educational institution in Odessa that accepted Jewish students, and it became a cradle of local Russian and Jewish intellectual giants.

My school #36 reverted, after Perestroika, to its proud name Richelieu Lycée

From as early as 1817, all classes were conducted in French by the best and often renowned European and Russian professors, such as Dmitri Mendeleev (creator of the first Periodic Table of Elements in Chemistry). The Lycée produced such classical writers as Ivan Bunin (poet and novelist, the first Russian to receive the Nobel Prize for Literature in 1933 and one of the finest Russian stylists), Sholom Aleichem (born Sholom Rabinovich, creator of classics in Yiddish literature), Isaak Babel (Soviet short-story writer considered an innovator in the early Soviet period and who enjoyed a brilliant reputation in the early 1930s), Haim Byalik (a leading Hebrew poet), and Vladimir Zhabotinsky (Zionist leader and writer). They all studied in this school. But who knew? We were not familiar with their works. Their writings were strictly banned in the Soviet Union until 1980. I learned about the historical fame of my school more than half a century later during a visit to Odessa after Perestroika.

This was when I discovered that after *Perestroika* (the economic and political reform of the Soviet Union), the school had abandoned its colorless Soviet title (Day School for Girls #36) and adopted its original name. It also listed its famous students on a large plaque in the school's reception area. It is a shame that I was unaware of its illustrious past; I would have felt such a feeling of pride in the school's accomplishments and would have been powerfully motivated by the feats of my forebears. Even the classic Russian poet, Alexander Pushkin, often visited the Lycée for readings of his poetry during his residence in Odessa.[57] The famous Polish poet Adam

Mitskevich and classic Russian writers such as Nikolai Gogol, Alexander Ostrovsky, Lev Tolstoy, and Alexander Kuprin also participated in the Lycée's literary meetings, which were a city tradition.

I was only six years old when I obtained an automatic membership in 'Oktebriata' organization during my first grade at school. Oktiabriata means the children of the October Revolution, and its purpose was to introduce children from grades 1 to 4 to the initial levels of communist political education. At the age of 10, all school children have again enrolled automatically into the second level of political education: the Young Pioneers organization. Then, at the age of 15, all high school children were expected to enroll in the next level: Komsomol.

I had a dreadful experience during my initial Oktebriata level. When I was seven years old, in the early autumn of 1952, at our regular weekly Oktebriata class (basic political education for the second-grade students), our teacher Vera Estafievna reminded us about the '*canonized patron saint*' of Oktebriata and Pioneers, the heroic Soviet child Pavlik Morozov who in 1932 bravely denounced his kulak father (peasant-farmer owner of his land) to the Soviet authorities.[58] The story of Pavlik Morozov concerned a 14-year-old boy from a remote village about whom the Soviet government created mythological propaganda aimed at the idea that children must denounce their families to state security for wrongdoing against the policies of the government. In the heroic example of Pavlik Morozov, the falsified propaganda version claimed that this righteous boy, being a Komsomol leader in his village, denounced his father to the authorities, for which he and his brother were in turn killed by their own family. Overnight, Pavlik's story became a subject of massive public meetings, readings, songs, plays, and public monuments all across the USSR in every town and city. Schools, clubs, and public squares were named after him.

My second-grade class with our teacher, Vera Estafievna. Paulina is second row, far left

Afterward, in the late 1970s, on-site investigations by a prominent Russian writer, experienced as a police detective (Yuriy Druzhnikov), demonstrated that the story of Pavlik Morozov was false; it was completely fabricated. The Komsomol organization did not exist in Pavlik's village of Gerasimovka, and Pavlik Morozov falsely denounced his father to punish him for abandoning their family for a younger woman.[59] His father was not a *'kulak'* (small landowner) but the chairman of a remote rural Soviet (locally elected council). He was arrested and died in a forced labor camp on the trumped-up charge of hoarding grain. But even in the late 1970s, Yuriy Druzhnikov was not allowed to publish any of his findings. The Soviet propaganda machine preferred to maintain intact the cult of Pavlik Morozov because revealing the lie would undercut the legitimacy of the Soviet State and its moral fabric.

During our Oktebriata class in the autumn of 1952, our teacher called on each of us to stand up and comment critically on our parents at home in memory of Pavlik Morozov. When none of the children demonstrated the capability of criticizing their parents, she suggested that we were simply too young to exercise the critical judgment of our parents. So, she said that she would help us if each of us merely repeated the conversations our parents held at home. In particular, she asked us to describe the discussions of our parents at home about recent public denunciations of the current plot by Moscow Jewish doctors.[60]

Allow me to describe this alleged Plot for readers unfamiliar with these details in Soviet history.

The Doctors' Plot in 1952, at the pinnacle of the aged Stalin's paranoid schizophrenia, ignited a national wave of barbaric anti-Jewish hysteria in the Soviet Union, involving mass false accusations of Jewish doctors and intellectuals to unmask the group of prominent Jews purported to be the conspiratorial assassins of Soviet leaders.

It started with the newly born State of Israel allying itself with the West in 1948. Stalin, who was counting on Israel becoming a Soviet ally in the Middle East, reacted with an obsessive vengeance against all Jews. His initial retaliation was the elimination of the Jewish Anti-Fascist Committee in 1948 and launching a campaign against so-called 'rootless cosmopolitans'. After the show trials of 13 internationally prominent members of the Jewish Anti-Fascist Committee, they were secretly executed on Stalin's orders. The episode became known as 'The Night of the Murdered Poets'. This event was followed by show trials of other Jewish intellectuals and anti-Semitic propaganda in state-run mass media. Many Soviet Jews were promptly dismissed from their jobs, arrested, sent to the Gulag, or executed.

Stalin's dread of his own death, aggravated by his advanced state of delusional paranoia, resulted in constant suspicions and fears towards medical doctors. In his later years, he refused to be treated by physicians and would only consult about his health with veterinarians. At this time, 37 of the most prestigious and prominent Kremlin doctors in the USSR were accused of taking part in a vast plot to poison top Soviet political and military leadership members.

The accusations began with 37 doctors, but the number quickly grew into hundreds. Outside of Moscow, similar denunciations quickly appeared. For example, Ukraine discovered a local 'doctors' plot' allegedly headed by the famous endocrinologist Victor Kogan-Yasny (the first in the USSR to treat diabetes with insulin and save thousands of lives). Thirty-six 'plotters' were arrested there.

To continue with this story, I was not warned ahead of time by my father or by anyone else about what I should say in the event of such requests. In my naiveté as a seven-year-old, I thought that I would make a good impression if I mentioned something positive about my father. When my turn came to stand up and tell, I said that I heard my father speak about Moscow doctors to 'auntie' Shura (an engineer from the Black Sea Institute who was Papa's friend). Papa spoke to her about doctors who practice in Moscow - doctors like Uncle Leonia.[61] I said that I was very glad that my father was not a Jewish medical doctor, and that we were not living in Moscow. I also said that I was worried about Uncle Leonia because he was a Jewish doctor from Moscow. It must be bad, I added, to live in Moscow; we are very lucky to live in Odessa.

At least, I had enough sense not to mention our neighbors in our communal kitchen, who were also saying that they were frightened by these reports about the Moscow doctors. Though we lived in Odessa and not in Moscow, it was possible, they said, that the persecution might spill over to other cities, as it tended to do so for Jews. I did not repeat their comments because, in my judgment, they were not positive but threatening to us in Odessa, while my father's comments referred to a danger that was only for the doctors in Moscow. This was safe, in my opinion, because we lived in Odessa, and my father was not a doctor; therefore, I was confident that there was no danger for him.

When I finished my brilliant presentation to the class, I returned to my seat, proud of my logical arguments. Our teacher took notes during each presentation by the children and congratulated us at the end of class for being good oktebriata. Afterward, I came home late from school because I had played with my friends in the neighborhood. In my apartment, I became alarmed about the delay in my father's return from work. I waited anxiously for him, but he failed to arrive home. Nor did he return home over the next two days. I went to the Black Sea Institute to ask about him, but nobody knew where he or Shura was. All I was told was that he must be very busy with work somewhere outside, and I should go home and wait for his arrival. Naturally, I made no connection with my clever reporting in the oktebriata class because, in my mind, my presentation was only positive. I waited at home, afraid and crying. I missed school over the next two days because I was now very frightened about my father's disappearance and wanted to be home when he finally returned. After two days of absence, he returned home. I ran to embrace him. He did not speak to me at first; instead, he just entered the room in a solemn mood and pushed me away from him. Then, he took his belt out of his trousers and, without speaking a word, grabbed me, sat on a chair, and laid me across his knees. He whipped me with his belt for the first time in my life, and it hurt a lot. Though I cried in shock from the pain, I was happy that he was back. Still, I thought that belting me was absolutely inexplicable and terribly unfair. I cried bloody hell out of insult and pain.

Returning to my punishment, I really can't say how long it lasted; probably, only a few minutes, but as a kid, I could never forget it. After I had finished resisting and mopping up my tears, my father sat me down to explain in all seriousness his reason for such unusually cruel punishment. My teacher, Vera Estafievna (in a twist of irony, Vera in Russian means trust), had delivered her notes about what her second-grade children said in class to security agents at the office of MVD (Interior Police).[62] My comments about Uncle Leonia, the medical doctor in Moscow, provoked their immediate alarm. The MVD agents came to arrest my father and his girlfriend, Shura, while they were leaving the Black Sea Institute at the end of their workday. They were interrogated for two days, mostly regarding the whereabouts of our relatives - particularly, the Moscow doctor whom I called Uncle Leonia. They were interested in knowing if my Uncle Leonia was his brother.

My father was able to demonstrate that Dr. Leonid Moyseevich was not our blood relative and that Paulina, being simply a child, called all adults 'uncle' and 'auntie' because this is how small children traditionally referred to adults, even strangers. Papa met with Dr. Leonid Moyseevich in Moscow only for medical consultation about a knee injury that he had suffered from since the war. The MVD detective interrogated Shura, checked our documents, checked with Moscow, and found no family registry of Leonid Moyseevich as our relative. It was also discovered that this particular doctor had already been transferred somewhere else in the North. The discovery that Uncle Leonia was not indeed a relative saved my father and Shura because the MVD agents released them. I felt awfully embarrassed and guilty for endangering my father with my stupid naivete. Still, I was confused and asked why it was so bad to be a family related to a Jewish doctor in Moscow.

Then, my father decided that it was better, despite my young age, to warn me of dangers than to allow the manipulations of my naiveté by others, which could mortally endanger our lives. He explained that according to the Soviet Criminal law, all members of the family of a Soviet citizen accused of 'anti-Soviet activity' could be arrested and sent to a Gulag labor prison camp for re-education with hard labor for five to ten years, even if it was possible to prove that the members of the family were not involved and didn't know about the actions or plans of the accused. If my reporting of events about Uncle Leonia could be confirmed as family relations, all of us could be arrested and sent to prison labor camps for five to ten years, while all of our possessions were confiscated by the state. My father felt that I was too young and too delicate to survive this horror. He said that he belted me so hard to make an impression on me forever: that I should NEVER AGAIN TALK to anybody about what I hear or what I honestly think. My answer should always be: “I heard nothing”. He also said that after losing my mother, he absolutely could not lose me; he would rather die. Shura, who later married my father, also spoke to me, teaching me her preferred popular Soviet expression: “Bigmouth - big problems! Keep your mouth small and your ears big, or we will not survive.”

Who could blame me when, after this experience, still a child of seven, I completely lost trust in the sincerity of teachers? But being only a small ‘roaring mouse’, I designed my own game to play with ‘cats’. Just as in the fairy tale of *Little Red Riding Hood and the Wolf*, I decided never again to trust the wolf, no matter what clever disguise it wore. I decided that my teachers would never be able to deceive me again if I stopped trusting them. The best way to do this, I determined, was to look directly into their eyes to make them think that I was listening to them while I would escape into daydreaming. I succeeded in deceiving them because I learned how to disconnect my mind completely from my facial expression. With eyes fixed on the teacher, I learned how not to hear what they said and instead, to engage in the process of fantasizing about stories I had read in books. Our access to books was very controlled regarding contemporary writers, both national and international. Only those writers who flattered Stalin were published, and their books were kept in private or public libraries. Fortunately, however, the majority of old literary classics were not forbidden. These provided for my mental escape.

I distrusted all contemporary humanities and social sciences because they were lies and, therefore, very boring. During classes with those subjects - communist/Soviet literature, history, geography, philosophy, and all other brainwashers - my mind would abandon my body and simply daydream about those adventurous but nonpolitical stories which I read at the library and at home, the stories of Lev Tolstoy, Basni Krylova, Brothers Grimm, Hans Christian Anderson, and later Jules Verne, Dumas, Feihtvanger, and so on; all those authors who were farthest from our reality. My teacher ordered me to take the front seat in the class so she could monitor my attention. Always improving my masquerading skills, I learned how to repeat the teacher's questions automatically when asked and improvise the answers without mentally processing the questions. This skill became very important for my mental survival because, except for mathematics and physics, I was bored out of my mind in school; so, I learned to escape, at least mentally, from the world of the walking dead.

Despite the crowded condition in our communal apartment, I never heard anyone complaining about our neighbors or those elsewhere in our building, who informed or might inform on each other despite a few small and rare squabbles. Maybe they did, and I just never heard about it. To me, it seemed like they acted protectively towards each other, despite occasional harassment by somebody with black humor like Fimka, the brother of my friend

Annushka. No one got seriously mad at him because everyone believed that he was psychologically affected. I only felt sorry for my friend Annushka, who had to shield him from complaining neighbors. So, in comparison to the countrywide Stalinist paranoia and treachery, our small communal enclave by the Port of Odessa was a haven of mutual trust, support, and protection. Lucky me!

7. The Lion Sleeps Tonight

Unlike other girls whose lives followed predictable habits, I was free from the supervision of protective parents running wild in the streets of Odessa, playing in 'partisans (guerrillas) and Germans' with my delinquent little friends in the Odessa catacombs. Later, I discovered reading opportunities in the city's public library, where I would find books unavailable in stores or in school, books that would take me to distant vistas and on fantasy trips.

My father was worried about my wilder adventures. He received some complaints from the parents of boys who reported being beaten up by me; after that, he would promise me a spanking but not resort to it. Instead, he enrolled me in the Fine Arts Club, which was a beautiful Greek-style palace belonging once to Governor Vorontsov of Odessa.

Fine Arts Palace of Vorontsov

In this club, I became involved in theater, music, and dance. Despite such fantastic possibilities, my damaged hearing was a liability, especially in music. Frustrated, I would often wind up hiding from my instructors among the Greek colonnades. Later, noticing that I became shy and embarrassed to speak up publicly, my father tried his best to take me everywhere he went, including the sea. He believed such real-life adventures would boost my self-confidence.

The City Garden, the oldest park in the city, was created by Felix de Ribas, brother of the first builder of Odessa. It was only half a block away from our communal apartment, and we often went for strolls there. When I was about six years old, I experienced my first traumatic incident. I began to feel attracted to one of my playmates. His name was Victor, an older, tall, skinny Russian boy who lived just a few buildings away on our street. We often played together war games in the City Garden, into 'Russian partisans against German soldiers', just for the fun of running and role-playing without real anger.

Paulina with her father in front of one of the lion sculptures in the City Garden Park

One day, while we were playing in the City Garden, Victor suddenly began to act viciously toward me. He dived onto the ground, grabbing my legs. I fell to the ground as a stone near one of the numerous lions' sculptures placed throughout the City Garden. Victoriously, he sat on top of me, displaying very strange, hateful emotions, punching me in the face and shouting: "Dirty Jew, you deserve to be killed!" I was in shock. In desperation, I screamed: "Stop, or the lion will eat you!" Victor paid no attention to my frantic threats; instead, he firmly pinned me down and continued to beat me up.

We were only playing a game. Why would he display such simple-minded hatred towards me? Why would he hurt me so badly? I could not believe this was possible because we played together many times before and I liked him. I could not believe that the boy I liked could display such hate to hurt me. When the ordeal was finally over, and he left, I picked myself up and went home, utterly confused and with a bloodied nose and blue marks on my face. When my neighbor in our communal kitchen noticed me trying to wash the blood from my face, she asked what happened. I answered that I had a fight. I told her about Victor calling me a Jew and beating me up. She only shrugged her shoulder and dropped a single comment: "Your Victor is Ukrainian; stay clear of them." When my father came home and saw my bruised face, he questioned me immediately. I told him about the fight with Victor and my confusion.

"Victor beat me up, viciously, while we were playing war today in the City Garden. He did that for no good reason. I don't understand: who are those 'dirty Jews' whom he said deserve to be killed? And why? I was hoping that the park's lion would eat him for that, but the lion didn't help me as you promised, and Victor won the game."

Our games have often simulated the battles between Russians and Germans. Romanians were also the enemy; in an alliance with Germany, they invaded Odessa. Still, in my childish understanding, all evil foreigners were German. We children born in Odessa or elsewhere in the Soviet Union were on the good side.

"Papa, who are the Jews? Why do Jews deserve to be killed? Why did Victor make an enemy of Jews and me? Why did the lion, whom you call a guardian of the city, not eat Victor for beating me up? You said that the sculptures of lions in the City Garden were meant to protect us Odessans from our enemies. Instead, the lion was asleep."

My father decided that this incident deserved an explanation to six years old. He told me that the time had come to talk seriously, and he set me down to explain that, despite being born in the same country and the same city, people differ by their ethnic origin. He said that our ethnicity was Jewish, the people who came originally from Israel.

Papa said that Jews were the people of the Middle East who created the country, which they called Israel, over 3000 years ago. Israel was located on the major trade crossroads of that part of the world, and every nation in the region ventured, at one time or another, to attack Israel to get control of the strategically important trade crossroad."

"But Papa, I objected, we are not in the Middle East; we were born in Odessa. Why are we Jewish? Are the rest of our family and our neighbors Jewish as well?"

My father confirmed that Jews are all those who speak Yiddish. About 2000 years ago, the Romans conquered Israel, and they enslaved or expelled all the Jews. They were expelled from their homeland to migrate anywhere they could. Many found their way to Europe, others to Crimea, and among the Greek colonies on the northeast coast of the Black Sea, even before Odessa was established. Greeks, Romans, Tatars, and finally Ottomans (Turks) conquered and ruled the northern shores of the Black Sea. Then, about 200 years ago, Russia won this region in a war against the Ottoman Empire. The Russian Empress Catherine the Great founded the city center in the place of the Ottoman Palace Hadzhibey and renamed it Odessa. My father pointed out that the Vorontsov Palace and its Colonnades were built where the Palace of Hadzhibey was before. After that, people from every country around the Mediterranean settled in Odessa to participate in trade opportunities after Empress Catherine the Great granted 'free port' status to Odessa. This is why so many people in our city speak other languages besides Russian; not just Yiddish but also Ukrainian, Greek, Turkish, Armenian, and even Tatar.

He said I was right to ask why Victor hates only the Jews, with such a diversity of people in Odessa. The divisions between different ethnic groups started when most of the other migrants who wanted to stay in Odessa adopted Christianity. The Jews were also offered a choice to convert to Christianity or to be expelled. Those

Jews who did not convert became the targets of hostility by the state, the church, and the ignorant masses.

"Papa, why all this fuss about religion?" I asked. "The people of the Soviet Union are not religious; we are not religious, and I don't speak Yiddish with my friends or in school."

Papa explained that the Jewish religion began thousands of years ago in the Middle East. The founders, Abraham and later Moses, created the Jewish nation from the primitive nomadic tribes of the region. They needed to organize and discipline these tribes into a moral society, but they could not expect the tacit obedience of these primitive people without a unifying idea that it was God who visited them and gave them the laws for their people; there simply was no other way to discipline these people. All other religions do the same; they also invoke their God to give laws to the people. Without these laws, there would be anarchy, he said."

"Papa, I don't hate or insult or beat the Christian or Muslim children of Odessa, and we are not religious Jews, so why does Victor hate me?"

Papa suggested that Victor was too young; he didn't know what he was doing. The ignorant and stupid adults taught him to hate his Odessan Jewish friends and neighbors, even when they don't speak Yiddish and are not religious. These kinds of people are called anti-Semites, he explained.

"Where do anti-Semites come from? I asked.

My father explained that anti-Semites could be ignorant and angry people from anywhere. Their color or religion does not matter. What makes them anti-Semites is irrational hatred. It all started when Jews were expelled from Israel and forced to migrate elsewhere. Usually, nobody wants refugees, and nobody wants the Jews, but even when they were invited to come and settle in the remote and undeveloped regions of Europe, they were often taken advantage of and enslaved or robbed by local rulers. When these rulers needed to prevent public revolts against misrule, they looked for somebody to blame, to be made guilty for their mishandling of the welfare of the people. Jews were an easy target to blame for social/economic problems because they were outsiders. So, local rulers would blame the Jews for all their internal problems and incite the local poor to attack them to appease the anger of the mob by allowing them to loot the possessions of Jews. This practice temporarily resolved the anger of ignorant and abused populations. It was like throwing a bone at a rabid dog. This ignorant, hateful behavior is called anti-Semitism, '*dochenka*' (daughter), he confirmed.

"When did that happen, Papa?"

The father said that I would later learn in school that during the Great Patriotic War (WW2), German and Romanian aggressors executed all Jews who were left in Odessa after the Soviet Army retreated. That is because the Soviet Army could not provide transportation for everybody, especially for mothers with young children, the sick, and the elderly. All the men and young women were serving in the Soviet Army or were partisans. Over 300,000 civilian Jews were killed in Odessa alone just a few years ago. The victims were mothers, children, and old people.

"If you are wondering why this stupid boy called you such an insulting name? When you notice anyone acting like an anti-Semite, don't waste a second if you can; leave immediately. There is no use in arguing with such people. Let the anti-Semite boil in his poisonous juice. These people are vile and ignorant", he said.

Being stubborn by nature, I objected: "I want to be like my friends. I don't want to be different. Nobody believes in any religion anymore, so why do the anti-Semites hate us and call us Jews? Why did Victor say that I was dirty? Why dirty? Our neighbors take me every Sunday to the public bath, just like all other girls on our street. I am as clean as they are."

"The anti-Semites manipulate people with their lies, hatred, and senseless violence. They call the Jews by these offensive names to dehumanize them. It is easier to commit violent crimes against non-humans; these are the effects of ignorance, stupidity, and fear," answered the father.

"Victor is not stupid, Papa, and he is older than I am. Why did he become an anti-Semite? Our communal neighbors told me that it was because he was Ukrainian. Is it true?" I asked, still unable to believe that my friend could have behaved in such a hateful and absurd fashion.

"I know the family of Victor, and they are Russian, not Ukrainian. Don't repeat nonsense because then you will be no better than the anti-Semites. Tell me, who is your best friend in school and our building?" asked the father, still annoyed with me.

"Nadia Mazko, Papa, you know!" I answered, still confused.

"Have you ever experienced an anti-Semitic offense from Nadia or her family?" asked father.

"No, Papa, Nadia is a very good friend, and her family is also very nice to me. Yesterday, her mama served me a hot potato from the oven, the same as she did for her other children. Nadia and her sisters and her parents are very good and kind."

Papa pointed out that Nadia and her family probably are mixed Ukrainians and Russians, but not anti-Semites, and I answered that I had never before heard of anti-Semites. Anyway, in my simple mind, all the children in our city were Soviet people; therefore, they are all good and on the right side.

To conclude this discussion, my father simply said that I was too young for these grim stories, but now, for the first time, he would tell me another story, this time, it is about Uncle Joseph and Aunty Niusinka.

At this point, he told me for the first time the story of Uncle Joseph (the only brother of my mother) and his wife Niusinka, who lived not very far away from us. Uncle Joseph was a prestigious architect in our city and was usually very busy. His wife Niusinka was a housewife - a rare situation for a young Soviet woman. She was sweet but usually introverted and rarely spoke, especially to other my mother's family members. I did not know why; I thought it was simply her nature.

But now, my father revealed a secret. He said that Uncle Joseph (brother of Berta) was an officer during the war, and he was wounded in three places, including in the stomach, during a battle with the Germans in Ukraine. He was left unconscious to die on the battlefield. When he came back to consciousness, he found himself in the attic of a house belonging to a young Ukrainian peasant woman to whom partisans brought him in secret. This Ukrainian peasant girl saved his life under the extreme danger of being discovered, arrested, and executed by the Nazis for hiding the wounded Soviet officer. A German bomb had recently killed her husband and her new baby, but she was still lactating and was able to breastfeed my uncle back to life. Being wounded in the stomach, he could not digest any solid food, and there was no meat or chicken to make a nutritious liquid substance for him. He recovered, united with the partisans, and survived until this region was liberated by the Soviet Army, which he joined again.

After the war, he returned to that village and went straight to the house of the Ukrainian peasant girl who saved him. He married her despite strong opposition from his mother, Mania, and his sister, Eva. My parents were the only members of our family who kept friendly relations with the newlywed. My Uncle Joseph and Auntie Niusinka were lovely people, and I visited them occasionally at their apartment in Odessa. I felt that they cherished and looked after one another with love and understanding despite the illnesses and physical traumas they contracted during the war and despite their cultural differences. They did not have children because of their state of health, and I had nobody to play with when I visited them. My father revealed to me their story as an example that Niusinka risked her own life to save the life of my Uncle Joseph, regardless of differences in ethnicity. The conclusion of his story was that not all Ukrainians or Russians were anti-Semites; some of them were true friends who, like Auntie Niusinka, risked their lives to save Jews, or, like my friend Nadia Mazko and her family, who treated me as their own child because my mother had died.

The photograph below is damaged but still reflects the happy spirit of the relationship between my parents and the newlyweds Joseph and Niusinka, celebrating Victory Day on the seashore. My father was on leave in Odessa, visiting my mother, who was expectant with me, her first child, in her last month of pregnancy.

My parents (forefront) with Uncle Joseph and Niuisinka

"Anti-Semitism is like any kind of intolerance." Papa concluded, "It is not an exclusive privilege of Ukrainians, just as stupidity, ignorance, and superstition are not the property of any particular group. Anti-Semitism results from manipulating the ignorance and religious superstition of poor people for the political and economic benefit of ruling elites. This was the practice of the Russian Tsars Alexander III and Nicolas II, who intentionally ignited pogroms in the Pale of Settlement, where half the global Jewish population found refuge from European anti-Semitism and were restricted to live without civil rights until the Revolution took place."

Then, he added that if he could teach me how to fight so that I could defend myself the next time against any attackers, it would be more helpful to me than depending on the City Garden lions. Over the next few months,

Papa began teaching me how to box and how to a street fight. It became very useful because, from that moment on, I started to defend myself and my friends from frequent attacks from boys from the neighboring elementary male school or other kids who were divided on the streets of Odessa not only by their age but also by their neighborhood gangs.

I stopped depending on the lion and became a furious boxer and a local hero for girls in my elementary school until one day, when I was nine years old. That was when our attackers took their revenge. They waited for me when I was alone on the street, going home after school. I was surrounded and overpowered. Holding me, they pulled out tufts of fur from my new fur coat, which I was proudly wearing to school for the first time. I did not know at the time that the fur of my coat was not real and that this was the reason why tufts could be easily pulled. I only knew that I was embarrassed and frightened to face my father, who had bought me the new coat at some sacrifice.

Another important event was school reform. When I was ten years old, it was decreed that all schools become mixed (previously, my school was for girls only). About 15 new students, all boys, joined our class. We, girls, were still a majority with a ratio of less than 2 to 1. There was competition among the girls to impress these boys. However, thanks to our young age, we were still in a pre-romantic phase, and the competition was more fun than fierce. I began to enjoy our classes in mathematics not only because I had an aptitude for solving problems, but also because two of the boys in our class were not just good at math. They were brilliant at it.

One of the boys, Dodik Balmin soft, thoughtful, and very considerate soul, seemed to live in his own better world, the world of mathematics. He was always thinking about inventing new methods for calculations. I admired him for his creative abilities and his kindness; he was always willing to help everybody who asked. From some maternal instinct, I also felt that he needed my protection because of his physical vulnerabilities: he was small in size, often sick, and too thin, but not afraid of bullies. He gave me a purpose. I developed a protectionist attitude, defending him with my fists against those "bullies" who often ventured to attack him, knowing that he couldn't defend himself.

Fima Ziberman, another boy who was very good with mathematics, was stronger physically and did not evoke the same protective feelings in me. I informed everybody that Dodik was my adopted little brother and that they would have to deal with me if he was attacked. Dodik was grateful for my protection and often shared with me his mathematical ideas. Our new teachers were now much more interesting, especially the ones in mathematics and physics, as well as our teacher of German. It became much more challenging and fun to study.

My father was always very tender with me and soft-spoken with others despite being a commanding officer by training. He was also curious by nature and independent in thought. He had his own mind and did not bend under pressure from women, friends, or his bosses. He always managed to find his own rebellious but not provocative ways. For example, I caught him listening to foreign language radio stations under his bed when I was older. He was covered with blankets to muffle the noise. Shortwave radio reception was strictly prohibited by Soviet law. None of the commercial radios could receive shortwave signals. He built the shortwave radio by himself and tuned it under his bed to hear prohibited news broadcasts. He did not know that I was aware of him listening and reacted alarmed when I asked him:

"Why are you doing this?"

My father looked at me with a serious expression and signaled me to stop talking. He invited me for a walk in the City Garden. When we walked outside, he warned me that he could be arrested if I mentioned this to anybody. He explained that he believes that only one source of information when the world is so big and has many versions of the truth is not sufficient. He listens to at least two or three stations and makes his own judgment about the facts. He asked to keep this secret.

"Papa, did you learn foreign languages? If not, how do you understand them?", I asked, surprised.

He said that when he was a little boy, he learned some Yiddish and Hebrew, and French, but Esperanto he learned on his own. This is because the broadcasts of programs he was interested in were translated into Esperanto.

"What is Esperanto? We were never told of this language in school", I continued questioning him.

He said that this language was invented by Dr. Zamenhof for the sole purpose of improving communications among people who speak different languages. This kind of language does not belong to anyone's specific culture or political system. People who learned this language called themselves Hillelists.

"Esperanto is very simple and very practical," he said. He learned it quite fast and by himself, but soon after, both Stalin and Hitler called this language a Jewish conspiracy. My father was forced to stop practicing it except when he listened to his programs in secret on his shortwave radio. Again, he stressed that I should never tell anybody at all about what I have just seen or heard.

"Understand! Please don't say anything about the radio or Esperanto to anyone, or you will endanger yourself and all of us", he repeated.

8. Coming of Age in the Vegetarian Epoch

Paulina with her new mother, Shura

After Stalin died in 1953, the carnivorous monster known as the Gulag began to devour fewer people. In recognition of the monster's evolving diet, the Russian people dubbed the post-Stalinist era The Vegetarian Epoch.[63]

In the fifth grade, when I was ten years old, I enrolled automatically, like all other children of that age, into the Young Pioneers, which is similar to Boy Scouts or Girl Guides in the organization of outdoor activities for children. In matters of instilling political ideology, it differs radically from the Scouts or Guides.

I enjoyed all the Pioneer outdoor activities but hated formal political meetings, which were absurdly boring except for the rewarding social assistance activities. For example, in one school program, my duty as a Pioneer was to undertake responsibility for visiting, every third day after school, a female Odessan pensioner who lived alone to assist with house chores or reading tasks. Our Pioneer organization coordinated with the city to provide school assistance for solitary pensioners. I liked this voluntary work; it gave me a feeling of being needed. The elderly ladies I visited were sweet and grateful. The idea of extorting money from these impoverished women never came to my mind or to the minds of anyone else who was with me in the same program. We also had responsibility for cleaning the school and washing its windows. I loved washing windows. It was so much fun. We were permitted to stand on the open window ledge and spray water on the glass. I remember horsing around on the second level of my class window ledge, scaring the passersby on the street. I still don't understand how we did not have a single accident!

Another challenging but happy event in my life was the announcement of a marriage between my father and Shura. They decided that I had become accustomed to the presence of Shura and was becoming more independent from my father. They said that I needed to learn how to become more like a lady. I felt that they were using me as an excuse to get married. Not that they needed such an excuse since, to my eyes, they had a sufficiently strong relationship on their own.

From a romantic and sexual standpoint, my father and Shura have always been discreet around me, not even kissing - an activity I learned from some movies and books. Shura never stayed with us overnight until the day they were married. As a result, I never witnessed any of my father's intimate relationships, and nobody had ever explained sex to me or any of my girlfriends. To tell the truth, I don't remember being interested in female physiology until one day, when I was 13 years old, when, on my return home from school, I discovered bleeding, and it was strong and persistent. I completely panicked because I had never presumed that a person could bleed without being cut. I was so terrified that I could not figure out how to ask any of our neighbors or my friends for help. Instead, I hid in the corner of my room, waiting for my father and crying because I was convinced that I was dying. I did not want to die just yet.

When my father arrived, he found me terrified and in tears. I confessed to him that I was dying. That scared him. However, when I told him where I was bleeding, he started to laugh loudly with relief. It was now my turn to become utterly surprised and offended. What a strange reaction when his only child is bleeding, probably to death! After he had recovered from his bout of laughter, he said that what was happening to me was only normal. It meant that I had entered the age of a young woman. He added that now I should ask our female neighbors to explain what I should do about it, and to stay clear of boys or men because now I could become pregnant with a baby. He did not explain any further details. When asked, our female neighbors advised me only about hygiene during the days of menstruation. Our neighbors never talked to me about sex or elaborated on the physiology of reproduction more than my father's useless version. None of them explained to me this men/boys business with any clarity.

I felt guilty and was embarrassed to ask any questions about menstruation as if it was my fault that I had come of age when I could become pregnant. I did not know anything, nor could I understand the real-life biology of it all. During the famine in Odessa, all dogs, cats, and horses were eaten; as a result, I never saw street animals engage in sex. My father only mentioned that to avoid becoming pregnant, I should stay clear of boys and men. I was embarrassed to ask or to talk more about the subject. Presumably, my father meant that if they touched me, I could become pregnant.

Searching through my experiences, I recalled a frightening incident with Mila's father. The previous summer, the father of my school friend Mila, a tall and athletic middle-aged officer with a confident, commanding attitude, invited me to join Mila and him on their trips to the beach for a swim in the Black Sea. On one occasion, while in the water, he tossed Mila away and went after me, grabbing me tight and running his fingers over my body. A sudden, inexplicable panic gripped me, and I fought him hard to get free. Once free, I swam quickly to the coast. Instead of waiting on the beach for Mila and her father, I ran straight home. Never again did I meet with the father of Mila, and never again did I visit her at her home or speak to anybody about this incident in the water. Honestly, I was quite embarrassed by my unaccountable fear. Simply, I didn't understand what really happened or why I reacted so wildly. My fear was purely instinctive, nothing else. Now, I fretted about my father's warning that if I didn't stay clear of men and boys, I could become pregnant. I began to suspect that the touch of Mila's father's fingers had made me pregnant, and that made me cry again. I could not sleep, so I got up and went to wake my father. I was even more embarrassed this time while telling Papa the news that I was pregnant. This time, it was my father who almost had a heart attack.

"My God, what are you saying? How? When?"

"This summer, Papa," and I told him what happened. This time, he did not laugh; he was serious.

"How come you didn't tell me this before when this incident took place? Next time, if something similar happens, you must report it to me! If he didn't do anything else before you escaped, you are not pregnant. Thank God you did not share this story with anyone because the father of your friend Mila works for state security. If you had not escaped from him, he could have abused you and then found it convenient to get rid of you to protect his secret. Don't worry; you are fine now. There is no pregnancy, no problems. You must always avoid such situations. I will ask Shura to talk to you about these things. This must be explained to you by a woman. But the most important thing to remember is this: you will be safe if, when you suspect someone of wrongdoing, you run away immediately without wasting time thinking or worrying. Just get away and don't talk to anyone about it before you talk to me first. Tomorrow is Sunday, and I will start teaching you a fighting technique that will disable your attacker temporarily, facilitating your escape."

The next day, Shura came with my father to talk to me. Both of us felt uneasy. She explained that when girls come of age to become pregnant, they ovulate every month, and if they have a physical relationship near that time, they would become pregnant. Still, she didn't explain any details about the physical relationship itself, and I was ashamed to ask. She warned me that it was necessary to get married first before such a physical relationship occurs, or the lives of the future mother and child will be ruined. I felt cheated because I expected more. I wanted to understand how this relationship is physically carried out, but felt embarrassed to ask. The actual physical event was still an enigma, and our school programs never touched this subject. My girlfriends also felt uneasy even talking about it, so we pretended that it didn't interest us and resigned ourselves to our collective ignorance about this aspect of life.

Still, my recounting of the event with Mila's father and my total ignorance about female physiology and matters of sex probably brought the attention of my father to the timely requirement of female guidance and influence: to convert me from my rough and tumble life and to teach me how to become a proper female teenager. He discussed this problem with Shura, and they decided that it was important for me to have a positive female role model and mentor in our own home. It was then that my father proposed marriage to Shura. After discussing his proposal with Larisa, her mother, Shura, agreed to marry my father and convert me into a little lady.

Papa and Shura registered their marriage but did not invite any family members to witness their registration or attend the celebration afterward. Probably, my father was just cautious, trying to avoid a backlash from the family of Berta, my deceased mother. My grandmother Mania was still very resentful of my father's refusal to marry her other daughter, Eva. At home, Papa simply separated off a corner in our room with floor-to-ceiling wallboard, which provided visual, but not sound insulation. This small boarded-off room became the bedroom for three of us: Larisa (Shura's mother), Nadia (Larisa's maid), and me. Shura and Papa didn't have their own bedroom. They slept in the main room, which served as a living and dining room for everybody. The rest of us quietly respected their privacy and never entered the main room if the door to that room was closed.

I recall a few of my rebellious explosions when the disciplinary rules imposed by Shura collided with my traditionally free activities. She was a strong disciplinarian, and I found myself in a subordinate position, forced to ask for her or Larisa's permission for all my outings. I was resentful of such curtailing of my freedom. On one occasion, when I was punished for evading the rules, I promised to run away. The thoughts of running away became my fantasy at home and in school for some time. These mental escapades helped me handle the stiff and dispiriting disciplinary obligations at home and in school. However, I never attempted to escape because deep in my heart, I was confident of my father's love for me and Shura's best intentions to train me as a young lady. There was a lot to learn from her, and she was an intelligent and giving woman. She started introducing me to proper social manners, hygiene, and aesthetic choices in art and fashion. I was also instructed in basic cooking and housekeeping routines.

Civilizing Paulina was not an easy task for any of the three women who came to live with my father and me. Sometimes, all four females of the household could break out in tears of desperation. Then my father would wisely go out for a walk just to cool down. Afterward, we would all rejoice in reconciliation and share hugs and kisses without even reaching a final agreement on the contentious issue. The truth was that I did not want to hurt my father. My love for him and my desire to see him happy was greater than my little adolescent ego.

Though Shura was never cruel to me, she had no previous experience with children of her own. In many ways, it was a difficult experiment for all of us, but I recognized the integrity of her efforts and, most importantly, the need for the emotional stability of my father.

Unwillingly, I submitted to her authority for my father's sake and came eventually to appreciate the resulting harmony and learning opportunities. Shura was the very opposite in every aspect of my character. Like the mothers of my friends and our female neighbors, she lived most of her life as a hardworking and compliant member of society, where everything, from rules to rooms, was restrictive. She compensated for feelings of being powerless, a cramped existence, and hunger during the war and post-war years by overeating starchy and greasy food. I was appalled by the quality of these comfort foods.

All that said, I have to recognize that Shura demonstrated flexibility and resilience in her understanding of our differences. She even learned to cook for me the light and spicy food I preferred. Ultimately, she abandoned her attempts to reform me and reshape me into somebody unrecognizable. She let me be. I felt grateful for this recognition of my personal needs and tastes, with the result that I curtailed my jealousy and downsized my ego. In the beginning, I was resentful about sharing Papa with both Shura and her mother, Larisa, new rivals for the attention and affection of my best friend and only parent. Yet, I was also embarrassed by the pettiness of my jealous feelings. With time and maturity, I learned to show my appreciation for the efforts of both women. Not that I didn't miss the unrestricted freedom I enjoyed before my father's marriage to Shura, but I was learning to respect other people's needs as well.

Shortly after their marriage, Papa bought our first television set, which magically appeared from the prototype production in the Soviet Union. It did not have any programming at all, only a test pattern. Everybody came to look at this miracle. Friends and neighbors lined up in the corridor in front of our apartment just to enter my parents' living/dining/bedroom, where Papa kept that TV set. When their turn came, they would stand in front of the set just to marvel at its test pattern.

To the dismay of my parents, our apartment became very busy. When, six months later, the TV station started broadcasting for several hours at night, only a couple of times per week, very few people took an interest. Presumably, their curiosity had already been exhausted by the test pattern. Then, a year later, it became popular once again when my father attached a transparent plastic screen cover consisting of three separate colors (blue, red, and green) to the TV display. This brilliant Soviet invention served to satisfy a popular quest for color programming.

Larisa, the mother of Shura with whom I was now sharing my corner, was the widow of a Hero of the Soviet Union, assassinated by the Nazis. Saveliy, her husband, was a medical doctor and the father of Shura. During the war, he saved the lives of his patients (wounded Soviet soldiers) by defending the hospital on his own against Nazi occupiers to allow the last delayed evacuation of the wounded from the hospital. The Germans captured him alive and hanged him in the public plaza. Thanks to him, most of the wounded soldiers escaped from the German Army.

In my eyes, Larisa, in her late fifties, was too old to relate to me. Also, she was the wife of a national hero, which, in my mind, made her act like *a prima donna*. She attempted to discipline me and teach me manners, but I refused to recognize her authority and behaved like a little brat. Then, one time, she told me a story that softened my resistance to her. She told me a story about a drunkard who killed her little dog while she was walking it outside on the street after she and Shura returned to a liberated Odessa following the war evacuation.

Her heroic husband had been killed, saving the lives of wounded Soviet soldiers. Her daughter, Shura, was working very long hours, and Larisa rescued a little dog (a miniature pincher) to keep her company during her long and sad hours alone in a small room they were given after the building they lived in before enemy bombs destroyed the war. One day, when she was walking her little dog along their street on her own, a drunkard confronted her with vicious insults, shouting that it was too bad the Germans and Romanians failed to kill all the Jews of Odessa, that their job was not finished because not only was she still walking on the streets of Odessa but even her Jewish dog feels that he owns the street. He knocked Larisa to the ground and seized the leash of her dog. He grabbed the little dog and smashed the dog's head against a tree. Larisa lost consciousness and was brought home by neighbors to recover, still smeared with the blood of her dead dog. The drunkard was not arrested. This is why Larisa was afraid to go outside.

Her story reminded me of how Victor had beaten me up, shouting that I was a dirty Jew and must be killed. This was the familiar story of anti-Semitism. Now, Larissa and I were on common ground. From that moment on, our relationship began to improve.

Larisa had high blood pressure and often stayed in bed, even during the daytime. It is why she needed help, and to that end, she employed Nadia, an illegal migrant from the countryside. No person in a healthy frame of mind could understand why Nadia was an illegal migrant in constant fear of arrest. The Soviet law prohibited peasants from abandoning their *kolkhoz* (collective farm). To prevent their escape from the *kolkhoz*, the state denied them internal passports. Those captured peasants would be arrested and sent to prison or a labor camp, only to return to their native kolkhoz after completing their sentence.

Nadia, a strong and good-looking young Ukrainian peasant woman in her early 20s, had not migrated from another country or region but from the nearby collective farm, a two-hour bus ride from our home. She slept on a folding cot, which would be put down beside my single bed every night. Nadia chatted with me in the evening, especially when Larisa was asleep. Her answers to my questions about her and her family situation in the *kolkhoz* utterly shocked me.

She told me that her extended family was always poor and that many of them died from hunger. They lived in a small earthen floor hut. They never had electricity, and her parents were illiterate. The two surviving children, Nadia and her little brother, could read but with difficulty. The family has always been hungry or starving. Payment for their hard work in the kolkhoz was negligible. When Nadia attended the regional school, she was forced to stay after classes to do her homework because the walk back home took several hours, and by the time she returned home from school, the daylight was gone. Without electricity, she was unable to do her homework. In bad weather, she couldn't walk to school. As a result, she did not graduate; nor could she leave her home on the farm to try to find work in a city because all members of the families of *kolkhozniks*, even the children, were forbidden to leave the *kolkhoz* by Soviet law.

To ensure that *kolkhozniks* don't escape, they have not issued identity cards or internal passports, documents available only to the officially registered residents of cities. Police always checked the streets and transport terminals for escaped *kolkhozniks*. Because the peasants lacked identity documents, they did not stand a chance to avoid the police, acquire even a badly paid temporary job, or obtain a temporary residence. Nadia was working for Larisa illegally and, if caught, would be arrested. She was frightened of the police. She had no rights of any kind. She was an illegal migrant even though she was Ukrainian-born and was living in her own country.

I could not understand this cruelty. Who made these laws? Why were *kolkhozniks* so poor? What was the motivation to make a revolution, if not to improve *kolkhozniks'* rights and living conditions? Why were they kept as slaves or prisoners without documents? Why, if they escaped, would they be arrested, imprisoned, and then returned to *the kolkhoz* against their will? I learned in school that the Russian Tsar Alexander II abolished the slavery of serfdom in 1867. Why did the modern Soviet State find it acceptable to enforce slavery on peasants? Can it be true? What did Nadia tell me amounted to a description of inherited slavery, enforced by the Soviet State?

Before the Revolution, many peasants were extremely poor (as we read in school in the short stories of Chekhov), but at least they were free to migrate to the cities. Wasn't the Russian Revolution intended to improve the lives of peasants and laborers? That being the case, why are the lives of the majority of them now worse and not better? This was very confusing. Life was very good for the bosses but not for the majority of peasants and workers. Why so? Didn't they make a revolution and create a Soviet society to get rid of this injustice? What is the Soviet system then? Has it created a new privileged ruling class?

When I expressed my confusion to my father, he answered that Nadia was living and working with us illegally, and if the police ever discovered her, all of us would be punished because by employing her, we also are breaking the law. Therefore, I should be clear that she stays with us in strict secrecy for my own good. He implored me not to mention anything about her to anyone and never again ask any kind of political questions. Never, or all of us will be punished severely! I understood his answer. It confirmed indirectly what I was thinking about the slave status of peasants and the privileges of the bosses, but it was forbidden even to question.

Shura was doing her best, trying to civilize me despite the constant criticism of her by our neighbors and the family of my deceased mother. In the act of loyalty to my father, I always took the side of my new mother, whom these jealous people slandered at every opportunity. To their credit, none of our neighbors denounced Nadia to the police. Nadia was voluntarily doing a lot of cleaning in our communal apartment and the whole building. I never heard anyone complaining about Nadia, but some of our communal neighbors often behaved resentfully towards Shura. To avoid all the wrangling and to take advantage of the warmer months, my parents would close our city apartment for the summer and move to Arcadia, a beautiful resort area high in the hills overlooking the sea, located 15 minutes from Odessa. As the widow of a Hero of the USSR, Larisa was awarded a very modest accommodation consisting of one mid-size room with a terrace on the second level of a communal house belonging to a Cooperative of Workers in Science.

The major advantage was, of course, its location in Arcadia, high above the rugged coastline of the Black Sea. The house had a small land parcel attached to the property for gardening. Life there was so beautiful that I thought that I had fallen asleep and awoke in paradise. From the early morning to the late hours of the evening, my Odessa girlfriends and I roamed along the coastline, driven by our curiosity about the newly discovered wilderness of the seacoast and its history. We ventured to dig for ancient Greek, Ottoman, or Scythian artifacts and stories of conquest. It was a beautiful and imaginative time.

In midsummer, poor Larisa had a sudden heart attack and died. She was only 60. Everybody in that period lived only until their 50s or 60s. It seemed to be normal. I could not understand how somebody who was here one day could suddenly disappear the next day. Shura, who inherited the dacha, was grieving over the death of her mother. To deflect her mind from her loss, she created vegetable and strawberry plots in our garden, which, until then, consisted only of mature fruit trees and grape and black-currant bushes. My parents and I worked together in our garden on weekends. On weekdays, when my parents went to work in the city, I was assigned gardening tasks each morning. My girlfriends from Odessa (only 15 minutes ride by the tramway) would often come to distract me from this duty, and together we ate more fruits and vegetables than we harvested. We also went swimming daily at sea and stole corn we ate because we were very hungry after swimming, and we didn't have pocket money to purchase any food.

Coast of Arcadia, where Larisa had her summer dacha

I don't know how my parents tolerated all our abuses. Despite my repeated disobedience, they were patient with me and kind to my reckless friends. My only complaint at this time was that they categorically refused to buy me a bicycle. That's because they understood that if I had one, I would venture too far afield. They said, "You would disappear to the moon." We had a few possessions but did not feel their absence. I had only one pair of sandals, one dress, and one uniform for school, but I didn't mind because most of my friends were in the same situation.

The bicycle was very important to me since I always dreamed of traveling far away along the seacoast. Unfortunately, this dream was never realized. My parents also used other excuses to keep me close to home; for example, a bicycle was just too expensive. Despite the absence of a bicycle, I felt very fortunate to be able to swim and dive into the refreshing, salty paradise of the Black Sea. I loved the sea breeze, which was always present on our terrace. Sometimes, feeling highly energized by the strong sea smell of iodine delivered by the wind, especially after rain, I would fantasize about life aboard a ship. I also loved the smells from the jasmine and rose bushes surrounding our dacha. The ever-present musical rhythms of the sea waves soothed my nerves and brought tranquil and healthy sleep in the evening.

Fishing and swimming at the Arcadia cliffs

In midsummer, poor Larisa had a sudden heart attack and died. She was only 60. Everybody in that period lived only until their 50s or 60s. It seemed to be normal. I could not understand how somebody who was here one day could suddenly disappear the next day. Shura, who inherited the dacha, was grieving over the death of her mother. To deflect her mind from her loss, she created vegetable and strawberry plots in our garden, which, until then, consisted only of mature fruit trees and grape and black-currant bushes. My parents and I worked together in our garden on weekends. On weekdays, when my parents went to work in the city, I was assigned gardening tasks each morning. My girlfriends from Odessa (only 15 minutes ride by the tramway) would often come to distract me from this duty, and together we ate more fruits and vegetables than we harvested. We also went swimming daily at sea and stole corn we ate because we were very hungry after swimming, and we didn't have pocket money to purchase any food.

I don't know how my parents tolerated all our abuses. Despite my repeated disobedience, they were patient with me and kind to my reckless friends. My only complaint at this time was that they categorically refused to buy me a bicycle. That's because they understood that if I had one, I would venture too far afield. They said, "You would disappear to the moon." We had a few possessions but did not feel their absence. I had only one pair of sandals, one dress, and one uniform for school, but I didn't mind because most of my friends were in the same situation.

The bicycle was very important to me since I always dreamed of traveling far away along the seacoast. Unfortunately, this dream was never realized. My parents also used other excuses to keep me close to home; for example, a bicycle was just too expensive. Despite the absence of a bicycle, I felt very fortunate to be able to swim and dive into the refreshing, salty paradise of the Black Sea. I loved the sea breeze, which was always present on our terrace. Sometimes, feeling highly energized by the strong sea smell of iodine delivered by the wind, especially after rain, I would fantasize about life aboard a ship. I also loved the smells from the jasmine and rose bushes surrounding our dacha. The ever-present musical rhythms of the sea waves soothed my nerves and brought tranquil and healthy sleep in the evening.

Every day was an adventure. The mornings brought happy anticipation to seeing my school girlfriends, who came to visit me almost daily. The most exciting past time was our coastal hiking expeditions. The coast was dotted with ruins of ancient Greek settlements known as Olbia, where my friends and I would hike. We lived out our youthful fantasies among the abandoned archaeological sites by staging ancient Greek plays and other theatrical games of our own unique production.

We explored the city's dangerous catacomb network built over the years by sea pirates, contraband traders, and notorious criminal groups. The Odessan resistance defenders (partisans) hid in the catacombs during their fight with the enemy invaders. These catacombs run under all downtown streets across the city and lead to the coastline.

Odessan catacomb

At the end of summer, when we returned to Odessa, my father took me to fencing classes, which I particularly enjoyed. I became enthusiastic and competitive in training in my age group. I practiced with the foil for one hour every day in the Vorontsov Palace fencing school. I began winning all regional competitions in the middle school group.

Then, one night, my trainer told me to wait for him, and he would take me home after the end of the fencing class. I idolized him because he was already famous for fencing in his early 20s, and I was fanatical about fencing. On our way home, he asked me to sit with him on the bench in the park because he wanted to explain to me something very important. He said that he was interested in dating me, but it had to be done in secret from everybody because I was only a child (I was14 at the time), and he was my official fencing trainer.

I was surprised and deeply insulted. I

understood that he does not care about me as a fencer, only as a female attraction. This was not how I wanted to be perceived by people, especially those I needed to trust. By their example, my parents were instilling in me the values of hard work and high academic achievements, which I assumed were important for a young person, regardless of gender. Shura was my only female role model, and I wanted people to take an interest in me for my achievements and merits, for my intelligence and athletic physical abilities, to which end I was willing to work hard to get good results.

My fencing trainer, however, demonstrated more interest in my growing body than in my talents. This was a blow to my self-image. It disillusioned me and destroyed my enthusiasm for fencing and tarnished my self-respect. I felt so sad that I started to cry and could not stop crying, tears washing my face. I was speechless. He attempted to calm me down, but he made it worse until I found the strength to stand up and run away with my face all wet from tears.

He probably did not follow me. I don't know. I never looked back. When I came home, I could not bring myself to tell my father or anybody else what happened to me. I simply never again went to the fence, and I explained it as losing interest in fencing, being busy with schoolwork, and so on. But deep inside, I felt hurt and despondent because I loved fencing and wanted to be recognized for it. At the same time, I secretly felt guilty for abandoning my trainer.

Like any other normal teenager, I was also curious about human sexuality. I knew all about the romantic side of relationships because they were an integral part of our culture. What I did not know about relationships was the sexual side. I knew a woman's body wherein the secret must be guarded and where men and boys shall not see. But now, I was already menstruating and still had no idea how sex is executed, and even less how children are made. Neither I nor any of my friends had observed anyone doing it, not even animals, because we were city girls in conservative Soviet society. The prospect of sex also seemed to be intimidating and scary.

When my close girlfriends and I asked Shura to enlighten us on this subject, she laughed and said, "This type of high math will be easily mastered by all of us when it is the right time and place. Now, we have more pressing issues and do not need to know about it yet; instead, we shall worry about our schoolwork."

That was it. But for the time being, I was hoping to learn more from the great adventures and romantic relationships described in the exciting library books of French and other European writers. During those years, books published in the Soviet Union were screened for political and moral content, but the classics were admitted. Those on which I could get my hands were probably quite puritanical. This was a confusing time in my life. All of us were socialized at home and in school with assertive female role models. However, any information about sex was non-existent. How we were to square this puritanical lifestyle with the provision of babies was a mystery to all of us, which no one bothered to explain.

Shortly after the death of Larisa, her maid Nadia announced that she was leaving to become married to a sailor. Now, I had my corner of the room in our Odessa apartment all to myself. It wasn't much space: crowded with my single bed serving as a sofa during the day, a small desk with a bookshelf, and an antique mirrored wardrobe where the whole family kept their belongings. To me, my tiny, liberated room became incredibly important because I learned to appreciate my privacy. My Pioneer projects often became home-based: receiving younger children for volunteer tutoring at home and writing letters to a girl at an East German school as part of the correspondence school program, which helped practice and develop foreign language abilities and cultural understanding.

I was content with my situation: loved by my parents, treated kindly by our neighbors and by the parents of my girlfriends, doing well in school, and dreaming of becoming a sea captain when I grew up. I also valued my volunteer work as a young Pioneer, enjoyed my art classes, and felt free to do anything after school I wanted because all of the city's services and facilities were free to the public. For each program, students were accepted on the merits of their talent. The sky appeared to have no limit for young dreamers. I was confident that Odessa was the best place on earth to be born and that I was a very lucky girl.

9. The Proletarian Handbook for Success

Suddenly, in the early spring of 1958, before we graduated from grade 7 in middle school, our carefree youthful existence was rudely interrupted by a government announcement of school reform. The Soviet government decided to extend our academic program for an additional year (from 10 to 11). More ominously, the government would also introduce an additional grade 8 into an obligatory middle school education, which consisted previously of 7 grades. This grade 8 could be considered a total waste because it was dedicated to the dreaded Komsomol political brainwashing.

The rationale for reform was that Soviet students were graduating from middle schools lacking 'communist ethics'. The reform took place because the current educational system was blamed for the insufficient political education of youth: *Many young people from the age of fourteen who were allowed to enter the workforce after grade seven proved to be undisciplined, lacking the political instructions and proletarian conscience required by real-life needs.* We interpreted the wording of this reform to mean that strong pressure will be exerted on us to become members of Komsomol, and the whole year of grade 8 will be squandered on the political indoctrination of Komsomol youth.

The pressure to join Komsomol would normally start in high school at the age of 15. Approaching our graduation from grade 7, we were all expected to attend a Komsomol assembly meeting at which we were informed of the procedure of Komsomol enrollment for those students who would attend the next grade in our school. I figured out that this new political campaign to enroll all young Pioneer students in grade 8 would threaten my small freedoms. Our country once again was experiencing an economic downfall, this time, because it began to release masses of Gulag prisoners - now deemed innocent victims of Stalinist terror - who were officially exonerated by the Soviet government in 1958.

According to our new leadership headed by Nikita Khrushchev, the country needed a fresh, young, able-bodied workforce to replace the unproductive incarcerated slaves to develop the resources in the Far Eastern regions called Virgin Lands. This geographical region was well known for its extremely harsh climate, remoteness, totally undeveloped infrastructure, and infertile desert soil. The first pioneers to open up these Virgin Lands were the prisoners of the Gulag; now, they had to be assisted by masses of young people sent by the Komsomol. These youth were persuaded to interrupt their studies under the pretense of patriotic enthusiasm for developing the Virgin Lands, but the majority of these young people knew the truth and would invent all kinds of illnesses and handicaps, permitting them to stay home.

Compared to the Young Pioneers, Komsomol (for youth between the ages of 15 and 28) was altogether a very different species. It assumed an almost military discipline of membership on direct orders of the Communist Party, involving Communist Party assignments and responsibilities on all matters affecting political, social, and even private lives. There were 40 million young people enrolled in the Komsomol in my generation. The official propaganda pretended that young people joined the Komsomol voluntarily. In real life, everyone was aware that it was a requirement for the continuation of high school and college studies. However, I was keenly aware of its dangerous disadvantages, such as an obligation to comply with the orders of Komsomol superiors, including orders to inform friends and relatives.

Komsomol controlled all education but was responsible for nothing, creating a perfect future for *Homo Sovieticos*, the passive and obedient Soviet creature, which we called Sovki in Russian slang.[64] If the Komsomol organization of a school or college voted to volunteer for work in the Virgin Lands, everybody had to drop their studies or work and allow themselves to be transported to the middle of nowhere in conditions that seriously endangered their health and resulted in thousands of ruined lives and untimely deaths. It was a completely wasteful exercise because the urban youth have often been helpless - lacking proper tools, skills, housing, and nutrition - particularly in the agricultural opening of the Virgin Lands. Many contracted serious illnesses from which not a few died.

After my childhood trauma over how I was tricked into informing on my father and under the influence of my politically skeptical parents, I developed a strong distaste for all political instructions, an antibody against political manipulations. It was as if I had been vaccinated against political engineering at the age of seven. It was the case of my teacher deceiving me to obtain compromising information about my father. At our school, we were ordered to describe the discussions of our parents at home regarding the alleged Doctors' Plot in front of our class. My misguided report on my father's commentaries almost got him and Shura imprisoned. After my father had explained to me how dangerously I had been deceived, I learned to be vigilant in my observations, independent in my thinking, and secretive with my opinions.

The situation, however, was very different for the members of Komsomol of the members of the Communist Party. Members of Komsomol of the Communist Party were obliged to report perceived wrongdoing. Those who refused were committing a serious crime. I was revolted by the idea that all young people over the age of fifteen have been forced to attend long and boring brainwashing Komsomol meetings after classes. The kids who attended those meetings told me that the Komsomol discipline required absolute obedience to the orders of the Communist Party even when those orders were completely idiotic. I decided for myself that I would avoid joining the army of young *Homo*

Sovieticos at any cost. To that end, I needed to find a loophole in the educational system. I needed an escape from this trap before it was too late. Yes, I wanted to continue studying in high school, but only if I could avoid the brainwashing as well as the menacing and unethical obligations.

Additionally, under the new rules, it was virtually impossible for a young girl with my ethnic background, straight out of school, to obtain admission to the university, even if I became a member of Komsomol. To be admitted for the entrance exams at university, apart from Komsomol, the candidate was required to have two years of labor experience after school and a proletarian family history (for which my parents, working as engineers, were not qualified).

My Jewish ethnicity also automatically reduced me to a status of "undesirable for the university," blocked by strict quotas limiting the admission of Jewish students. All those who satisfied the acceptable conditions (non-Jewish ethnicity and two years of post-high school experience) still needed a recommendation from the Komsomol organization of the candidate's labor unit and a recommendation from a Communist Party organization from the workplace of their parents. A prohibitive screening regimen!

The KGB agents attached to the universities would screen all applications for the entrance examinations. They would disqualify all those they suspected of lacking the essential political merits, including the correct ethnicity. Everybody knew that Jews were prohibited from entering various prestigious academic institutions, even though no Soviet law supported this discriminatory practice. It was done simply on Party instructions. There was, nevertheless, a narrow quota gateway (2%) for acceptance of exceptionally gifted Jewish students in some less important provincial universities or colleges in careers related to food, agricultural, or service industries; of course, always on conditions that the Komsomol recommended them, and the KGB approved. However, I was not interested in those careers. As a child, I wanted to be a marine captain like Papa. Though he told me that this was not possible, the best I could do was marry a captain. Still, I continued to dream, at least, of a career in the marine field. To my mind, there could not be an alternative.

My close girlfriends and I spent long hours inventing scenarios and arguing about different solutions to avoid the Komsomol meat grinder. Some of our propositions were completely impractical, such as hiding in the countryside; other ideas had more realistic prospects. Finally, we agreed upon one solution, which presented a good compromise for the continuation of our schooling, but outside of the standard educational system. After graduation from grade 7, the plan was that we simply quit our school and join the municipal workforce, initially to learn a skilled trade as apprentices and, after that, become skilled workers. At the same time, we would apply to "The Night

School for Working Youth" to continue our education. The Night School for Working Youth did not have a reputation as a strong academic institution. Nevertheless, it permitted students to carry on with the same ten-grade program, which continued at night school just as before the educational reform. That is because its aim was mainly to improve the educational level of adult workers and not to politicize the youth.

This is why, upon completion of grade 7, four of my closest girlfriends and I decided to leave our school and seek employment with an authentic proletarian labor brigade in the city. It seemed to us that this was the best way to outsmart the system and save at least three precious years of our time before we were allowed to take the university entrance exams.[65]

In 1958, the four of us went to the city's municipal office seeking the city's labor employment vacancies, which adults did not want because of low pay. My friends were already 14 years old and, therefore, they had a legal right to become employed (Soviet law permitted formal employment as an apprentice starting at the age of 14). In the municipal office, we were told that after graduation from grade 7, we had to bring written consent from our parents. The city could offer us employment as apprentices in any industrial sector where and when a job would become available, but the pay would be very modest.

Shortly after grade 7 graduation, I turned 14, and later that summer, my friends and I, secretly from our parents, went to the municipal administration office to apply for apprenticeships. The city office offered us a chance to learn various skills in different industries. I selected an apprenticeship as a bricklayer at one of the Odessa municipal construction brigades because their current construction site was near my apartment. My girlfriends preferred apprentice positions in the retail textile trade. They were very surprised by my choice.

Paulina, 7th-grade graduation

"What a stupid job choice you made," they told me. "Wouldn't you rather stay inside a nice fabric store that offers an opportunity to steal cuts for a dress?" No, I was not interested in textiles, and that decision shaped my future career.[66]

I needed the permission of my father. My most challenging task was to convince him that this would be the right move. After our long argument about it, he surprised me with a story that I could never forget in a lifetime:

"My dearest little one, there is nothing of value that I could leave for you when I die; nothing, except to share with you my experience in survival. Remember, I told you how in 1920, drunken looters killed my parents during a pogrom? It happened that the Russian employees of my mother hid me, my small brother, and my sister in a village near Odessa. I was twelve years old; my brother was seven, and our sister was five. The family in the village who allowed us to stay with them expected me to work on municipal road construction in place of their son, who would rather help his father in the fields. The state required peasant families to contribute one member each toward local road construction.

My job was very hard, digging the earth from sunrise to dusk every day. I could not imagine a worse kind of work in this world. But I persisted in that job, and it brought us a surprisingly good fortune that I never expected. I had to walk every day to the road construction site. In this period, civil war and famine were ravaging the country. There were checkpoints everywhere on the roads of the countryside. The revolutionary guards, drawn from every walk of life, were often simply bandits and looters. Still, they were in charge of screening all passersby for their class affiliation. This was how our new chaotic society divided itself: only by social class. All the Russian people were divided simply into only two classes.

"The divisions were not about rich or poor or about Russian and non-Russian. The new divisions were the working class, who were allowed to pass, and the bourgeoisie, who were arrested. Those who were arrested were sent, without a hearing, to be shot or to concentration camps where they were decimated by starvation and illness. The revolutionary guards at the checkpoints were illiterate, and they did not trust the documents of the passing people. Their only criterion for class judgment were the calluses on the palms of people's hands. They demanded that everybody show the palms of their hands. If their palms were covered, like mine, in calluses, they could pass thanks to my job of digging the earth; they could pass. They were even given some bread, which was removed from those who were arrested because they did not have calluses on their palms. I was fortunate; not only did I pass freely every day by just holding open the palms of my hands, but I was also often given some bread that I could share at night back in the village with my sister and brother. Many people died from famine in those years, but we survived, thanks to the calluses on the palms of my hands. It is why nobody ever knows what will allow him to survive; so, I must not stand in your way, but help you if I can, always on one condition: if the work becomes too hard or too unbearable, you will leave."

I knew that the municipal administration of the city was not my father's area of work influence. Neither he nor Shura was a member of the Communist Party. His connections were mostly in the field of marine transportation and port operations. Even if my father wanted to corrupt somebody in the municipal construction company, he would need much more money than my parents had. They always told me that they did not have any savings because, despite their merits, they were not promoted any further in their careers for two important reasons: Jewish background and no affiliation with the Communist Party. Neither did they belong to the commercially savvy and corrupt '*apparatchiks*' (bureaucrats) or the politically powerful '*nomenklatura*' (ruling class created by Stalin).[67] It was clear to me that I should accept my father's conditions, but should not count on him. I knew that my parents' salaries were modest, and they did not steal, like many others, who enjoyed the correct ethnicity and the protection of Party membership.

At the municipal construction company Number 8, where I was sent to work, my coworkers (the adult bricklayers) bossed me around because I was just a kid. I accepted the punishment because I understood that, being the youngest, I was to be beaten up by the 'old dogs' (who were often drunk during work).

Despite their friendly verbal or physical abuse, I was never offended. I was so anxious to become accepted on the day of my initial salary; I permitted them to buy vodka with the first money I earned. They insisted that I join them in raising a toast with a full glass of vodka. Never before in my life had I tried to drink alcohol. It smelled revolting. Seeing my hesitation, they told me that I should upend the whole glass of vodka without stopping; otherwise, I would never learn. Anxious to prove to them that I could become a member of the brigade, I overpowered my natural resistance and threw the whole glass of this awful liquid fire into my throat. After that, the floor under my legs caved in, and I fell unconscious. I assume they carried me to my home, where I awoke only late at night after my parents returned from work. I could not remember how I landed at home. My repulsion toward alcohol began at that moment. Now, I knew that I could not pass the vodka test (by which, presumably, all Russian boys qualify for manhood). The next time we were paid our salaries, I gave them my salary for the vodka, but categorically refused to drink vodka myself. They decided to forgive me since they, too, were frightened of my reaction. Still, they insisted that I smoke with them a *papirosa*, a Russian cigarette made with strong tobacco designed to kill a horse. I learned to do it to please them, even though these stinky and primitive cigarettes made me choke. Of course, my parents never learned about this side of my apprenticeship. I spoke to them only about my progress with my working skills and how well I had adjusted socially to my brigade.

I learned to mix the appropriate mortar for different jobs, to carry it without spilling it, not to harm anyone while doing it, to climb construction scaffolds carrying large concrete blocks (one at a time) in my hands, and to lay straight walls neatly and without squeezing or dropping mortar. My workday would start at seven o'clock in the morning and finish between four and five in the afternoon at the open-air construction site regardless of weather conditions, including winter cold with snow. Every night after work from seven to ten-thirty in the evening, I attended the "Number 12 Working Youth Night School" for the full three years until my graduation from the 10th grade.

It was tough not to fall asleep during the night school classes after the daily hard physical labor exposed to the elements, but I was a stubborn kid who decided to beat the system. I did not complain about working conditions to my father, except just once at the beginning, but only on the condition that he would permit me to continue this experiment. I never even complained to my father about the verbal abuse I had to put up with. My co-workers were ordering me around and calling me *Koziavka* (shrimp), which offended my sense of dignity and conditioned me for the rest of my life. I never again wanted to be demeaned with epithets such as *Koziavka.* To that end, I was willing to work very hard and strive to be respected for my work.

Our municipal construction workers' organization was established to employ adults, but not adolescents. Bricklayers were an aging group because it was a job shunned by young people. As a result, they had no local Komsomol, only a traditional Communist Party for adults. It is how I managed not to fit into their setup. The Working Youth Night School Number 12 was responsible only for the delivery of academic high school programs; political matters were the responsibility of the working organizations within each industry.

Paulina at 16 with her friends above Odessa port

Lucky me, once again. Not only did I avoid Komsomol, but I also benefited by obtaining permission to take university entrance exams because I was the chosen delegate from my municipal construction company to qualify for the educational upgrade at the university. It meant that, despite being Jewish, I was permitted to take exams at university. In contrast, graduates of Jewish descent from traditional high schools were not accepted at all, not even for entrance exams at prestigious universities, unless they were exceptional.

Since I did not consider myself a genius, my tactics were aimed at becoming an exceptional worker. This exceptional rule consisted of the requirement for state universities to respond to petitions from the Communist Party organizations of any authentic proletarian labor company (like my municipal construction company). The Communist organization of the Municipal Construction Company Number 8 requested that I be accepted to take entrance exams at the University of my choice on the grounds of being their best young bricklayer.

This is how, in 1961, I was permitted to hold

exams at the National Marine University, from where I graduated in 1967 as an engineer in the Faculty of Coastal and Offshore Engineering. The competition was strong: 50 student candidates competed for each place, but I managed to do well on the exams and was accepted.

The Komsomol organization at the Marine University tried to force me to join a good number of times. I always promised to do so at a future date when I become more proficient in my studies, because that was my first responsibility as a nominee of the Communist Party of my construction company.

Our Komsomol leaders at the university were not stupid, and they knew that my answers about Komsomol were not sincere, but they were busy with their own academic programs at the university, and my responses were satisfactory from a bureaucratic point of view.

I felt triumphant and clever to be able to circumvent the enrollment expectations with these political organizations without causing any harm to myself and my family. So, taking the circuitous academic route of a construction worker, I managed to stay clear of political responsibilities, but at the price of missing my normal adolescence.

This is why, as soon as I was accepted at the university, I felt like a prisoner thrown out of jail. I was eager to investigate the world outside my cell and to discover whether I could be attractive to boys.

Paulina in front of the State Marine University of Odessa in 2011

I lacked confidence in this area and was very shy at the beginning. But the student body of our university was largely male (in my faculty, the ratio of women to men was 1/50), and, naturally, I soon enjoyed some contenders and developed a friendship with two nice boys from my faculty: Vanechka and Sasha. Both my new friends were well-received by my parents.

The parents of Vanechka knew my family well. Vanechka Romanov was a typical good-looking Russian prince, tall and well-built on the heavy side with blond hair and blue eyes. Intelligent, well-read, elegantly dressed, soft, polite, and considerate, with a gorgeous deep baritone voice, he came from a very good family of important intellectuals in the city. Vanechka frequented our home and deeply impressed my parents. Papa gave me his recommendation to consider Vanechka as a boyfriend since he was half Jewish. Despite all these sublime affirmations, I rebelled against the prospect. I felt the high status of his parents was too rarefied for my rough-and-tumble life. I also believed that he was over-protected by his parents. For whatever reason, I was romantically indifferent to him. I would enjoy him as a friend or a brother, but I could not feel the spark that ignites a friendship into a romance. When he asked me for a date, I turned him down.

Sasha was different. He was slim and very shy with a handsome, sensitive face, which made me seek his friendship. However, when he suggested more than friendship, I had to act cruelly towards this sweet boy simply because I was not physically attracted to him. He was a single child of a single mother. His father died from illness while Sasha was young. His hardworking mother was also, in my view, overprotective of him, and this was the reason for his shyness. Both boys - Vanechka and Sasha - were quite good-looking but too docile and obedient for my taste. Both were Odessan Russian boys who graduated from day high schools and were members of Komsomol. They were safe conformists while I was a closet rebel. Our friendships were terminated when I excused myself in a clumsy and embarrassing fashion following their timid invitations to date. I had no alternative because after becoming familiar with the passive characters of these boys, I could not feel attracted to either of them. They were good friends but, but romantically, they bored me. I sent them both packing without even experimenting with a first kiss.

Then I was punished for my arrogance when I met with handsome Emlise Guriev, a third-year Azerbaijani student from our University. After a couple of months of dancing dates at University parties, both of us believed we were in love. Then one day, he told me that he spoke to his parents about me, and his parents forbade him from seeing me again. I was shocked and asked why. He could not explain; he just said that he believes his parents want him to marry somebody local. I was hurt and went home crying. I told my parents all about Emlise. Instead of feeling sorry for me, they were relieved. They said: "This *goyishe* (not Jewish) boy must have been a Muslim."

I tried to argue with them, saying: "Nobody in the Soviet Union has a religion any longer; if we don't have religion, if nobody I ever met has a religion, if religion is prohibited, and if those who secretly practice religion could get arrested, then it does not seem logical that his parents should prohibit him from seeing me only because they are religious and we are not." My parents told me to smarten up. Papa concluded: "Even if the family of Emlise did not practice any religion, they still would not like their son to fall in love with a Jewish girl because the ethnicity of Jews is considered undesirable in our country."

"You are *meshugah* (crazy) to fool around with boys, especially from Azerbaijan, outside of our circles. It would be better if you first finish your studies at the university and only then start to worry about your boyfriends. I will introduce you to the best young Russian engineers from our Black Sea Institute. These will be the boys that are right for you to marry, and we shall all be happy that your Azerbaijani was forbidden by his parents to date you," said Shura.

Still, I could not understand why Emlise took the prohibition of his parents to heart. If both of us were falling in love, how could his parents dictate to him what to do with his girlfriend? I was emotionally bruised and insulted. Then, I understood it was very simple: Emlise was also the obedient and over-protected son, a typical *Homo Sovieticus*! That was the end of this story.

My university course contained many new subjects which I enjoyed. I thought of our professors as experienced and knowledgeable. They tried hard to interest us in science and technical subjects, which I loved. As usual, I disliked "political" subjects, which, unfortunately, formed a large part of our obligatory early curriculum.[68] I especially detested these ideological subjects and used my traditional tactics to dream up escape routes or to do something else instead of listening to the professor. Finally, I failed miserably in the exams for Marxist-Leninist Communist philosophy. I caused a very embarrassing incident when I stood up to hand my exam paper to the professor, and the manual fell to the floor from under my skirt. I was incredibly fortunate that the professor forgave me. He could have expelled me from university permanently for such an outrageous crime. The hard science subjects, especially technical ones, were enjoyable and stimulating.

Most of our professors were skillful teachers. I always rushed to occupy the front desk in order not to miss a word from them. All that said, I learned most when in practical terms, I had to face real-life construction problems in our field and search for and implement solutions to these problems. Eventually, I became recognized as a good student.

10. Destiny's Prince

Training in Cuba | Eduardo, student in Odessa, 1960 | Visiting Moscow

Eduardo - my destiny Prince

The omen was there from the beginning. I had lived my entire life thus far on the street called Havannaya. In English, this name means it belongs to Havana, translated to Russian as a harbor. Then, what a stroke of fate that I should meet and marry my first serious romantic partner, a young man from the City of Havana. I had never even been out of Odessa, not to mention the USSR; so, what were the chances? Providence, destiny, call it what you will. Of course, my heart was seeking an alternative to the local male variety. I was disillusioned with the Soviet type of boys, with their nearly robotic obedience to the authorities. Weren't we Odessans, the rugged, rebellious survivors? The *Sovki* or *Homo Sovieticos* did not appeal to my romantic imagination. I was left to cherish the enchanting dreams of a different kind of man who would be independent, adventurous, and determined. This was how I thought of Eduardo, a student at my university in the Faculty of Naval Engineering.

For a young woman on the lookout for a mate, the Marine University of Odessa was a happy hunting ground with a gender gap that was off the charts. The university had five faculties, three of which had some female students, while the other two had none. Only one faculty, Transportation Management, was especially popular among women, and Shura, my stepmother, was a graduate of this faculty. The Ship Mechanics Faculty and the Faculty of Naval Engineering were less popular with female students; in Mechanical, there were none, and in Naval Engineering (Shipbuilding), only one female student. My Coastal and Offshore Engineering Faculty, consisting of about two hundred students, had only four females.

Our meeting could not have been better scripted by a dating service. The year was 1963, and our university was ordered to conduct a “Cultural Solidarity” event with Cuba. Five Cuban students were asked to assist with presentations. The national Soviet KGB was headed then by Alexander Shelepin, former chief of the Soviet national Komsomol. Many Komsomol leaders were promoted at that time into the KGB. Komsomol also had unrestricted power to monitor and control the activities of all Soviet students, especially among those groups, which included foreign students. Komsomol sometimes met with me to invite me to participate in their trips to Moscow or Leningrad, during which they sponsored all costs of transport, accommodation, and cultural programs. These organized trips (or traps) never interested me, and I always found excuses, accompanied by profuse apologies, to avoid these invitations. Some of the students who went on these trips told me that they were given a good time to seduce them with the added promise of attending the Higher Party School (VSP), after which their careers would skyrocket -but at the cost of collaboration with the KGB. They would tell me that by seeking excuses, I was endangering my career.

The opportunity to do something for Komsomol presented itself when Komsomol organizers picked up a few students from different faculties to form a dancing group that was supposed to be composed of volunteers. Eduardo was giving this group dance instruction to provide a musical contribution to the "political theater" addressing Soviet solidarity with the Cuban Revolution. The Komsomol representative approached me with a request to volunteer for dancing because the dancing group lacked female participants from the university, which had so few female students. I liked the idea since it was convenient to do something for Komsomol, which I might even enjoy while avoiding getting entangled in more serious commitments with them. It could be an easy "credit" for me with Komsomol and less politically boring than usual. This is how I was introduced to Eduardo, a student from Cuba. We spent a week or two practicing Cuban dance movements. At the end of it and during the event itself, when I danced with Eduardo on stage, I felt inadequate and clumsy; there was no comparison of my movements with his. When, afterward, behind the stage, he asked me what I thought of our dancing, I replied how embarrassed I felt about my awkward performance. He asked me to meet with him again to learn more about Cuban dancing.

Odessa, at the start of the 1960s, was unfamiliar with modern Western music. The best was our wonderful Odessan music leftover from the period of NEP (New Economic Policy).[69] It was fun decades ago, but quite outdated for the mid-sixties. Unlike my father, I had an aversion to Soviet popular music with its false patriotic sentimentality. Mariners may have brought some swing and popular American jazz to the city, but its influence was isolated, and I was unacquainted with such new trends, including rock and roll. All my time was spent at the university, and most of the foreign students there were from developing countries who shared the Soviet antipathy toward popular Western English-language music, which they regarded as a product of decadent capitalism.

Ignorant of Western pop music, I was enthralled and fascinated with the Cuban popular music that Eduardo brought on LP vinyl records. The music had a fresh, rich, and free melodic sound. The dance movements were exotic and very sexy. My imagination went mad. My clumsiness on the dance floor was largely due to the crush I developed for

Eduardo. I was very attracted to this 19-year-old, middle-class Cuban who danced brilliantly and had the exciting experience and romantic aura of the Cuban Revolution in which he participated while still only a high school student. There was only one problem with him. I heard from Natasha, one of my girlfriends from the city, that she was dating Eduardo. Unwilling to betray a valued friendship, I spoke to her honestly about my liking of Eduardo and asked for her opinion. Natasha reacted generously and said that she would set up a meeting in her communal apartment for the three of us to allow her to observe Eduardo's reactions when both of us were present.

Eduardo was invited by Natasha to come over. He had no idea that we had conspired to set up this meeting. When I arrived as well, he was under the impression that my visit was coincidental. We chatted about dancing and drank tea with biscuits. Shortly, Eduardo stood up to leave, probably because he felt ill at ease, and excused himself on some rather banal pretext. After he had left, Natasha said that she could see that Eduardo was embarrassed. She reacted generously to me by suggesting we leave this matter entirely up to Eduardo and me to decide. Thanks to our frankness, we remained the best of friends for years after this incident.

The next time, when I met Eduardo at the University (both of us were in the second year of our five-year program), he asked me out again, and I agreed. We started meeting outside of our university, trying to learn about each other as much as possible. He assured me that he was not a communist nor, in general, was the Cuban Revolution, which he described as a national-democratic liberation movement. Eduardo did not like politics and preferred to become a professional engineer rather than a politician. His political stance (libertarian) at the time was similar to mine. He never, in the course of his life, joined any Cuban political organizations despite the pressures.

I found Eduardo stimulating, romantic, exotic, and good-looking; he was fair-skinned, of slim build, with softly curled light brown hair. He was happy in character, enthusiastic, and idealistic. He was also quiet, introverted, and soft-spoken, qualities that did not prevent him from expressing his affection for me. I was impressed by his modesty and moderation, including his abstinence from alcohol, which was a very serious problem among young men in the Soviet Union. When my university friends, probably jealous of Eduardo, asked me why I preferred a slim and modest Spanish boy when we had so many tall and strong athletic Russian students, I answered that if height and mass were my criteria, I would rather choose an elephant.

In retrospect, my sarcastic answer reflected the inadequacy of a growing Jewish girl with a Semitic complexion in a Slavic society where the icons of beauty are blue eyes and rosy, white skin covering large-framed, thicker-boned women. My self-image was of the alien stranger in an imaginary beauty contest in Russian society. Yet, I found local boys unappealing. They lacked individuality and higher aspirations. Too often, they were driven into an alcoholic stupor seeking to escape from our repressive culture.

Throughout Russian history, from the time of Tsar Ivan the Terrible, alcohol was an instrument of despotic governments designed to suppress rebellious leanings by corrupting the masses. After centuries, alcoholism became an inherited national addiction. Before the revolution, some of the religions practiced in Russia - particularly Islam and Judaism - protected their followers from alcoholic indulgence through forbiddance or social restraint. However, after the new Soviet government declared all religions to be dead, other ethnic groups also became seriously infected. For example, in our communal apartment, composed entirely of Jews, the young husband of Bella (Annushka's sister) and Fimka (the brother of Annushka) were often drunk. Both of them later met their early deaths in drunken fights. However, their alcoholism could be blamed not on ethnic origins but rather on Soviet culture.

Looking back and reflecting on the conditions of their existence (three generations of their family: 6 adults and a baby – all lived in one room of our communal apartment), anyone could understand their frustration. Though, interestingly, none of their women became alcoholics. Later, Annushka married a handsome Russian director of a large food processing plant where she was working as an engineer. Unfortunately, her husband had a terrible car accident while driving drunk and became completely paralyzed for the rest of his life. Annushka had to care for him and their son, and work as a cleaning lady in the building where she lived to be available to her family 24 hours a day. This was such a tragedy for a young woman who studied hard, lived righteously, and kept a bright outlook on life, whatever the circumstances. I detested the weakness of alcohol along with its tradition of escapism. This vulnerability was a serious flaw in the character of local boys.

Eduardo impressed me as a free spirit. By contrast, young Soviet men (independent of their ethnicity) are often overprotected by their mothers and socially conditioned to alcohol as a traditional test of their manhood. Soviet men often assaulted and humiliated their wives out of frustration and a habit of expressing despair through drunken violence. The custom was so ingrained that Russian women have a saying: "If you don't beat me, you don't love me." Soviet men, commonly born into single-child families, were often spoiled and immature, unable to deal with anger and frustration creatively and confidently. I witnessed such male behavior everywhere and at all levels, from the stevedores in the Port of Odessa (like Bella's husband) to the doctoral candidates in our student residence.

My papa was different. He would never raise his voice to a woman or threaten her. However, he had a very different attitude towards male delinquents, and I observed him personally expelling the drunks from our building and, if necessary, knocking them down and carrying them away. He told me that to avoid disappointment, I should marry a Jewish boy in preference to any other ethnic group. Jews, he explained, don't beat their wives. I was not so certain he was right. Annushka's brother and her brother-in-law both were Jews and often were drunk and vicious. I saw with my own eyes how Bella, the sister of Annushka, came one morning into the kitchen, her face black and blue and swollen. When I objected to Papa's racist comments with this example, he said, "Any family can have an anomaly. A *meshuga* (crazy person) can be born anywhere. Historically, drinking alcohol for the Jews was an anomaly. Remember before the revolution; it was forbidden by the Jewish religion while for the Slavs, historically, it was encouraged and became a common social malaise."[70] However, I still believe Papa was wrong: all of us, independent of our ethnicity, were victims of this oppressive social system and were seeking escape by one means or another.

I was frightened of my parents learning about my new boyfriend because of Eduardo's foreign nationality. Our relationship was a security "taboo" regarded as a danger in the USSR in the early 1960s. My parents spoke to me as soon as I was enrolled in the university about the importance of maintaining their reputation as reliable citizens and how I was to avoid any contact with foreigners to that end. Any contact with international students or foreign sailors arriving at the port was considered detrimental and dangerous. Those who broke this taboo would wind up on record with the KGB, depicting their immoral and suspicious for the remainder of their lives. Nor could their families ever aspire for some privileges, such as job promotions or attendance at an international event (conference) abroad or even nationally.

Eduardo was a true alien in our environment. He came to our country quite unprepared linguistically and culturally. (Later, his mother told me that his knowledge of Russia before he arrived was limited to the notion of bears roaming the country like the dogs in Cuba. Regardless, he swept me off my feet. I was two years younger than him, and in my youthful self-absorption, I could only daydream of our romance. He had many colorful and beautiful recordings of Cuban music, without which, it would appear, he could not survive. Everything about him was different: his speech, his posture, his dancing prowess. His body always moved with the music, and I felt like a tide swept me into the deep water of the Caribbean Sea. Eduardo had a very happy disposition most of the time despite the hardship of being so far away from his family and his Caribbean sun, culture, and lifestyle. He was always considerate, polite, and restrained, at least while courting me. Despite my privileged middle-class situation in Odessa, of which I and any other Soviet could be proud, Eduardo was shocked by the level of deprivation in our communal apartment. Though he never commented or complained, it was obvious that he was taken aback by the lack of elementary living conditions and hygiene, the crowded kitchen, the absence of a phone, and so on, which characterized our so-called Soviet middle-class paradise. By comparison, his life in Cuba was infinitely more comfortable as a member of the Cuban middle class whose living conditions in the 1960s were still quite American and had not yet degraded to their present level.

Russian was Eduardo's second language, and he had to pursue his professional studies with extraordinary effort, considering the complex technical terminology. In the beginning, when we started dating surreptitiously at the university or student residence, we used the pretext of my helping him with his studies. I was worried mostly about the need to keep our relationship hidden from my parents. Both of us acted as if we would lose our minds; despite the autumn season, we felt the full euphoria of spring, completely intoxicated with the happiness of shared young love.

Since dating a foreign student was not encouraged because it was considered unpatriotic, we tried to avoid being seen together at the University. The entrance to the student residence was fiercely guarded by *the babushka* (old peasant woman) at the gate to screen visitors. (She would also pass a list of all visitors to the university administration, which could get the visitors into serious trouble). To avoid harassment, we met either at my home or outside in a park while my parents were still at work most of the time. The late autumn weather in Odessa was cold, windy, and wet; we were periodically catching colds. Our meetings were always risky because one day, somebody could see us walking together on the street, or our communal neighbors might see Eduardo coming to visit me at home. Apart from that, my parents might return early from work and catch us like delinquents at a crime scene. Yes, we knew one day we would get caught. It seemed inescapable and the risk unavoidable.

Then, the inevitable happened. One afternoon, my father returned home early from his work. When I heard him opening the door with his key, I managed to hide Eduardo in the small wardrobe in my room. My father entered the apartment but did not notice anything strange except, perhaps, for my nervous appearance. He proceeded with his regular exercises (jumping and clapping hands overhead), which he was in the habit of doing after work in front of the wardrobe mirror behind which Eduardo was hiding. I almost died a couple of times when it became apparent that his jumping in front of the mirror could accidentally unhinge the wardrobe doors, and Eduardo might fall out right into the arms of my father. Happily, it did not happen. My poor father failed to notice anything. Finally, after finishing his exercises, he went shopping. I pretended to be very busy with my studies and declined his invitation to accompany him.

When my father left, I released Eduardo, who had spent over an hour hidden in the wardrobe. He did not look very good, and I was still in shock. We felt ashamed for cheating on my father. Embarrassed about our immaturity and mischievous behavior, Eduardo quickly left the apartment. The next day, when we met again, we discussed our pain from cheating my sweet and trusting Papa. We decided that it would be better to inform my parents by ourselves before anybody else told them. The guilt of letting down my parents, who were always caring and protective toward me, clearly conflicted with our romantic feelings.

In this confusion, Eduardo suggested that since we are both in love, we should marry. For such a legal union, both of us would need to request permission not only from our parents on both sides but also from both governments. In the early 1960s, such an idea would appear utopian to any Soviet with a rational mind (marriages with foreign citizens were legally prohibited), but we were in love and decided to take a chance. Eduardo told me that he would take the initiative. He proposed to come on Sunday morning when my parents will be at home and ask my father formally for my hand. I was happy but also worried about the health effects on my parents that this marriage proposal may produce (both had high blood pressure). I was afraid that they would forbid us to marry and continue romantic relations.

On Saturday, I asked my parents to stay home on Sunday morning. They demanded an explanation: “What is going on?” There was no escape for me any longer. This is how I ended up taking the first blow by myself. Both of my parents were upset with me for hiding the truth about having a boyfriend. Shura was even more upset than Papa. She demanded that I immediately break any contact with Eduardo because if I don't, our lives will be ruined: my parents will be expelled from their jobs, and I will be expelled from the university with a black mark on my records denying me any respectable future. Shura and I were crying and arguing all night. My father went "for fresh air" several times during the middle of the night. Shura was attempting with great determination to convince me that the ideal husband was any young Russian engineer who reported directly to her at the Institute. I could even choose from her selection.

In the end, they agreed to receive Eduardo the next morning, to meet with him, assess his character, and listen to what he has to say. I was terrified, imagining that they would shred Eduardo into pieces, but when he came and spoke, they didn't throw him through the window. Instead, they tried to discourage him from marriage, listing all the obstacles. Eduardo explained that we were in love, that our relationship was serious, and that if I agreed to marry him, we would be able to live together and not have to hide.

My parents objected that it is not even legally possible because of the Decree of the Presidium of the Supreme Soviet of 1947 called On Prohibiting Marriages Between Soviet Citizens and Foreigners. Eduardo said that his embassy informed him about this decree, but it had been recently revised to allow marriages in some legitimate cases with good pro-Soviet foreigners when the parents and their respective governments issue written permission for such a marriage. These revisions were not made public because the authorities arbitrarily conducted this process, and Eduardo learned about this revision of the Decree only through his diplomatic channels. Still, the special permission of the authorities for such a marriage was required.

After a whole night without sleep, my parents were so exhausted from crying and quarreling with me the previous night that they capitulated to Eduardo's charms. They tried to argue that we are only children and don't want to recognize reality. It did not matter how much we were in love and how noble our intentions were. The decision was not ours, but of the government. They explained to Eduardo how dangerous it was for them and for me to enter into a family relationship with a foreign national. It was dangerous not only for my future but also for my parents' work at the Black Sea Institute. My father informed Eduardo that he and Shura could be fired from their jobs as soon as my amorous relationship with the foreign student became known. I begged them that it was not the case because Cuba had become a Soviet satellite state, and Eduardo would never have been accepted into our University unless he was cleared by Soviet security.

All my relatives, friends, and neighbors were summoned by my father to come to talk to me, to convince me to drop my outrageous and dangerous idea and ponder the perils I am inflicting on my parents and myself by dating an international student. I was subjected to a powerful onslaught of close advisors: my uncle and my aunts (brother and sisters of my deceased mother Berta), all my cousins from both sides of the family (they were all older than me), friends and colleagues of my parents, our neighbors and their children, mothers of my girlfriends - all were summoned to visit me and to change my mind. I received them all and resisted their admonitions. I said that they were outdated, that the times had changed, that the citizens of those countries which the USSR took under its wing are no longer considered enemies, that I did not believe in their fears, and that I have decided to act according to my heart. I was young and in love, and this was the only reality. Their fears were out-of-date because they were still traumatized by Stalin's policies. The Soviet Union of today was not alone any longer but had won a whole new world of the colonies, which were now members of the Warsaw Pact. Cuba aspired to become a member of the Warsaw Pact as well. Therefore, there will be no danger to me and my parents, no threat of being classified as an enemy. I told them that they were all too old to notice the changes in the political and geographical situation of the Soviet Union.

Finally, it was Eduardo who made a fair compromise with my father that we should proceed with marriage arrangements only after a positive response from the security department in the Black Sea Institute. My father would file an inquiry with security at the Black Sea Institute regarding the feasibility of obtaining their approval for the marriage. Papa agreed to proceed with such an inquiry but only after Eduardo's superiors and the Cuban government issued a formal approval. The deal was struck, and Eduardo went to meet with his superiors at the Cuban consulate to obtain their permission first.

Eduardo was told by his counsel to write to his parents in Cuba and asked them to notarize their approval of our marriage formally. All these approvals and formalities took a good number of months, during which we both felt a bit nervous. Finally, when Eduardo received their approvals, we pressured my father again to consult with the security department of the Black Sea Institute. The security department told my father to submit the request in writing, and both my parents had to sign it. However, the answer to this request was returned only four months later and only in verbal form.

This bothered my father because it meant that he would have no evidence to demonstrate that he acted with the knowledge and approval of his security department. He felt that, in the absence of a written response from his security department, serious problems for him could be created in the future (for example, in case of the relationship between the USSR and Cuba degrades). Still, he was cautious not to nag security personnel since that might provoke only an adverse reaction. These consultations with the higher powers were a nerve-wracking exercise for all of us. There was still a possibility of approval rejection by the Soviet government because of the occupation of my parents. They could be suspected of endangering state secrets in the case of their daughter's marriage to a foreign citizen. At any rate, despite having to wait with anxious uncertainty for more than eight months for all these legal approvals on both sides to be realized, we now felt much better because we were no longer guilty of cheating my parents. We stopped hiding and pretending.

The first three years of our university program included 50% practical experience and 50% theory. For practical experience, we worked on actual construction projects in the Port of Odessa in different capacities, starting at the lowest proletarian ranks in the first year, technical in the second year, and ending as assistant junior engineers in the third year. The project on which I spent these three years (Odessa Passenger Terminal) was considered by my family as their major professional achievement.

This has been the most visible project in Odessa since the times of the founders of Odessa: de Ribas and Catherine the Great. The passenger terminal was built in front of the famous Potemkin Steps, on top of which the statue of de Ribas himself greeted the arriving passengers. This project was the pride and satisfaction of my family, who considered it their baby because the main architect of this project was my uncle, Joseph Alter. The civil design was led by my father, and the traffic design by Shura. Everyone in my family cherished this project, and we were very proud of our collective accomplishments. I, too, was very enthusiastic about working on this exciting project, which was transforming my city, even though my participation began at the level of a laborer. In the third year of our university program, we had to deal only with academic courses. The work practice in the Port of Odessa ran for the first two years.

Odessa Passenger Terminal

We met with Eduardo's Cuban friends and the Cuban diplomats who were stationed in Odessa. For the first time in my life, Eduardo and I took a flight to Moscow to meet with the family of my father's cousin and with Cuban students who were friends of Eduardo, studying at Patrice Lumumba University. This was an advanced educational center for foreigners from LDCs - less developed countries - studying how to make a revolution and overthrow their governments. Eduardo stayed with his student friends, and I stayed with my father's cousin Raya. She was a kind, middle-aged, simple, sweet woman. Unfortunately, her husband was quite upset and resentful of me because he was frightened about my proposed marriage to a foreigner. He believed it would endanger his job at the food processing plant near Moscow. As a result, my experience in Moscow was negative for this and other reasons. I disliked this vast, cold, and sterile city. Generally, I got the feeling that Moscow was not conceived for ordinary people, but in the distant past for the Tsars and in the present for the Soviet government. How lucky it was for us to live in Odessa!

Eduardo's friends appeared to be easygoing, open, and ingenious. They studied hard and loved music without consuming large amounts of vodka. The family of the Cuban consul in Odessa (husband and wife with two young kids) were personal friends of Eduardo, and we often visited them. From now on, we felt even more obliged to focus on our studies because we were anxious to validate the positive expectations of our parents, friends, and authorities. We were in the third year of our faculties, and there was no time to fool around. We already finished the general engineering program and now had to study the specialty subjects, which required a lot of technical terminology in Russian. Eduardo had a tough time with the terminology in Russian, but he was very industrious and determined. My studies in my native language were, of course, much easier for me than for Eduardo. I helped him with his language difficulties, and this gave me an excuse to spend more time with him and his Cuban friends, whose company I enjoyed.

11. Carry on Doctor: Soviet Torment/Cuban Farce

Registration of the marriage and wedding of Paulina and Eduardo in 1965, Odessa, USSR

For parents, the marriage of an only child, an only daughter, should be a moment of joy, especially in a society where the family is the sole refuge of happiness. Alas, for my poor papa and mama, the impending marriage was a quiet disaster, a deeply sad event. I was marrying a foreigner and would disappear, invariably, to a distant land. In a country where immigration did not exist, foreign travel was reserved for the few individuals who were selected and approved by the KGB: Soviet citizens traveling on state businesses such as diplomats, KGB agents, and members of the entrusted elite. For ordinary people, freedom of movement was tangled in an infinite web of restrictions. The future appeared bleak for my dear parents.

At the end of our academic year, we made the booking to register our marriage at Odessa ZAKS (municipal civil registry) on Primorsky Boulevard. We invited all of our friends and relatives as guests and witnesses to the marriage ceremony. However, only my parents and Natasha, a few Cuban diplomats, and the representative of MID (Ministry of Foreign Relations) showed up for the official registration ceremony.

I remember how forlorn my father looked. Shura arrived with eyes red from crying. She could barely control her tears. Sooner or later, their only child would separate from them for a very long time. The rest of my family, friends, or relatives did not come to the official registration because they feared being seen with foreigners, a situation that could create a security problem for them in the future. But they all came that evening to the garden of our dacha in Arcadia, where my parents, with the help of our neighbors, prepared large quantities of food to celebrate our wedding in the company of Soviet friends and relatives. Eduardo was the only foreigner there. Now that he was part of the family, they were less afraid of being seen with him.

I am forever grateful to Shura, not only for her abiding love and attention but also for the opportunity to enjoy this summer - a true honeymoon - at the dacha. On the second level of a communal house, her property consisted of one mid-size room separated into two rooms by thin wallboard. The new room gave us enough space for one bed and a common open terrace overlooking the garden. My parents had to go to work very early in the morning, so we were alone for the day, mostly outside at sea or in the garden. It was a wonderful and worry-free time. The first and the last holiday Eduardo and I ever enjoyed together.

Eduardo's mother sent us photographs of her family for me to start recognizing them. Eduardo was the firstborn, and he had a younger brother and sister. I was very impressed with the young and attractive family in the photos.

Parents of Eduardo are celebrating the birthday of Maria Elena

They were of a very different physical build and appearance: slim, small-boned, healthy, relaxed, and confident people. All of them: mother, father, their three children, and even the grandmother in the background - had an easy-going air about them that I thought was unknown to the citizens of my country. I was attracted to them and felt fortunate to become related to these beautiful and exciting people, apparently free to enjoy themselves. I learned from Eduardo that his father recently had to move to Havana, where he was offered a prestigious position with the government, and his brother left for Germany, where he was studying for a science degree. At the moment, only his kid sister stayed with the mother.

In September, we moved into the gloomy, prison-like, heavily guarded married foreign student residence of our university, which consisted of a separate floor for married couples in a building for foreign and postgraduate students, as well as for the new incoming teaching personnel. The rest of the building was reserved for individual Soviet students from different republics and cities across the Soviet Union. All rooms were of the same size and design, with only one window, so that the principle of equality was observed.

The best students at the university (those who had excellent academic records) were paid a stipend by the state. All foreign students were paid a stipend of 90 rubles per month, and Soviet students were paid 49 rubles per month on the condition of consistently high academic standards and only if they formally proved that their parents or adoptive families lacked the established minimum income to support their children.

My parents were high-income earners by Soviet standards, not even near as high as the salaries of Soviet communist '*nomenclatura*' (key administrative bureaucrats). Still, we could count only on Eduardo's stipend of 90 rubles per month as long as his academic results remained high. His stipend was only sufficient for purchasing very modest food for two weeks; my parents helped us financially for the other two weeks. Also, I carried Shura's cooked meals for the next day each time we visited my parents. Still, the foreign students had good reason to feel privileged. They were provided with beds in the students' residences and higher monthly payments.

Our student residence

In contrast, no Soviet students could manage their expenses without help from their families if it was available. However, many of them were working night shifts to get additional income. To give an example: the salary of my parents, who were the leading technical experts in their respective fields ("Senior Scientific Operatives"), was around 240 rubles each per month (the salaries of Communist Party nomenklatura officials were between 700 and 900 rubles per month plus paid expenses like cars, service personnel, and special luxury holiday resorts.

A Soviet student capable of keeping up excellent grades was paid a stipend of 49 rubles per month. These students needed help. It was especially true for students from other Soviet cities who did not obtain a bed in the student residence because the beds in the student residences were pretty limited. Most of them had to rent a bed illegally somewhere in the city, and that was very expensive. They were forced to work night shifts to pay for their rent and food. Their lives were much more complicated than ours. I don't know of anyone who managed to study for a professional career for too long on such a basis.

Despite our compassion for their plight, there was nothing we could do except invite them as friends for a meal. Everybody invited each other when the stipend was paid, and I tried many crazy spicy concoctions cooked up by friends of ours from many nationalities. I will never forget the Indonesian red peppers. I saw them for the first time in my life, and our Indonesian friends offered me a slice of bread with a topping of red peppers, which they had crushed and cooked, and were eating in the communal kitchen of our student residence.

After I bit into this bread, the fire that started in my mouth could not be extinguished with water or air. My shouts, tears, jumps - nothing helped. Desperate and not knowing what else to do, I ran out to the staircase and started running up and down while keeping my head down and mouth open. I don't know why, but after 30-40 minutes of this exercise, the burning pain stopped. When I finally lifted my head, I confronted a crowd from the entire student residence who had come to see who had gone crazy this time. Otherwise, it was fun to learn about the ordinary life of students from many foreign nations.

Our room was a narrow 3m x 6m (about 180 square feet) - just sufficient for our metal single bed, a couple of chairs, and one small table serving as a desk and dining table. Every room had one window. The gates at the entrance were closed to everybody except the residents. All visitors could come in only on certain days and hours after obtaining permission for the time of their visit. Sometimes, no visits were allowed at all, and we would start to feel like prisoners.

Conditions were extremely modest: we shared common washrooms (separate for men and women) and kitchen facilities (one on each floor) with the other 16-18 families of students and postgraduates living on the same floor as us. There was no radio, television, or telephone. We did not have an LP player either; no one would dream of having such expensive kinds of bourgeois equipment. Eduardo missed his Cuban music, so we would try to visit my parents' apartment when my parents were absent just to play Eduardo's LPs. But we did not dream of any better life, and no student would bother himself with fantasies about such impossibly luxurious items that were commonplace at that time, even in Cuba.

Despite deprivations by contemporary standards, we considered ourselves to be fortunate and privileged. Similar rooms on all the other floors of the foreign student residence were about the same size as ours, but each accommodated from four to six single students sharing two-level narrow metal bunk beds. Eduardo and I were ignorant about birth control; probably, I became pregnant on the very first day of our sleeping together. We often visited my parents and stayed with them to accommodate my suddenly enlarged appetite for home-cooked food during the pregnancy.

My parents were worried that the pregnancy and the baby would prevent me from continuing my professional studies. My father told me that he could die in peace only if I obtained a profession for which I had to graduate with a professional degree. He said that having a baby would endanger my graduation. He kept repeating that he had nothing to leave me for an inheritance, neither money nor property, but he would happily leave this earthly vale of tears if he knew that I had a profession. He said that a profession has a value higher than property and possessions because nobody would ever be able to steal it from me. This is why he felt that the only valuable assistance he could offer was to convince me not to drop out of my university program despite the baby.

I promised him not to abandon the university and to accept his help whenever we run out of money. Meanwhile, we were overwhelmed by baby gifts prepared and sent from Cuba by Eduardo's mother: a huge parcel with beautiful baby things, including a special baby basket, baby jumpers, shirts, and 40 hand-embroidered cloth diapers. My friends and I had never before seen such delightful and lovely fittings for a baby. Russian babies traditionally were simply bound or cocooned in ordinary single bed sheets. Of course, we had no concept of disposable diapers.

During pregnancy, I continued with my normal studies since the doctors from Odessa's sole maternity hospital, located only two blocks away, were satisfied with my physical condition and that of the baby. Suddenly, two weeks before the expected birth, a new doctor, preparing a delivery date, requested blood samples from Eduardo and me. A few days later, he announced that we should have been told before we even married that our blood types were not compatible. Mine was Rh-negative. Eduardo was type O. The doctor told us that the baby would not survive. We were utterly shocked and could not believe him. We were afraid to worry my parents, so Eduardo asked for help from the wife of the Cuban consul in Odessa.

After consulting with her doctor, she told us not to worry because Eduardo's blood type is considered universal, meaning compatible with everyone - the best possible situation for our baby. We decided not to alarm anyone. A week later, in early February, during a nighttime snowstorm, Eduardo and I rushed on foot the two blocks to the maternity hospital to await the arrival of our first child. Eduardo was never permitted to enter the premises of this ugly, dilapidated building. In Soviet maternity hospitals, fathers were not allowed inside.

A maternity hospital in Odessa

It was an experience I will never forget, intimations of Soviet torment. For the next 16 hours, medical students were ordered to drag me along the corridors of the hospital in the belief that this primitive procedure would help the baby to a drop off.

Not even the British cinema could script such a comedic scene in their hilarious film “Carry on Doctor” from the mid-sixties. For me also, it could have been very funny - if it had not been so painful. When I finally gave birth to a baby boy, he emerged with screams of protest, which sounded like music to my ears. The nurse who received the baby showed him to me from a distance and immediately took him away. Naturally, I was exhausted but even more frightened that something was wrong. I begged the nurses to show me my son at a closer distance. But they replied that it was not possible, that the baby was big, and they needed to clean and examine him.

The next day, when I awoke, I found myself in bed in a large hospital ward with another 18 women who were given their babies for feeding every 3 hours. When I asked for my baby, I was told that he was under observation and would not be allowed any contact with me. For an entire week, I heard the same story. I was devastated. I cried every day, fearing my dear baby was stolen (such rumors were not uncommon in the USSR).

Meanwhile, I was producing breast milk but had no baby to feed it to. It was physically painful. I squeezed the milk into a bottle every day and begged the nurses to take it to my baby. They refused, saying that it would contaminate the baby. Neither my protesting nor my pleading changed this nightmarish situation. The nurses always responded with the same answers: your baby is doing well but is under observation, and no contact is allowed because he might get contaminated with my Rh-negative blood. The tragic part of this Kafkaesque story was that our son turned out to have the same Rh-negative blood as I. Doctors only watched his skin color, whereas a simple check of his blood type might have prevented the horrors of those endless days.

All the other mothers gathered at the windows overlooking the street to share the happy news with their husbands waiting anxiously outside. February was especially cold that year, and windows could not be opened at all; they could only communicate by the use of sign language and drawings on the walls of the opposite buildings, which the excited fathers had to make at night, or they would be arrested for hooliganism - damaging the residential property of the city.

A week later, a nurse came to announce that my baby looked well and brought him to me for feeding. I was so elated to see my healthy and hungry son that nothing mattered to me any longer. Finally, later the same day, when the baby and I were allowed to leave the hospital, Eduardo, waiting nervously outside with floral bouquets, could see his son for the first time.

My parents and friends were also waiting anxiously for the first appearance of the mother and child. It was a cold February day, whitened with heavy falling snow. Shura was crying. None of them had been allowed to look at the baby or talk to me until this moment. We were all in wonder, gazing at the little cocoon - the way hospital personnel swaddled our baby in numerous sheets and blankets. The crowd of family and friends were standing, God knows for how long, in the heavy cold snow, staring in amazement at my baby. We all felt a sense of awe and admiration at this miracle of new life.

Eduardo and I took a taxi to the student residence. When we arrived at our room, I started crying because I was afraid of doing anything wrong for the baby. I did not even know how to unswaddle him. Shura could not help me either because my parents were not allowed to enter the foreign student residence after 6 p.m. and had to return home. The baby began crying loudly, and the atmosphere became desperate. Eduardo was pale as paper and in total panic. Only my friend Musia, who had never before in her life touched a baby, had the presence of mind to remove the infant from my hands and put him on our bed. She started to unwrap him, and her brave act brought me back to life. I went to help her, and we changed the baby. Then, I tried to breastfeed him. I was crying again, but this time from joy. The baby was very hungry, and that did the trick. Now, I was in the seventh heaven of happiness. We placed the baby basket beside our single bed, and our son became satisfied and happy.

The strangest part of this story was that after all the tortures in the maternity hospital, where neither Eduardo nor my parents were allowed even to look at our baby to prevent the possibility of contamination, the doctors never bothered to inject me with the antibody serum (immunoglobulin) to prevent any possible future birth complications. Despite the difficult winter conditions in the student residence (only cold water was available), our son was a healthy and agile little boy. He continued breastfeeding, and that kept his immune system strong against illness. Eduardo and I gave him the Russian name Eduard, but called him Edik, his Russian nickname. In the Cuban tradition, according to Eduardo, firstborn boys are named after their fathers.

The diapers and baby clothes that Eduardo's mother had sent to us were our salvation. I considered myself fortunate and proud to wash my baby's soiled diapers every day in our communal washroom. I could feel like a queen since no other Russian mother had ever seen or touched such soft and elegantly embroidered diapers. My father was delighted with his grandson and very proud of him.

My father with six-month-old Edik

Shura, however, was despondent since she could not stop thinking that the baby and we will leave the country after our graduation. The separation from my parents will be painful and prolonged because Soviet citizens could not travel abroad for private visits. She submitted to this fate but could not cease suffering and crying every time we were together. We would come for relatively short visits and rush straight back to the student residence because we were extremely busy with our studies and because it was hard for us to see my parents so forlorn over our imminent departure from the Soviet Union, especially Shura, who was now deeply bonded to the baby, especially during the summer when we stayed at Arkadia dacha together with my parents.

Most of our neighbors in the student residence were also our friends. They kindly accepted free babysitting as their natural obligation to allow me to attend courses at the university. Particularly helpful was Fatima, the wife of a Moroccan student. She was only 16 years old and was like a younger sister to me. Sadly, her husband often beat her, leaving her black and blue every other week. She looked after Edik and fed him from the bottle with my milk while I attended courses.

I sympathized with her and felt angry at her husband for beating her constantly. However, none of our interventions on her behalf were helpful. Such brutal treatment of wives was frequent in Russian families as well. Unfortunately, a year later, and after Eduardo and I had protested the treatment of Fatima, she was prohibited by her husband from talking to us. She even stopped greeting me when we encountered one another in the kitchen or corridor. Other Arab boys also began avoiding us. Poor Fatima!

Artistically speaking, the birth of my first child in the Soviet Union was a torment, a near-tragic drama of despair from the likes of Eugene O'Neill with musical overtones of the grotesque from a Shostakovich symphony. In striking contrast, the birth of my second child in Cuba two years later was like an Italian farce from *Commedia dell'Arte* with bright, inspirational melodies from a Rossini opera.

Our second child, also a boy, was born in Havana two years and two months after Edik. Eduardo suggested we name the baby after Cuba's recently martyred revolutionary hero, Ernesto Che Guevara. So, we named our baby Ernesto after Che. We called him Ernesto, with the nickname (diminutive) of Ernestico. The comedic farce began inside the Havana movie theater Payrete, where we went for a Friday night show after work. (I felt physically well until the very last moment of my pregnancy and did not take any maternity leave). First, though, we went to Coppelia, a famous ice-cream restaurant in the Vedado district of Havana, for a treat of Cuba's classic ice cream specialty - rich, delicious, and affordable. We had to line up there for several hours. After we had eaten huge portions of ice cream, Eduardo wanted to check if there were any movie tickets available at the Payrete movie theater in central Havana.

We lined up for the second time. We bought our tickets after two hours in line - me nine months pregnant and in high heels. The theater was showing a British comedy about a hospital, *Carry on Doctor*. Edik was seated on my lap, and together we laughed so hard that the unborn baby, perhaps curious to see for himself what was so funny, began to push his way out. The convulsions were so strong that Edik was knocked to the floor by constant kicking inside my suddenly agitated belly. Eduardo had to carry me in a panic to a taxi outside the theater that drove us to the Naval Hospital in *Habana Del Este*.

Our second child, also a boy, was born in

Havana two years and two months after Edik. Eduardo suggested we name the baby after Cuba's recently martyred revolutionary hero, Ernesto Che Guevara. So, we named our baby Ernesto after Che. We called him Ernesto, with the nickname (diminutive) of Ernestico. The comedic farce began inside the Havana movie theater Payrete, where we went for a Friday night show after work. (I felt physically well until the very last moment of my pregnancy and did not take any maternity leave).

First, though, we went to Coppelia, a famous ice-cream restaurant in the Vedado district of Havana, for a treat of Cuba's classic ice cream specialty - rich, delicious, and affordable. We had to line up there for several hours. After we had eaten huge portions of ice cream, Eduardo wanted to check if there were any movie tickets available at the Payrete movie theater in central Havana.

Payrete movie theater in Havana

We lined up for the second time. We bought our tickets after two hours in line - me, nine months pregnant and in high heels. The theater was showing a British comedy about a hospital, *Carry on Doctor*. Edik was seated on my lap, and together we laughed so hard that the unborn baby, perhaps curious to see for himself what was so funny, began to push his way out. The convulsions were so strong that Edik was knocked to the floor by constant kicking inside my suddenly agitated belly. Eduardo had to carry me in a panic to a taxi outside the theater that drove us to the Naval Hospital in *Habana Del Este.*

This was a large new elite hospital dedicated to serving only foreigners and members of the Cuban Navy. At the hospital, hardly waiting a moment, the baby forced his way out just enough to be picked up by nurses in a clean emergency room. I was lucky this time - the hospital was fantastic.[71]

Naval Hospital in Habana Del Este

This was a large new elite hospital dedicated to serving only foreigners and members of the Cuban Navy. At the hospital, hardly waiting a moment, the baby forced his way out just enough to be picked up by nurses in a clean emergency room. I was lucky this time - the hospital was fantastic.[72]

From the very first moment of his arrival, Ernestico was given into my hands to hold and, between feedings, taken to the glassed nursery room where admiring parents could gaze and goggle. Though Eduardo was not permitted into the emergency room to see us at the moment of delivery, still, when he came the next morning, the baby was brought straight away to both of us and was given to his father to hold. It was such a delight, such a contrast with Soviet practice, that I could not believe my good fortune.

Doctors never objected to the natural breastfeeding of our baby and explained that Eduardo's type O blood would not create any problems for our children. I wondered why the Soviet doctors in Odessa were so barbaric in their treatment of mothers and their newborn children. According to Cuban doctors, the knowledge regarding type O blood is common; so, why were our Soviet doctors ignorant of this subject? Fortunately, Cuba in the mid-1960s had not yet developed the same deadly bureaucracy in every area of life. But revolutionary Cuba would also age and harden with time.

Later, we had visits from everyone in the family and all of our friends to my private hospital room. The Naval Hospital, reserved for naval and foreign personnel, was large and well-equipped before the Revolution. Yes, in Russia, too, many beautiful things were produced before the Revolution. Generally, it felt like I was in paradise. The baby and I were healthy, free of torment and pain. We were really happy. This was the very opposite of my childbirth experience in Odessa. Only two days after Ernestico's birth, we were allowed to leave the hospital and went to stay with Eduardo's mother in her Havana apartment.

It was 1968, and conditions in Cuba had deteriorated greatly since Eduardo left for studies in Odessa in 1961, shortly after the Cuban Revolution. Normally, his fond middle-class recollections would have been rudely interrupted. Fortunately, however, life in a Soviet student residence had fully prepared Eduardo for the dismal conditions we encountered in Havana. Maria, Eduardo's mother, helped us the best she could during those difficult few weeks after the baby was born. She convinced me to return to work less than a month after the birth of Ernestico. She was very capable and experienced with children, and I trusted her entirely. Ernestico was adorable, healthy, always in a happy mood, and well-behaved.

Despite frequent interruptions with all municipal services, including lengthy absences of water and electricity, despite the crowded conditions (11 people in a small three-bedroom apartment, including Eduardo's sister and brother with his wife and their two-year-old child), we were warmly welcomed by Maria and her family. The only running water near Maria's apartment appeared at the industrial port and only for a few hours during the late morning. This water had to provide for cooking, drinking (after boiling), cleaning and washing, bathing for everybody, and washing clothes and

Ernestico's diapers. The three women - Eduardo's mother, the wife of Eduardo's brother, and I - had to each carry by hand two pails of water from the port area to the apartment under the midday Cuban tropical sun.

This was a five-block journey each way during which the men of our household were at work because the water from the port was available only during late morning working hours. I tolerated the heat quite well. Coming from Odessa, I was used to hot weather, but two pails full of water were more than my tender back could manage just after giving birth. I suspected that Maria felt sorry for my aching back, and this was the main reason she insisted that I return to work so early after childbirth, leaving both my children in daycare.

Eduardo's younger sister, Mary Elena, also adored our children and spent a lot of her time with Edik. Everybody in Eduardo's family, as well as the neighbors, was in love with "Russito" ("the little Russian" which is how they called Edik), especially after we left him for a few months with Maria, Eduardo's mother, before our graduation in Odessa, while we were preparing our theses, our final graduation projects. As a result, Edik became a favorite with his Cuban grandmother and aunt. Being left with his Cuban family also encouraged him to learn Spanish. His overly adoring Cuban family spoiled him, and he became very demanding. I could never have dreamed of people sweeter and more supportive of me than the family of Eduardo (except, of course, my parents). Since the electrical power in our residential area was off most of the time, Eduardo's mother cooked daily for 11 people on two '*reverberos de alcohol*' (alcohol camp burners) lit on the floor of the apartment (just like a wilderness camp) because they did not have access to kerosene for a more sophisticated burner.

Eduardo's mother took the initiative with "Russito" (Edik), and this allowed me to spend more time and energy with Ernestico, our new baby. It was important because Edik was an energetic and independent little boy. Edik now could understand Spanish, so I did my best to speak less Russian at home to promote his faster grasp of Spanish, unless I needed to say something privately to Eduardo in Russian.

I felt welcomed and appreciated by his mother, but at the same time suffered guilt for contributing to the crowded conditions in her apartment, and because our imposition was involuntary. Maria complained to me a lot about the terrible mismanagement of the economy in the country. She was always repeating to me that Eduardo and I must request our future employer to award us our own residence because that is what the Cuban government has done for all its valuable personnel. Poor organization and incompetent management of municipal services in the residential areas of Havana produced these new service shortages (unknown before the Revolution).

The failure to provide adequate services became a hallmark of the Cuban leadership.

Despite their proclamations to the contrary, it is conceivable that they never intended to resolve these problems. It is, after all, an effective method practiced by dictators to render their populations completely dependent on the government for every aspect of their survival. To that end, it was useful and necessary to keep them hungry and powerless.

Yet, according to Maria, the vast majority of the population supported the Revolution because under the military dictatorship of Batista, with the American mafia in close partnership with the corrupt government of Batista, a gangster-like climate was created, oppressive to the majority of the population. The needs of the poor and illiterate peasants and large groups of penniless migrants, particularly those from Haiti, were ignored, and the middle class was weary of corruption and gangsterism.

Maria didn't tell me, but her older sister did, that Fidel Castro, before he decided to run for parliament, was himself a brutal gangster. Nevertheless, after the Revolution succeeded, those who came to power had no experience in running an economy. As well, they were too arrogant to involve professionals. Instead, they experimented with the economy at their whim. Nobody was permitted to raise any criticism of their policies without immediately being accused of counter-revolutionary behavior and severely punished.

All these shortages and failures were blamed on "counter-revolutionaries" and Yankees, even though the mismanagement of industry and economy had little to do with the Yankees and everything to do with incompetence and corruption, which, when given a free ride, will ruin any economy. After the Revolution, political sloganeering always trumped productivity. Cubans were saying that the only people with a perverse motive to maintain the American blockade were members of the Cuban government. Without the blockade, they would have nobody else to blame for disasters in every sphere of the economy.

Meanwhile, Cuban revolutionary elites were living like yesterday's super-rich: the finest mansions, private and gated residential areas, classy cars and obedient servants, the highest quality of medical and communication services, the very best products supplied by exclusive stores, exciting entertainment, and luxurious resorts. The best part was that often they have not had to pay for it. None of this surprised me. In the Soviet Union, I was accustomed to this inequality and hypocrisy since my birth. The winner takes all. What's new? Ten years after the Revolution, Cubans had already become used to economic injustice, just like the rest of the desensitized population of the communist camp allied with the Soviet Union.

12. Graduation or Prison Break

By 1967, Eduardo and I were preparing to graduate from our university. We had completed the academic program and now required field practice, which meant that a Diploma Project was assigned to each of the graduates. Mine was the design of a Sugar Terminal in Odessa Port, and Eduardo designed a new dredge ship. We were given three months to complete and defend our Diploma Projects. It was the first time in our lives that we had personal responsibility for a creative mission of our own. I believe it was the most useful time in our six years of university learning. We experienced the personal freedom to manage our time. Initially, we wasted a lot of that time groping our way in the dark of a new challenge. Eventually, we had to learn self-discipline and how to organize work on our own. It was also the moment when I became pregnant again with our second child.

Each of us was given a Diploma Project Consultant, a professional from the field, to guide us in the new process of developing a project from start to finish. Many of the students spread out through the University and the Marine Design Institute libraries and archives to search for similar prototypes. If we found one, we tried to copy it by hand and distribute it among ourselves. We did not have computers, calculators, or even photocopiers. The university had one mainframe, which occupied an entire special hall. It was there simply as a museum exhibit, not accessible. We were brought to see it only once, but were never allowed to use it. Our work involved calculating large amounts of data, and we were using only a slide rule. All drawings and calculations were made by hand and recorded as a sole original without a single copy. If any part of this handwriting were lost, it would be dramatic because all the data were interdependent. I went to consult with colleagues of my parents at the Black Sea Institute in the department of my field. They were able to help me with developing the concept of a new specialized terminal.

During my first three months of pregnancy, I was frequently nauseous, which did little to help my Diploma Project. Pregnancy was not planned by us to occur at such a demanding and important period in our lives. But birth control in the Soviet Union was extremely primitive, and despite my consultations in a local clinic, we had never even heard about birth control pills. So, I had to give thanks for the blessing of an unplanned but welcoming new baby and started my hard work on my diploma project between sessions of nausea.

We completed and submitted our diploma projects at the very last moment to shorten the anxiety time before defending our projects in front of the appointed committee consisting of our academic professors and professionals from the industry. Our task was to present our projects and to answer all the questions from the committee convincingly. This was not so simple: we could anticipate the kind of questions from our professors, but we had no idea about the questions from the industry representatives. Their queries were often unexpected and fatal for those who lacked actual industrial practice.

Eduardo and I were fortunate. We successfully defended our projects, and that was a critical victory because the majority of students failed in the defense of their diploma projects. In my faculty, for example, (Coastal and Offshore Engineering), only 12 students out of the original 150 who started in 1961 graduated in 1967. The results in Eduardo's Faculty (Shipbuilding/Naval Engineering) were even worse. I believe the high failure or dropout rate was due to the difficult economic conditions for the majority of students. Too many of them had to work night shifts just to eat. These jobs were temporary and low-paid, and impacted the health and performance of these youngsters negatively. To claim that professional education was open to everybody is not entirely true. Kids without economic help from their parents or some assistance from the Communist Party (to that end, they had to be members of Komsomol of the Communist Party) rarely graduated on time, if at all.

At the official graduation speech, our Dean asked the crowd of graduate students: "How does it feel about graduating as a professional after all these years of toiling?" Somebody from the crowd shouted, "It feels wonderful; we will never again have to study. We can start working for pay!"

"You are wrong, *tovarisch* (comrade)," answered our Dean. "Your real studies will start only from this point on. Everything you have learned by now, overall, these academic years, is how to search for the right information. Real life will demand that you do this constantly over your career! Good luck to you, but don't fool yourself: constant learning will be necessary for the rest of your lives."

To be honest, in retrospect, I should say that we took the support from my parents for granted. Don't most kids? Was I truly sad about leaving my parents upon graduation? No, I was excited and could not wait to start our new life as adults, leaving behind this gray, authoritarian Soviet system that could squelch anyone of us, at its convenience, at any time, and we could do nothing about it. Graduation felt like a prison break!

Still, the last image of my parents in tears when we were departing was just too traumatic for me. I believe that my 'memory keeper' wiped out all details of it from my brain's hard disk as a measure of emotional protection. I don't even remember the farewell from my parents, family, and friends. Nature has its ways to block out memories that are just too painful for us. Generally, though, everything went well. The Cuban government paid for Eduardo's air flight to Havana, and Eduardo gave his flight ticket to me. He departed for Cuba by cargo ship. I was very uneasy about coming to Havana by myself. I had been to Havana twice before on a ship as part of marine training in our summer university practice program. But I had spent only brief periods onshore and most of the time on board in the harbor. I could not remember much about the city. This time, I was apprehensive but managed to switch off, at least temporarily, my emotions over the pain of separation from my family, friends, culture, and my beloved Odessa Mama. I put my emotions into a deep freeze, an unconscious anesthetic, in a forced effort to cut myself off from my loved ones and everything familiar to me. It was all too painful. Every immigrant on this planet is familiar with this feeling.

Everything about Cuba upon my arrival was overwhelming for me: the heat, the old colonial architecture, Eduardo's large and wonderful family, the motley crowds of noisy visiting neighbors, and the annoying, persistent shortages of power, food, and water. The shortages were not as hard for me as they would be for the average Westerner. Most Cuban people struck me as very good-looking, especially Maria, Eduardo's mother, and her three sisters. They were all very friendly, attractive, and elegant. My preference has, though, been for Eduardo's 12-year-old sister Maria Elena. She was beautiful with angelic looks and an equally angelic character. She looked more Russian than I, with her very light skin and curly blond hair. She was always sweet, cheerful, obedient, and willing to help. I never met such a well-behaved little girl before. All the girls I knew in Odessa were mischievous rascals who would not think twice to venture together into dangerous local surroundings, such as caves or boat escapades. Maria Elena was always beside her mother. I never observed her running off with her little friends without her mother. This was quite a contrast to my childhood. Eduardo's father also impressed me with his fine appearance and civilized manners. Only later, I learned about his cold determination and *machismo*.

In early 1961, Eduardo left his parents to undertake professional studies in the USSR at 18. During his absence, there occurred significant changes in the life of his family. After the Revolution, Rolando, Eduardo's father, due to his administrative knowledge and industry experience, was appointed to a newly created high government post in Havana. For this posting, he moved to Havana from the city of Sagua La Grande (in north-central Cuba), where his family lived on a large estate. Rolando asked his wife, Maria, to donate the family estate in *Sagua La Grande* to the Cuban government in exchange for a new small three-bedroom apartment in the center of Havana. After Maria donated her estate and moved to Havana, a dramatic change occurred in Eduardo's father. He stopped coming home and finally dropped his wife and three children altogether for his young secretary. His wife and children were in shock. Eduardo and his brother were both studying for their careers abroad and felt guilty for not being beside their mother to help her at such a difficult moment.

I could not comprehend Rolando's behavior. I was too young and inexperienced to be aware of the promiscuous nature of men. To me, it was a matter of loyalty, and I was spoiled by the chaste example of my father. The Latin revolutionary culture in Cuba encouraged the promiscuity of men: “a macho is a Caballo” (the man is a stallion). I learned later that promiscuity in Cuba was a normal standard, a socially accepted phenomenon of the male character. Promiscuity was not acceptable socially in our Soviet society and was further inhibited by crowded communal living conditions. No doubt, it was often simply repressed and unleashed covertly in a more violent form. Also, a puritanical and asexual culture was easier to control. Brainwashed Soviet masses were constrained by the northern climate and scarcity of residential space. Privileged elites were exempted from such limitations and prohibitions, but we have never learned the truth about their secretive personal lifestyles.

Maria, Eduardo’s mother, was a beautiful, slim woman in her early 40s, a classy and elegant lady in addition to being modest and kind. She used to cry at night because she was still in love with her ex-husband. Despite that, she astonished me by behaving with self-restraint and civility in his presence. With me, she was always very diplomatic and generous. When, on my arrival, she noticed that my luggage contained only a single dress and one pair of shoes, she did not comment. It had never occurred to me that it was necessary to own more than one decent change of clothing. In my short Soviet life, I never met any female who aspired to own more than one decent dress for public wear. Maria told me that I needed various dresses and matching shoes with handbags. She gave me one matching set of her own as a gift because, after we finally had sufficient money to shop, Cuban stores received instructions not to sell any goods without Cuban ration cards, to which I had no rights. Later, all goods, except for food staples, disappeared from stores; having rights under the Cuban ration system lost any sense for Cubans as well. I didn't mind those shortages while I enjoyed the sun, the sea, the people's happy disposition, and their exuberant temperament. Life was sparked by Cuban music and Cuban dance. At the age of 22 and after the dreadfully stale Soviet society, all this vibrant Caribbean culture got under my skin. Then, there was the ultimate ecstasy drug - *café Cubano.*

Cuban coffee is very strong, very black, very sweet, with a deep aroma, and percolated for intensity, espresso-style, with an Italian stovetop coffee maker. It was utterly irresistible. Cuban coffee became my obsession. It could stimulate my energy to such a degree that all tiredness would disappear, and I would be filled with fresh and lasting energy in a positive, upbeat mood. Just the aroma of roasted, uncooked coffee beans would lift me into euphoria. I was always ready to stand in a long line for a petite cup of coffee at the street corner store. Cuban rations were so small that Cubans could not afford to percolate more than one very small portion of coffee at home in the morning before leaving for work, and even that was not every day. Like me, they had become addicts of this wonderful 'black spirit of the angels', a shortcut to paradise for which they were willing to wait in long street lines to purchase one small cup of Cuban espresso.

Unfortunately, many delicious and nutritious Cuban fruits were no longer available: sweet mangoes, frutabomba, mamay, papayas, guyava, coconut, pineapples, guanabana, cherimoya, carambola, granadas, caimito, and many others. I did not even get to taste some of them while we lived in Cuba. This was not so hard on me because I did not know what I was missing. Even the Cubans seemed to have forgotten them.

They explained to me that all farmland was private before the Revolution. Fidel Castro implemented his agricultural land reform during 1959-1963. Land expropriated from foreign owners was subdivided among 200,000 peasants, with each family parcel limited to 67 acres. The rest of the agricultural land became the property of the state. It was a very clever masquerade for implementing Soviet Kolkhoz (collective farms) without anyone understanding what was going on. The key element of this reform was that the new peasant owners of these land parcels could not sell or mortgage them. As well, they were only permitted to plant crops ordered by INRA (*Instituto Nacional de Reforma Agraria*)[73] , which decided that all peasants should join Agricultural Cooperatives (Cuban name for Soviet Kolkhoz). INRA ordered the cooperatives to plant only approved crops and dictated the selling prices. These reforms converted all Cuban peasants into powerless employees of the state. Then, after Fidel Castro made a deal with the Soviet Union for sugar, INRA decided to use all agricultural land solely for growing sugar cane, which the Soviet government demanded as part of a trade deal in exchange for Soviet armaments.

When small farmers and small local vegetable retailers protested, the Cuban state just took possession of their property. The previous owners could continue working as employees on their farms or at street stalls, but they did not get to decide what to plant, what to sell, or how to price products in local street vegetable stalls, which were called *bodegas*. Eggs and milk were so scarce that they were rationed only for children. Meat rations were savored once a week, and families gave them only to their children. The Cubans did not even remember the meaning of cheese. Ordinary fish was eaten as a delicacy, and this was on a Caribbean island surrounded by fish. Corn was not so common in Cuba and was consumed only in restaurants in the form of Mexican tamales. I always wondered why there was no tradition of corn and potatoes, as in the rest of the Latin American countries. Why no green salads of any kind? Cubans would answer that this situation came about because Cuba's native people were eliminated from the island, and the local food traditions closely followed the customs of Cuban peasant immigrants, the bulk of whom came from Spain's cooler and poorer northern regions. Foods that were natural for those regions of Spain proved less suitable for Cuba's tropical climate. Besides, Spain forbade any Cuban commerce with countries other than Spain and refused to allow immigrants from other European countries to settle in Cuba or the other Spanish colonies.

The staple foods, many of which were difficult to buy, included rice, all kinds of roots unknown to me (*yuka*, *bonitos*, *cassava*, *plantains*), and very colorful beans of all sizes (a Cuban favorite), such as black beans, *garbanzos*, *habichuelas* called *Moros y Christianos* (black and white beans), and many other varieties. I loved most of these foods as well, except that they were difficult to prepare at home without the necessary ingredients (such as garlic, tomatoes, onions, and potatoes), most of which completely disappeared after the Revolution, according to Eduardo's mother, our cook. Still, Maria managed to prepare delicious *salkochos* and *potajes* (thick Spanish bean soups) made with *mojitos,* a marinade of grapefruit, lime, red peppers, and garlic, because she was a master in Creole cooking. She always had on hand marinated pimientos and other spices from the Cuban countryside, where she had some family. The preferred dish was *Arroz congris* which is rice cooked with beans. All these dishes were very heavy Spanish peasant food that did not suit urban activities in a tropical climate and ultimately led to an unacknowledged epidemic of painful hemorrhoids among Cubans.

What I adored were seafood cocktails, but they were served only in the best and most expensive restaurants. To a degree, all these Cuban foods were tasty but very heavy for a tropical climate. I had a difficult time managing without our traditional Odessan Mediterranean salads and light vegetarian dishes. Generally, though, I did not care so much about consuming the food so long as I had access to my favorite drug, *café Cubano.* I was bewildered by the strange indifference of the Cuban government to the incredible wealth of Cuban natural tropical produce. To me, this appeared insane. With such a favorable climate and fertile soil, Cuba should be able to cultivate at least three harvest seasons per year. In Odessa, we collected only one harvest per year, and still, we were expected to ship food from Odessa to Cuba: incredible but true.

After the Revolution, Cuba stopped traditional agricultural production in favor of producing sugar cane (for export to the USSR) on all fertile agricultural land. Fishing was forbidden because fish and seafood were government-controlled cash food for export or the Cuban elite and hotels. The people of Cuba were not happy about these prohibitions, but they were powerless. It was a nation where all decisions were made by one man only: Fidel Castro. He was "re-inventing the wheel" because he always knew better and always had to win at any price. Everyone was afraid to contradict him. The result was the destruction of fruit and vegetable agricultural production and the nutritional deprivation of a nation.

Many Cubans I met were seriously frightened of government trickery and retaliatory punishments. I heard of mysterious disappearances and legally absurd accusations against those who attempted to express critical opinions. Right or left was of no difference; all opposition to or competition with *Fidelismo* was wiped out. Those who aspired to survive in Cuba also had to learn our Soviet 3Us: '*ugadat, ugodit, ustoyat*' (to guess, to oblige, to withstand). The Cuban variation was: *'Ordename Commandante'* (Order me, my Commandante), meaning total submission and obedience without questioning. But after all, who am I to criticize Cubans? We had lived like this in the Soviet Union for half a century. The Cuban situation was not unique. I did not blame them, though, occasionally, I was annoyed by the excessive and naive revolutionary enthusiasm of my husband. In the Soviet Union, we were indoctrinated but had already lost any idealism. What remained were the fear and the instinct to survive.

My mother-in-law and her sisters were serving reluctantly at the local CDRs (Committees for Defense of the Revolution) created by the first brigade of Soviet-Spanish advisers (*Niños*) who had introduced, trained, and helped to implement the first public security surveillance in each local residential neighborhood. Maria explained to me that it was an obligation for all residents who aspired to be accepted as supporters of the Cuban Revolution. In real terms, it could be translated into something quite similar to our Soviet experiences back at home. Everyone had to spy on their neighbors and report all wrongdoings to the CDR. Culturally, Cubans despised '*chivatos*' (informers), and now the Revolution made them all '*chivatos*'. Yes, it was an obligation to participate in the CDR.

Maria's apartment block

I know that because as soon as I arrived, the CDR sent their delegate to Maria's apartment to request my participation in 'the *Guardia*' of our neighborhood (night vigilance guards of CDR who were expected to do all-night surveillance of the neighborhood). I was able to escape the criticism of locals for not joining '*chivatos*' only thanks to my Soviet citizenship, which I used as a reason for my completely cynical excuse: the Soviet government wouldn't want its citizens to interfere in Cuban internal matters. CDR had to swallow my excuse, but other residents were caught in the web of CDR.

Of course, not everybody I met in Cuba was a young and enthusiastic, idealistic dreamer like Eduardo. I also met individuals, mostly from the middle class, who were much less passionate and who felt weary and disillusioned. Some of them even complained to me in secret that they felt completely deceived. Many of those who participated in the Revolution from the very inception and were early *compañieros* (comrades) of Fidel Castro were now confused, frustrated, and frightened. Some of them were connected to the few surviving members of *Juventud Ortodoxa* from the University of Havana who survived the Moncada suicide mission of Fidel Castro and became members of M26J - *Movimiento de 26 de Julio* (a name invented by Fidel to commemorate the attack on Moncada); others became members of the *Directorio Revolucionario*, principally in Havana. None of these movements were communist. Their members were nationalistic liberals who wanted only to introduce reforms. Fidel Castro found no further use in the Orthodox Party (the majority of them were killed in the Moncada attack). One woman, who was an ex-member of Juventud Ortodoxa, told me that Fidel secretly arranged with Batista to trade their parliament seats for his amnesty, and then he became the leader of M26J. Initially, Cubans believed that Fidel was a non-ideological leader and a Democrat because that was the message of his emotionally charged speeches.

Cubans told me that the PSP (the Communist Party of Cuba) has existed legally in Cuba since 1925 but was not popular because it was allied with the worst Cuban dictators: first, with President Machado and then with Batista.

Spanish communists, trained by the Soviet KGB, ran PSP long before the Cuban Revolution. Many of the original members of Directorio Revolucionario and M26J were anti-communists. They trusted Fidel's promises of an independent, democratic national government. Many of them suspected that Raúl Castro, Che Guevara, and Ramiro Valdez were pro-Soviet communists even before 1959. However, they did not believe there was any danger because Fidel and his movement, named *Fidelistas*, had always announced publicly that he was not a communist but a democrat and the leader of M26J. However, the M26J stood for mild reforms, which could not be achieved because of Batista's dictatorship and the domination of American imperialism; hence, the necessity of guerrilla war. But to start the large-scale expropriation and nationalization in Cuba, Fidel Castro, being a non-communist, needed to find scapegoats to justify his decision.[74] He had always been an exceptionally good actor, so his theatrical portrayal of the two guilty culprits was nothing less than a brilliant and dramatic manipulation of the facts.

One of these scapegoats, not hard to imagine, was the Yankees. Fidel succeeded in deceiving everyone in the world about the reason for the refusal of the American petroleum refinery industry in Cuba to process the new Soviet supplies of heavy oil from Siberia, with which Fidel decided to replace the light Venezuelan oil. The true reason was that the existing processing plants were designed and equipped only for light Venezuelan oil and, technically, could not process the heavy Siberian oil without major modifications that were recognized as technically and economically unfeasible. But Fidel, in his declarations, neglected to mention this aspect; instead, he denounced the refusal to accept heavy oil as Yankee sabotage. This strategy served to justify the expropriation of the oil processing industry in Cuba without compensation to its American owners.

The second scapegoat constituted all other political parties. Suddenly, again without consulting with anyone, Fidel announced the fusion of the M26J with other political parties. The fusion took the form of a takeover of the PSP (the old Communist Party) by the Fidelistas to form a new party, namely the *Organizacion Revolucionaria Integrada or briefly ORI*, a project which caused considerable conflict with old-guard Stalinists. Fidel was also a brilliant tactician in consolidating his power. He would put potential competitors or leaders he had slated for elimination in charge of unpopular programs or political parties. For example, Anibal Escalante, the veteran Stalinist who had been given responsibility for organizing the ORI (Organizaciones Revolucionarias Integradas), ensured that trusted Stalinist staffed the leading positions in the towns and provinces. There was a huge public outcry as a result of the numerous assassinations and expropriations of properties (ORI was trying to clone the history of Stalin's expropriations, which we Soviets called The Great Terror). In March of 1962, Castro finally used this public outcry to accuse Anibal Escalante, who was acting on Fidel Castro's mandate of sectarianism and creating a counter-revolutionary monstrosity. Escalante was expelled from the Directorate and hastily departed for Prague. This is how the brothers Castro found their perfect scapegoats: the Yankees and the alternative political parties.

Such tactics are not new in the history of revolutions. The Bolsheviks in Russia declared that all alternative revolutionary parties - Mensheviks, Trotskyites, Cadets, SRs (Socialist Revolutionaries), and others - were the worst enemies of the Soviet state[75] and spared no effort in hunting them down and exterminating millions of them and their families up to the third generation.[76] Consolidation through elimination is the way of all dictators and tyrants as soon as they obtain power. The Castro brothers were neither unique nor original; most charismatic dictators are loved by the crowds.

By the time my husband Eduardo left Cuba early in 1961, Fidel Castro had assumed absolute power and control in the country, though he was still declaring that he was not a communist and that the new government in Cuba was not going to become communist. However, at the end of December 1961, Fidel delivered a special surprise for his collaborators and the people of Cuba. On that night, eight months after his victory at the Bay of Pigs, he delivered a speech on national television, declaring that he had become a communist and that he would take Cuba onto the communist path. Of course, nobody consulted with the Cuban people about whether this was a path they wished to pursue.

The way Fidel went about this change was not democratic, as he pretended, but authoritarian and despotic. He declared illegal all other political organizations in Cuba except ORI, which was later renamed PCC (Partido Comunista Cubano).[77] After this, the absolute, indisputable monopoly of the Castro brothers, Ramiro Valdez, and Che Guevara, within the PCC became a reality in the drama of the Cuban political theater. All other participants of the Cuban Revolution now lived in fear of reprisals, of being accused of counter-revolutionary activities for which the common sentence was 20 years in prison; unless, of course, they too joined the PCC and submitted to its authority. Long-time comrades of Fidel were upset because nobody consulted them about their fate and the destiny of their country. They felt as if they were being kidnapped. Any expression or suspicion of discontent was punishable either by firing squad or a long prison term.

The young and charismatic Fidel Castro always made his public declarations of his plans in such a passionate and theatrical fashion that few listeners doubted the nobility of his intentions. He learned to deliver his speeches with the musical guile and prowess of a snake charmer. The Cuban populace was driven into a state of hypnosis by these performances – probably, not less than Germans during speeches delivered by Hitler, Italians by Mussolini, Soviets by Stalin, Libyans by Gaddafi, Chinese by Mao, and other talented strategic manipulators of crowds that were ready to die for anything their spellbinding leaders called for. The hysterical exaggerations in public speeches of these leaders provoke excitement and trust in mass audiences. Like most other revolutions begun with the best intentions, this one also created the necessary chaotic conditions for a hijacking by a local tyrant. Idealism turned to cynicism, hope to mistrust. In the Soviet Union, we learned not to trust anybody at all, only the whip! Cuban friends and members of my new Cuban family, who secretly shared with me their outrage, expected that I would be shocked by their stories. However, their distressing tales failed to produce in me the expected effect.

My attitude, grounded in Stalin's reign of terror, was always: "It could have been worse." Despite my sympathy for disaffected Cubans, I knew better than to get engaged in a political conversation. I kept quiet in the best Soviet tradition. I heard their complaints but did not comment on them. 'Keep your ears open and your mouth shut' was something I learned early in childhood. This self-discipline and discretion are essential for survival in an absolute dictatorship, communist or fascist; it doesn't matter. The price of a careless joke or a thoughtless remark could be paid in personal and family misfortune if your listener is an informer or provocateur.

But such suspicions and fears were still ahead of me as I relished my Cuban coffee in the soft Caribbean ambiance and waited for my husband to arrive by ship in the Port of Havana. When Eduardo landed, he took me out to walk that night through the main entertainment area in Havana (*Av. 23 entre Av. De Paceo y Av. de Los Presidentes*), where we spent most of our money on one dinner at the famous restaurant Polinesium. This restaurant was still offering exotic tropical-style food. Eduardo ordered two dishes of frog legs with cocktails. The frog legs were very tasty, but it was culturally shocking for me since I had never before imagined that frogs could be eaten.

The next day, we went to the beautiful Santa Maria Beach, and that was our introduction to Cuban tourism. We felt elated, rented a tent on the beach, and stayed there overnight. We even experienced the excitement of nature's spectacle: after swimming all afternoon and evening in the warm, lightly salted Caribbean Sea, we fell deeply asleep in the night blackness of our tent. Suddenly, in my sleep, I felt somebody's touch. When I opened my eyes, I could not see who was touching me since we did not have a lamp. I screamed in terror after my eyes adjusted to the dark, and I could distinguish shadows. We were surrounded by large specimen land crabs that started their night migration. The large crabs were crawling on top of us and covered the beach. I became hysterical. Eduardo had to fight the crabs away and then reinforce the tent in total darkness, which was an astoundingly brave accomplishment, in my opinion.

In the morning, we walked back to the bus stop at Tarara, a gated community of large beach houses for pre-revolutionary elites and later the exclusive home to Cuban VIPs like Che Guevara and Enrique Oltulski. Never before had I seen such sumptuous private villas. That was our brief and only Cuban holiday. We were not given much time to relax; a week later, we were handed assignments to begin our employment in management positions at the Ministry of Transport in Havana. Eduardo and I were very happy with such an auspicious job allocation. After settling into my new surroundings, I started feeling homesick. The emotional anesthetic I had self-administered to dull the pain of separation from family, friends, and the city was wearing off. The loss of family love and familiar attachments became more painful and infected my mood with deep sadness. The best medicine against immigrant syndrome was to become very busy with my growing children, new professional work, and fresh learning challenges.

13. Back in the USSR

I could never have imagined that flying from the USSR to a balmy Caribbean Island would deliver me into the virtual lap of the Soviet State. I mean that not long after we landed, we began to work with a Soviet team transplanted to Cuba under the supervision of our 'big brothers' - the Soviet embassy, Soviet Navy, and Soviet intelligence services, courtesy of GRU and KGB!

That was early in January of 1968, the same year the Beatles released their political musical parody *Back in the USSR*. Life imitates art.

A small group of senior coastal and offshore engineers, colleagues of my parents in Odessa, was sent to Cuba at about the same time that we graduated from university. Their mandate was to design and build a new deepwater approach channel and general cargo port in Cienfuegos, a city on the Caribbean coast of southern Cuba. My father and Shura were working in the Black Sea Institute as senior technical managers for over twenty years, and I considered the colleagues of my parents my extended family.

Some of Shura's girlfriends, female managers from the Institute, often visited our apartment. House parties for colleagues were held in our one-room apartment on festive occasions. These were self-confident, determined, and optimistic professional women who became role models for me. I felt that many of my parents' colleagues respected them both technically and personally, and I trusted them.

When the small technical team from the Black Sea Institute was sent to Cuba, my parents asked Boris, the team leader, to look after me, *in loco parentis*. His small team consisted of only three engineers, but it needed more because their mandate was extensive. Boris secretly confided to my parents that he possibly would have a job position for me because he could not count on the productivity of his two colleagues, who were from Moscow, and he feared that they would spend more time at the embassy than at work because he suspected that their principal function was political (possibly informants).

Due to a shortage of design personnel and the promise he made to my parents, Boris officially solicited permission to employ me as a designer and a member of his team for his assignment in Cuba. When Eduardo and I were sent to report to the Cuban Ministry of Transport (known as MITRANS), the matter was already decided, and I was given the title of Soviet Technical Assessor and sent to join our Soviet team from the Black Sea Institute of Odessa, mandated to design and to build a deepwater multi-purpose port in Cienfuegos.

Eduardo was sent to work with the Ship Building and Maintenance Department of the Ministry of Transport (MITRANS) together with an older, experienced Polish assessor in naval architecture. The team of Boris was working in the same Ministry.

The building of MITRANS in Havana

The 7th floor in the MITRANS building was secured and dedicated to the work of the Soviet group. Officially, it was called Port Engineering, but the Cuban personnel of the Ministry called it *el piso Sovietico* (the Soviet floor). Most of our staff were Cuban: the translator, technician, draftsman, and secretary. Our Cuban manager-coordinator with MITRANS reported directly to the Minister, Comandante Faure Chomón, who, previously, was Cuba's first ambassador to the Soviet Union. Our design team of technical assessors from the Black Sea Institute was sent to Cuba on a three-year mission and allowed to bring their families along with them. It turned out to be a fantastic opportunity for the Soviet personnel and their families: a part-time holiday in the tropics. Instead of winter cold in the USSR, they were enjoying beautiful, warm Caribbean waters where they went snorkeling off Cuba's best beaches. Their Cuban assignment was considered a fabulous piece of luck; others could only dream of getting on the

Cuban team. Only the most reliable personnel were selected for it. On arrival in Havana, the Soviet technical assessors with their families were accommodated in a specially built, restricted gated complex - a walled Soviet compound in the village of Cojimar (Ernest Hemingway's old fishing haunt, 20 minutes east of Havana). The singles and the Spanish *Niños*[78] were accommodated in Havana's best hotels. Initially, we lived with Eduardo's mother in her Havana apartment; later, when I agreed to help our naval colleagues in Cienfuegos, our naval coordinator solicited the Ministry of Transport to arrange better accommodation for us.

The Soviets could not house us in Cojimar's Soviet compound because Eduardo was a Cuban citizen. The strict rules prohibited Cubans from even entering the military-guarded gates of this compound. This meant that Eduardo could not reside there with me. The Cojimar compound was unacceptable. Accordingly, the Ministry of Transport was asked to accommodate us in the fashion normally reserved for the Spanish Soviets (*Niños*). MITRANS sent us to live in a double room suite at the Hotel National, famous for its location and luxurious conditions. It was supposed to be a temporary arrangement since the hotel was not the best place to raise young children.

The Ministry promised to arrange for us more appropriate permanent family accommodation when it becomes available. The hotel was not far from MITRANS, and we could travel to work by taking a public bus near the hotel. The public transportation in this area of Havana was still quite decent in those years in comparison with other parts of the city. On the second floor of the building where we were working in the Ministry of Transport, there was an excellent daycare center for the employees of the Ministry.

The daycare center was well-equipped and staffed by cheerful young Cuban personnel. This was a free service where both our children were looked after and fed while we were working. I could even afford to come down from the seventh floor, where I was working on the second floor twice each day, to breastfeed our youngest son, Ernestico. Eduardo was working in the Ship Building and Maintenance Department located on a different floor in the same building, but we traveled to and from work together. Eduardo and I were happy with our jobs. We liked our technical superiors and our colleagues. We were enthusiastic about learning from them as much as possible.

I was working directly under Boris, a friend of my father, in my professional field. Boris was a tall and heavy-set middle-aged fellow with fair skin, a round face, green eyes, and reddish hair. He was a self-assured, resourceful, and street-smart survivor of the Soviet political system who often acted in a manner I found both calculating and dispassionate. He and his wife were perfect icons of a healthy Soviet middle-aged family: ethnically Russian, members of the Communist Party, street-savvy and competent at work. I kept friendly relations with his wife and trusted both of them as my only link to my parents, to whom Boris promised to look after me. Their daughter was close to my age, but she was attending university in Odessa because children older than 18 could not accompany Soviet personnel on their foreign travel.

Between ourselves, Boris and I often spoke in the "Odessan jargon" or local Odessa slang, sharing the intimate feeling of being back home as well as some privacy because Odessan expressions (a mix of Yiddish, Russian, Greek, and Ukrainian) were not understood by other Russian speakers. We Odessans consider this language, which is full of humor and irony, to be our true identity and privilege. All Odessans, independent of their ethnicity, learned this language at home, since birth, from their parents or neighbors; later, they would enrich it on the streets with friends. It became a sort of membership in an exclusive club of Odessans, and we were proud of this collective but exclusive invention, which made us feel more at ease.

The other two Soviet engineers who came with Boris were friendly with both Boris and me, but were often absent from the office. I was told they had other responsibilities. I suspected that they simply could not resist the temptation of the beach. I could have been wrong, but the Caribbean waters are incredibly beautiful, and no one could blame my colleagues for all the time they spent snorkeling while pretending to investigate the bottom of Jagua Bay.

Snorkeling was an important component in the Jagua Bay bottom studies.

Jagua Bay, surrounding Cienfuegos, where we were designing a new large port, is a huge bay completely protected by nature from the waves and winds of the open Caribbean Sea. It is located on Cuba's south-central Caribbean side, 250 kilometers opposite Havana, with the access road from Matanzas. Its geology is unique, with its complex limestone rock formation spread out over tectonic fractures. It was a complicated task to design and construct a modern port, and especially difficult to provide the deepwater draft required for a modern bulk cargo terminal in Cienfuegos.

Shortly after we collected some of the essential data and began the preliminary design of the numerous terminal facilities in Cienfuegos, two new senior Soviet designers from Leningrad joined our team. I found these two men, Alexey and Yuri, to be insular and uncommunicative, a type which we often called square heads. Both belonged to the Soviet Navy and were reserved, poised, and self-controlled. They did not mix with us socially for lunch or on weekends. I asked my boss, Boris, why they behaved this way, and he speculated that normal social relations were probably forbidden to them. Our design hall became subdivided. At the far end of our Ministry floor, a separate space was walled off and securely locked. Alexey and Yuri were working there.

Except for our Cuban translator, no one was admitted into their walled compartment, not even my boss Boris. During our first introduction to them, it was mentioned that they were naval designers from Leningrad and would be taking care of a new classified portion of the project in Cienfuegos. Only the personnel with appropriate security clearance could be involved in this work: Alexey, Yuri, Nora, and their translator. They were taking care of all their work by themselves.

The rest of us continued working on the design of commercial cargo terminals in the merchant port of Cienfuegos. To take advantage of the natural shape of the bay, the new port facilities would be widely spread along the coastline on both sides of Cienfuegos. My contribution was the design of an open terminal for general cargo such as gravel, sand, metals, wood, etc. Others in our group worked on designing different terminals for sugar, grain, chemicals, container cargo, general cargo, a deepwater oil terminal, an oil tank farm, an oil refinery, and some facilities for specialized cargo.

Returning to our new colleagues from Leningrad, no one from our group attempted to question them any further, as far as I witnessed, because we were familiar with the meaning of classified work. It is prohibited to ask, and it is better not to know. We simply kept apart from them; after all, they lacked the charm and humor to mix with Odessans.

Oil, sugar, bulk, and general cargo marine terminals designed in Cienfuegos by our team

My boss Boris expressed a note of envy when he said that these two men were certainly paid double salaries compared to ours, but such were the privileges of classified work. To obtain a commission like this, one had to have a high-security clearance, a filtering process that even Boris could not pass, even though Boris was a communist and of Russian ethnicity. Regardless, he thought that it would be difficult even for him to obtain such clearance because the KGB would filter back three generations to approve the reliability of the candidate.

If this was difficult for him, it would be impossible for me. Jewish ethnicity in "the fifth graph"[79] written into our passports and many other personal documents was the major obstacle. This racial or ethnic discrimination in the Soviet Union was justified by the argument that "Jews are cosmopolitans by nature; therefore, they will always be connected through Judaism to the international community, rendering their national loyalties suspect." This bigoted argument was the absurd fantasy of a delusional and paranoid Stalin. Why our leadership continued to carry on with this nonsense after Stalin's death, when his psychopathology was acknowledged, I don't know.[80]

Still, there were many other reasons why I could not be considered a likely candidate for high-security clearance: starting with not having proletarian roots going back three generations, not being a member of Komsomol, being married to a Cuban, and not being even recommended either by Komsomol or by the Communist Party or by other KGB operatives.

Then, some months later, an unexpected and dramatic event occurred with Nora, our Cuban technical translator. Nora disappeared, and nobody knew where or why. We never officially learned what happened to her. The rumor was that she was arrested by Cuban security. Her abrupt departure left the naval group linguistically lost. Our Cienfuegos civil design team could always have my assistance with translations when they needed it, but our naval colleagues could not allow anyone without first obtaining the appropriate security clearance access to their work.

Our sweet Cuban translator, Nora, was security cleared and respected by both Soviets and Cubans for being effective in her job. Already in her late fifties when we met, she was also initially born in Odessa and left Russia for Europe with her parents during the Revolution when she was still a child. Her family continued to speak Russian at home, and during the Second World War, escaping from the Nazis, they immigrated to Cuba, where she studied at Havana University for a professional career in simultaneous translations in Russian and Spanish. When the Revolution took place in Cuba, she was sent by the Cuban government to Moscow as a Cuban revolutionary for specialized security training and technical translation training, after which she was awarded Cuban and Soviet security clearance. When she returned to Cuba, she was assigned to work with the Soviet assessor groups of MITRANS, where she and I became friends.

Nora was a serious middle-aged Jewish lady with curly white hair. She often asked me for help when she had doubts about technical translations. Nora was modest, kind, and compassionate with a soft smile and a slow gait. She was interested in my well-being and often advised me about Cuban traditions and rules. We chatted a bit about ourselves; she asked me about my life in Odessa, and I was learning about her life in Cuba. I felt very grateful for her entrusting me because I was only a young puppy compared to her. She was the same age as my parents, but her experiences were very different. She enjoyed freedoms my parents could never dream of.

Once, she asked me what I liked to read. I don't remember my answer, probably something about adventure stories. I complained that it was difficult to find interesting books in Cuba.

Anyway, she offered me, making clear that it was to be kept secret, the Spanish edition of the Soviet magazine *Novy Mir* that included the publication of *One Day in the Life of Ivan Denisovich*. This was a groundbreaking contemporary short story written by Alexander Solzhenitsyn, which I, in my youthful ignorance, had never heard of before. It was cleared for publication by Nikita Khrushchev in October of 1962 (he was using it against his opponents in a Kremlin power struggle) and was not re-published after selling only 96,000 copies. When Khrushchev was ousted in 1964, Solzhenitsyn was declared an enemy of the people. *One Day in the Life of Ivan Denisovich* became prohibited from circulation or distribution in the USSR. However, it continued to be reproduced by photocopied and hand-written *Samizdat* (underground writings distributed secretly during the Communist era). The punishment for possession of a *Samizdat* publication could be a seven-year prison sentence and subsequent remote exile for two to five years under Article 70 of the Russian Criminal Code for anti-Soviet propaganda.

Being physically located in Cuba, so far

removed geographically and culturally from the Soviet Union, made me feel safer and more protected from KGB surveillance. I appreciated Nora's invitation and readily accepted. She begged me to be very careful. I promised to read the book in secret and not tell even my husband because it could be dangerous for Nora. Eduardo left for a business trip somewhere in Europe, and in his absence, I read *One Day in the Life of Ivan Denisovich* in Spanish during the night, with dictionaries when necessary.

When I began reading it, I understood the reason for its prohibition immediately. The work had shaken the conscience of Soviet citizens across the nation because it was written in honest language as a story describing just one day in the life of an ordinary Soviet political prisoner in the Gulag. This book really spooked me because it made it evident that I was a citizen of a nation kidnapped by ruthless and omnipotent tyranny. *One Day in the Life of Ivan Denisovich* is a story about Ivan Denisovich Shukhov, who has been punished, ostensibly for becoming a spy, after being captured by the Germans as a World War II prisoner of war.

Though innocent, he is nevertheless sentenced to 10 years of forced labor by the government on the false charge of spying. Brilliantly written, it impresses the reader with a sense of the brutality, torturous conditions, and utter waste of human abilities in the Soviet system. Millions of innocent and often the best and most talented people suffered and perished in forced labor concentration camps in the Northern and Far Eastern regions. Isaak, my father's younger brother, who was a professional violin player, died from starvation in such a prison.

I was always skeptical of Soviet propaganda, but I never knew the truth about the country's dark underside. To be honest, none of us truly could imagine the degree of cruelty of our evil system as it was described by Solzhenitsyn in *One Day in the Life of Ivan Denisovich*. I also understood that neither my family nor I could ever dream about justice from such an insane, cannibalistic system. We were merely insignificant flies caught in the flycatcher or "little bolts and screws in a giant machine of our state," as Stalin himself put it.

There was nothing we could do to help ourselves to avoid being burned and discarded when the state no longer needed us. We were less than slaves because slaves had economic value to their owners. We did not have an economic value in our homeland. On a whim, we simply could be wiped out. No, I could not forgive the reality, and sadly, I could not change it. I returned the book to Nora, thanked her, and commented that I read it in total secret from everyone at night while my husband was away on his business trip in Europe because I knew how dangerous it was to be caught with it.

A few weeks later, Nora did not come to work. Our Soviet colleagues did not know why nor where she was. Our Cuban coordinator was equally in the dark. I questioned my Cuban colleagues, and initially, they did not know either. However, several days later, I was told by some Cuban friends that she would not return because something very bad must have happened to her.

A few days later, my boss Boris asked me to temporarily help our group with translations because possibly Nora may not be working with us any longer. I was scared because I had heard from my father that the Soviet law provided seven or eight years of forced labor camps for reading and distributing banned literature. *Was it the book she gave me? Has somebody learned that I read it? Who could know that I read it? How?* I was also confused why Nora, being a Cuban citizen, would be punished under Soviet law. Something did not click, but whom could I ask when I was the guilty Soviet citizen reading a banned book?

Initially, I was shocked by the news about Nora, and later felt frightened because of my guilt for borrowing the Solzhenitsyn book from her. I have not disclosed my reading of Solzhenitsyn to anyone, even to Eduardo. Still, I was having nightmares that the culprit was the prohibited book she gave to me, and that this incident was the cause of her arrest. Now it will be my turn to become arrested. In the Soviet Union, such a gesture would suffice. I did not know enough about the rules in Cuba for the Soviets, and I was even afraid to ask. I expected serious trouble for myself and tried to control my anxiety. After a few sleepless nights wondering how to find out about what happened to Nora, I decided to stop this pointless worrying.

Probably, I would never learn the true reason for her arrest. I also wondered why educated middle-class Cubans were not revolted by these constant arrests, disappearances, and unfair accusations that were now taking place regularly in Cuba. When I privately asked my husband and some Cuban friends for their opinion, they would always come up with the same excuses – such as temporary excesses - reflecting their own fear and hope that it will not continue.

14. Nuclear Chicken Redux

In October 1962, during the Cuban Missile Crisis, the two superpowers confronted each other in what was memorably referred to as a game of 'nuclear chicken'. The two sides were on a collision course, 'eyeball to eyeball', with enough nuclear arms to destroy much of the world. Each opponent hoped the other would blink first ("chicken out") and thus avoid MAD (Mutually Assured Destruction). This was the most dangerous nuclear-armed confrontation ever to occur between the superpowers. The crisis was settled when the USSR agreed to remove its nuclear arsenal from Cuba and defuse the standoff. By 1968, however, the Soviet Union had begun a second and very secret nuclear arms build-up in Cuba, setting the stage for another game of "Nuclear Chicken - Redux" (resurgence).

The autumn of 1968 became chaotic for my Soviet colleagues. The arrest of Nora created problems for the engineers on our naval team. Unlike ourselves, they were limited in hiring new personnel to help them with the Spanish language because of the high-security clearance requirements. They asked their superiors for an urgent translator replacement. But the answer came back that, at present, resources were limited. Our navy colleagues were informed that going forward, they would have to use only Soviet translators with appropriate security clearance. This was inconvenient because they were forced to wait until our security organs, GRU (Soviet Military Intelligence) or the KGB (Soviet State Security), sent to Cuba the appropriate Soviet translator who was familiar with our technical terminology. Meanwhile, the Soviet embassy was asked to provide a general Soviet translator with proper clearance. The embassy replied that they too were short of Soviet translators because they were looking after the needs of thousands of Soviet military and civil "assessors" who were currently stationed in Cuba.[81] Meanwhile, our naval designers, Alexey and Yuri, were stuck, unable to interpret or understand the essential technical information in the Spanish language.

Until now, I have been working only on the Cienfuegos commercial project. Our naval colleagues had consulted with Boris about the possibility of co-opting me to their group, but at the time, Boris failed to mention anything to me. Clearly, it was difficult to obtain a replacement for Nora in a reasonable time. It would have to be a Soviet-Spanish technical translator with marine and coastal training. Meanwhile, I was a Soviet engineer who specialized in this field; therefore, uniquely technically qualified.

When one morning, while working in the office, Boris informed me that an embassy car was waiting to drive me to a meeting at the Soviet embassy, I became alarmed at the news of this sudden, unscheduled meeting. I had overheard rumors before about the traditional method of arresting Soviet culprits abroad inside the Soviet embassies and then delivering them back to the USSR in military craft. To live a frightened life was a normal state for all Soviet citizens who were conditioned to be afraid much of the time on a very primitive survival level. My own generation of Soviets, born during the 1940s, was brought up by our families and schools in the same vice grip of fear which produced cynical conformers - the fresh genetic construction of a new Soviet people who were never expected to question any decisions of the Soviet Government or its Communist Party.

Those who were careless enough to make political jokes or simply to be in the wrong place at the wrong time could become the subject of persecution. Permanent fear of torture if arrested, like an exposed nerve, controlled the psychological state of our society. All other moral values and emotions were secondary to this fear.

This type of socialization was possible only because we didn't know anything else; we were brainwashed from the moment we were born - proper zombie material. This process was not a matter of converting our ideology into a religion, as the West believed; rather, it was a phenomenon of mechanical obedience from traumatized and terrorized hostages who were born in a societal prison without windows to a different cultural or social landscape. It was mainly thanks to my father's open mind and emotional objectivity that I did not fall into a state of dogmatic fanaticism. Of course, my character played some part, but under my father's wise guidance, I was less brainwashed than others and, to survive, learned to pretend obedience. An open revolt would be madness.

When I asked Boris about the reason for the meeting, he answered that he didn't know. I was feeling very anxious, suspecting that the meeting could be the result of my most recent crime: for the first time in my life, reading a book by Solzhenitsyn, which was now prohibited in both the Soviet Union and Cuba. It was possible that, following the arrest of Nora, she had revealed that I had borrowed from her the forbidden subversive literature. The book had been permanently banned, removed from all stores, libraries, and personal use, with a prohibition against publishing or reading, together with all other works of Solzhenitsyn. Those who were caught reading banned literature were arrested and sentenced for anti-Soviet propaganda to labor camps for anti-Soviet propaganda.[82] Working in Cuba as a Soviet citizen with a Soviet team, I could be accused of organized anti-Soviet propaganda if it was linked to Nora, who disappeared and, according to rumors, was arrested.

By 1968, the invincible virtual version of Stalin was back, totally exonerated. During the Brezhnev era of 'Stalinism without Stalin', I could anticipate arrest, return to the Soviet Union, and a prison sentence for reading the banned literature. Especially now, after reading Solzhenitsyn, I understood the degree of inhuman tortures Soviet prisoners are subjected to. A charge of anti-Soviet propaganda usually brought seven years in a labor camp. As a result, paralyzed by fear, I imagined all kinds of bloodthirsty dragons who might attack me alive as they did in the case of Ivan Denisovich, the hero of the Solzhenitsyn novel.

On my arrival at the Embassy, security led me to a private meeting room where my naval colleagues were already seated at the table. Everyone appeared quite relaxed and friendly. The meeting was chaired by two political officers from the embassy (nicknamed “Pompa” by us; in reality, they were KGB operatives). They invited me to take a seat with them at the table. I was ready to invent all kinds of excuses for, as yet unannounced accusations; however, to my relief, I was not accused of reading Solzhenitsyn. Instead, they asked me to temporarily help my naval colleagues with technical translations from Spanish to Russian required for their classified project work.

They said that, due to extenuating circumstances, they would be appreciative if I could help, for the time being, with translations for both groups (those working on civil projects and those working on the naval project), until the arrival of a technical translator from the Soviet Union dedicated to it. It was clear that their determination not to use a Cuban translator might have to do with Nora. God knows why Nora was arrested. Obviously, her arrest was unrelated to my reading of banned literature; maybe there was something wrong on the Cuban side. This situation led my Soviet colleagues to the idea of using me temporarily despite my lack of the required security clearance and formal academic qualifications in Spanish.

Later on, I discovered that there was another problem with the Cuban side, and not just because of Nora. The problem was rooted in serious Soviet mistrust of the anarchistic antics of Fidel Castro himself, who was constantly manipulating events to provoke a Soviet pre-emptive nuclear strike against the USA from Cuban territory. During Cuba's post-revolutionary alliance with the Soviets, his principal objective was to court Soviet nuclear arms for Cuba. Castro nearly got what he wanted when, on October 27, 1962, he manipulated the Soviet operator of an anti-craft battery, Major Ivan Gerchenov in Camaguey Eastern Division (under General Stepan Grechko), to shoot down the single American U-2 reconnaissance aircraft which appeared on their radar despite clear orders from Moscow to abstain.

The American pilot, Rudolf Anderson, was the only person killed by enemy fire during the Cuban Missile Crisis. It was not possible to justify the shooting down of a single small reconnaissance aircraft with the excuse that the Soviets believed it was an American preemptive attack on Cuba. Daily over the previous week, American reconnaissance airplanes were flying over the island, taking pictures of Soviet missile sites in Cuba. These aerial photos enabled US Ambassador Adlai Stevenson to address the UN Security Council and his Soviet counterpart Valentin Zorin on the 25th of October, decisively demonstrating the presence of Soviet missiles in Cuba, notwithstanding Zorin's denials. On the same day, immediately following the downing of the U-2, Fidel Castro telegraphed Khrushchev with an urgent request for a Soviet preemptive strike. Khrushchev realized the danger and ordered the removal of some missiles from Cuba.[83] This was the official Soviet version.

Truthfully, this version of the Soviet military shooting down an American U-2 was difficult to believe. A Soviet operator cannot disobey the orders of his commander, who in turn would never disobey the orders from the military chain of command in Moscow, only because he was influenced by a foreign leader. If it were true, this operational officer would be court-martialed; instead, he was awarded the title of general. He was not demoted but was simply transferred back to Ukraine and then promoted, presumably to bribe his silence.

Fifty years after the October Missile Crisis, various Soviet participants published electronically, on an officially approved website, their memoirs of the U-2 incident and the death of Rudolf Anderson. It was noted that there was a high-level Cuban inspection at the moment in which the incident took place. Clear and expressed orders from the Moscow Central Military Commander not to shoot at aerial targets were breached on that occasion. None of the Soviet participants specified who was inspecting the battery and who breached the Moscow orders. Later, Moscow scolded the commander of the anti-craft missile division for coming under the Cubans' influence and disobeying Moscow's orders. The next morning, the official Cuban Government periodical *Revolución* claimed that it was the Cuban army that shot down the aerial intruder.

A more detailed version of the deadly event is presented by Carlos Franqui, who was a long-time comrade-in-arms with Fidel as well as the chief editor of *Revolucion* (later known as *Granma*) - the main newspaper of the new revolutionary Cuban state. Carlos Franqui was a nationalist and widely respected for his integrity.[84] Some of Franqui's reporters were permanently attached to Fidel, including on that fateful day when the American U-2 was shot down. Carlos Franqui's version was that on October 27, 1962, Fidel visited the Soviet anti-aircraft batteries in Camaguey. Fidel paid daily visits to the Soviet batteries during these decisive days of the October Crisis.

When the American surveillance plane suddenly appeared on the radar, Fidel asked the Soviet operator how he would shoot the enemy attack plane. The operator explained that the target was already automatically pinpointed and showed him the ground-to-air missile launch button, which would be used if the operator was shooting at a target. Fidel immediately pressed that button. This is how the U-2, flown by Rudolph Anderson, was shot down personally by Fidel Castro. The Soviets had to cover up this extremely dangerous and embarrassing incident by transferring the Soviet officials involved back home and awarding them with higher ranks to keep them quiet.

Franqui's account has the air of plausibility.

He was, after all, the Chief Editor of *Revolución,* which had announced the following morning that it was the Cuban military that shot down the U-2, and nobody denied this claim. Additional circumstantial evidence can be gleaned from an appreciation of Fidel's volatile and aggressive personality, coupled with his often-stated determination to strike at America. Finally, an understanding of the strict chain of command in the Soviet military would render an alternative explanation highly unlikely.

According to Franqui, Fidel commented, following the U2 incident: "Well, now we shall see if we will have the war or not." Then, he jumped into his jeep, returned to Havana, and sent numerous telegrams to Moscow, through the Soviet ambassador, with his request for a Soviet pre-emptive strike against the United States. As a result of this misadventure, Soviet anti-missile batteries became off-limits to all Cubans, no matter their rank.

Following the missile crisis, the Soviets announced their decision to repatriate their nuclear missiles from Cuba. Fidel's reaction was an explosion of rage. Both he and Che Guevara had cast suspicion on the seriousness of Soviet intentions because of the Soviet refusal to bother to camouflage the missile batteries. For what reasons? Did the Soviets intend all along to be discovered? Would that mean Cuba was only a pawn between the two world superpowers in their theater of power politics? Fidel was furious and even attempted to prohibit the actual removal of missiles following the "October Crisis" resolution.

He bombarded Moscow with telegrams trying to convince the Soviet leadership that a Soviet pre-emptive strike against America was an act of daring for which all Cuban people were willing and ready to die. However, this series of reckless tirades unnerved the Soviets, who now regarded Fidel as an unpredictable, unbalanced, and dangerous partner who almost burned their 'theater' down. Nikita Khrushchev wrote a reply to Fidel Castro on October 30, 1962, with an explanation to calm him down.[85] He followed up with a special envoy, Anastas Mikoyan, to temper Fidel's anger. Mikoyan made a valiant effort, even sacrificing himself personally to this end when he came to Cuba for three weeks to quench the raging fire while his wife was dying from cancer in Moscow.

Khrushchev intended to withdraw from Cuba the Soviet strategic nuclear weapons but leave smaller tactical Soviet missiles with nuclear warheads under Cuban control. However, when Mikoyan personally experienced the fury of Fidel in Havana, he understood that the Soviets could not afford to leave any nuclear warheads under Cuban control. For the sheer sake of demonstrating his power, Fidel was ready to use them. At their last meeting, Mikoyan neglected to inform Fidel that a decision had been reached to remove all Soviet tactical weapons from Cuba. On the same day that he returned to Moscow (November 24, 1962), Mikoyan visited the private home of the Cuban Ambassador to the USSR. He met with Faure Chomón Mediavilla before he even saw his own family.

The surprise visit to the Ambassador's Moscow private residence and the discussion during their meeting are described in a letter from Faure Chomón Mediavilla to Fidel Castro, sent the next morning on November 25th.[86] With many lines redacted in the archival version of the letter, it is still evident from the readable content that Mikoyan was very worried and had to throw a bone at his Cuban mad dog, that was an explanation that the Soviet missiles already served their objective: Kennedy promised not to invade Cuba which the Soviets believed Kennedy would honor as long as he is in power and that is certain for another five to six years. If Americans act aggressively toward Cuba, the Soviets will deploy their long-range missiles from the USSR against the US. Faure also implied that Mikoyan promised to sneak the Soviet nuclear weapons back to Cuba five or six years after the Americans calmed down.

When the deal was agreed upon, Fidel was invited to visit Moscow in the spring of 1963, during which the Soviets promised once again to return the Soviet missile base. However, this promise had to wait five years longer until the Soviet Government sacked Khrushchev in a coup and installed its new pro-Stalinist leader, Leonid Brezhnev. This new Soviet leadership had developed a new plan involving deceptive techniques necessary to effectively and secretly restore the Soviet base in Cuba for strategic and tactical nuclear missiles.

Brezhnev began implementing his promise to

Fidel in 1968. However, this time, the Soviet leaders intended to ensure their exclusive sovereign control over operations, blocking any possibility of Cuban interference in operational matters.

We never found out what happened to Nora. The rumors reached me that our security officials were reprimanded for previously using a Cuban translator on a sensitive military project. Nevertheless, obtaining sufficient Soviet technical translators on short notice was virtually impossible because many thousands of Soviet assessors and troops in Cuba required technical language assistance.

The embassy officers assured me that I was being asked to assist our naval colleagues only temporarily, which would not require a formal transfer to the Navy. I was so exhilarated at the mere fact of not being accused of any wrongdoing that I abandoned my habitual caution. In my youthful inexperience regarding the manipulations of the KGB and the ambiguities of Soviet law, I succumbed to their pressure and agreed to provide interim assistance, hoping that it would have no negative consequences for my future. Following the arrest of Nora and after my fright over the Solzhenitsyn book, I felt intimidated and was anxious to finish on a positive note with all of these negotiations inside the walls of the Soviet embassy. There was also an urge to get out of the embassy building as quickly as possible because of its oppressive atmosphere. I knew only too well that it was not advisable to turn down the *security organs* (the unifying name for all Soviet security institutions: KGB, GRU, and MVD) because they would retaliate viciously, sooner or later.

I expressed my reservations about the increased workload while my family and I were suffering from inadequate living conditions. I thought this was the right moment to request better accommodations. I told them that I also did not want to quit my design work for the commercial port of Cienfuegos because it was a unique opportunity to learn and grow as a professional. They all smiled at my naiveté about the importance of my professional work and treated me attentively by promising to consider my other needs and responsibilities. They suggested that they could help to improve my living conditions and provisions.

This additional help was very enticing to me because we continued living in a cramped apartment with Maria, Eduardo's mother, and the other seven family members, in addition to the four of us. Maria never wasted a moment reminding me daily that only Eduardo and I could resolve this unsustainable situation by demanding from MITRANS a family residence. Consequently, I agreed to help my naval colleagues the best I could - despite my scant understanding of what was entailed.

After we had come to the initial verbal agreement, I was told to sign a confidentiality agreement, a traditional requirement for any security-related engagement. They brought the standard form ready for my signature. I asked if I might read it first at home, where I could better concentrate. They refused me permission to take it home for reading and offered, instead, to leave me alone in the room because this Agreement should not be removed from the embassy. I reluctantly complied. I was afraid that it would be hard to concentrate in that atmosphere, but a cursory reading revealed nothing threatening or risky for me. The document had to do with the commitment not to disclose any aspects of classified work to anyone, including my closest family: my husband, my parents, my relatives, friends, etc. It mentioned that a breach of this Confidentiality Agreement would be punishable under the Criminal Code of the USSR.

Probably, such a confidentiality agreement was normal. Surely, they had to protect classified information. At the time of signing this confidentiality agreement, I was certain that I would never, under any circumstances, want to disclose important Soviet military information to anyone, not even to members of my family, for their own sake. I was also advised by all present to take advantage of this opportunity to improve my credentials and gain advantages. Additionally, one of the KGB officers at the embassy promised to talk with the administration of the Ministry of Transport about my complaint regarding our living conditions in Cuba, which were not yet resolved. This was very convincing, and I signed the confidentiality agreement. I had no idea at the time that a breach of this agreement could bring charges of treason against the Soviet homeland under Article 64 of the Soviet

Penal Code (1960) and put me on the KGB wanted list.

"Life", John Lennon famously wrote, "is what happens to you while you're busy making other plans."

From then on, I was obliged to attend the embassy's regular political briefings called '*politchas*' (political hour) together with my Soviet colleagues to be briefed on the latest Soviet version of current political events. We were advised that these briefings reflected the only correct interpretation of world events, and we could trust only this version and not Cubans or other foreign nationals (French, English, or Spanish) who were traditionally subservient to the USA, which was designated as 'the main enemy and a true empire of evil'.

In general, I learned that Soviet navies by the 1960s had developed capabilities to increase their presence in the world's oceans, but the American Navy, following our Soviet version, kept interfering aggressively with the Soviet fleet to limit the Soviet presence and intimidate them by constantly harassing them at sea and from the air. The result was the constant interruption of planned Soviet naval exercises. The head of the Soviet Navy, in response to this arrogant aggression, ordered an increase in the number of naval expeditions in the Norwegian Sea, north-eastern Atlantic, Mediterranean, and the Middle East, and to conduct naval exercises in the Mexican Gulf jointly with the Cuban Navy, thus establishing our presence just a few kilometers away from the territory of the United States. However, joint Soviet-Cuban exercises in the Gulf met with a serious obstacle: the lack of a naval base for refueling, resupply, repair, and change of crew.

During our briefings, Cuba was described as ideally situated in the region for such a mission. However, after the October Missile Crisis of 1962, the USSR and the USA verbally agreed to some kind of deterrent, which limits the Soviet presence in Cuban territory, claiming that the presence of Soviet arms threatens the security of the United States. This verbal agreement, according to embassy officials, had nothing to do with international law. The Soviet military presence in Cuba, in the Soviet view, was completely legal even in 1962. The Soviet government kept some of those Soviet tactical missiles in Cuba as an affirmation or gesture of our legitimate presence here.

The Soviet press continued to deny the presence of any Soviet missiles in Cuba. They even said that American aerial photos simply confused agricultural equipment, mainly Belarus's tractors, for missile batteries. They claimed that the US reaction to the Soviet military presence in Cuba once again represented a 'typical example of American aggressive and bullying militaristic attitudes'.[87] This American aggression initially provoked the appeal of Fidel Castro to the Soviet government for protection. To prove this point, our political officer handed us a copy of the Cuban newspaper *Revolución* from October 5, 1962, which quoted on its first page an article by the Associated Press Agency about an imminent

American naval attack against Cuba during the second half of October. This was the main reason, according to our Soviet version, that war with the United States was enthusiastically solicited by Fidel himself during his internationally organized campaigns around the world. We were also warned that the pressure from Fidel himself on Soviet divisions in Cuba is intensive and persistent and that our military personnel in Cuba are always vulnerable under his spell particularly, during his passionate speeches.

To avoid getting caught again by the US, as was the case during the 1962 Cuban Missile Crisis, the Soviet government decided to find an alternative route for the Soviet Navy and an alternative location for the naval base. To that end, they took extra precautions by sending Soviet hydrographic teams, beginning in 1964, to prepare for future naval activity in the Caribbean region by deploying an oceanographic research fleet to survey the area around Cuba, including Mona, Windward, and Anegada passages. The resulting data facilitated the development of a carefully staged plan for surface and underwater submarine service base facilities to be designed and built by our team in Cienfuegos. It offered the following three advantages:

A location where the Americans would not expect it: Cienfuegos is located on the southern coast of Cuba, not so visible from the US. It has a long, narrow, and shallow rock bottom entrance channel that would not permit the submerged entrance of submarines unless it was excavated at great effort and cost. The Americans would not expect an underwater submarine base to be built in such a geologically hostile location.

The construction of the naval base was

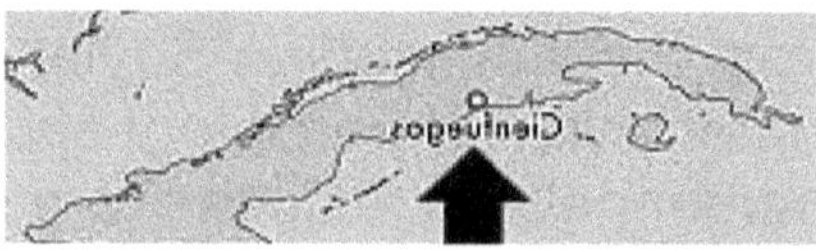

Cienfuegos Soviet navy base and commercial port

camouflaged by the construction of a new commercial port of Cienfuegos, which was already underway.

The naval project in Cuba intensified the requirement for Soviet development of innovative stealth technologies permitting the Soviet submarine fleet to operate silently and undetected.

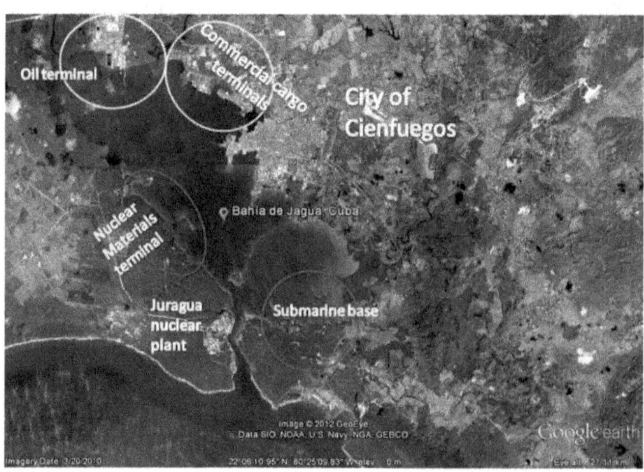

Bay of Jagua (Cienfuegos Bay) is on the southern coast of Cuba.

All this work related to the naval base should be carried out in total secrecy, especially before and during the epoch of '*razryadka*' (Soviet name for *détente*). According to Pompa (our political officer), this policy was understood differently by the two sides and misinterpreted by the rich and easy-going Americans. In the Soviet Short Political Dictionary, *razryadka* means a steady strengthening of the position of the countries of the socialist camp and defeat of capitalist forces. For the American leadership, however, *détente* usually means, according to Pompa, business at any cost. Of course, when the American administration is using taxpayers' money for multi-billion-dollar credits to the Soviets, it is hardly capitalism.

The Soviet leadership intended to create a strategic military advantage with its Cuban base to be prepared for an armed conflict with the USA. There could be no greater advantage or better opportunity than a secret Cuban naval base for submarines equipped with ballistic and cruise missiles with nuclear warheads. These submarines could approach unnoticed and attack most of the American territory.

I learned that the really important instruction was to make sure that the Soviet military in Cuba would act exclusively on orders from Moscow. The political officers concluded my crash course in politics on a bright note: "I hope that you will enjoy working with our naval personnel, and don't worry, it is only temporary, and if anybody inquires about your job, you should always answer that you are working with a Soviet team designing and building sugar terminals in Cienfuegos."

My access to information was supposed to be limited, but my curiosity, as usual, had free reign. My job was to translate from Spanish to Russian all data and information required for the design and to translate from Russian to Spanish for the periodic briefings of the Cuban leadership. Still, my situation as an insider permitted me to create, over time, a jigsaw puzzle pattern from the different pieces of information, overseen and overheard.

The new naval base in Cienfuegos was to combine berth and service facilities for both the naval surface fleet and submarines (diesel-powered and nuclear-powered). Our mandate was to provide for accommodation, service, and supply of submarines equipped with nuclear warhead missiles: ballistic or cruise and/or torpedoes. This is how Cienfuegos became the only Soviet Navy base in the entire region of the Americas.

The beautiful and very large Bay of Jagua and its long entrance channel presented very serious construction problems for our mandate. Its bottom formation consists of coastal limestone rock, which required dredging from 15 meters draft in the first phase and extended to 18 meters draft in the second phase to provide for underwater service stations.

It represented a staggering amount of very difficult underwater rock dredging required for the passage of submarines through the long access entrance channel and maneuvering inside of the Bay of Jagua. The dredged bottom also required periodic maintenance because of heavy sedimentation due to strong currents. I was involved in the first phase, which provided diverse pier and harbor berth facilities for the surface fleet, in addition to the specialized piers for submarines in Punta Movida and Cayo Alcatraz, as well as anchored buoys for tenders (floating plants for service, repair, and maintenance of submarines) and specialized tankers required to refuel both types of submarines.

The first stage of naval infrastructure also provided for accommodations of Soviet administrative service personnel and marine crews. The residences, workshops, storage, and recreation facilities were built in Cayo Alcatraz, Punta Movida, and Jaruqua in the restricted military areas in the Bay of Jagua.

Some of the remaining specialized submarine terminal facilities and special heavy cargo terminals for nuclear materials can be observed today in Punta Movida and Cayo Alcatraz.

Remains of the submarine base can be observed today on Google Earth

Such a large naval base required a significant draft and a huge amount of bedrock excavation, including special areas for service ships, used to store nuclear and other military materials and nuclear debris barges. I left Cuba before the start of the second phase of this project, involving even larger excavations to provide underwater service stations for refueling and servicing submarines. Our work was given a fast-track priority. Yet, due to its challenging geology, it was very difficult to work and required costly specialized equipment.

Pier for submarines in Cayo Alcatraz

There were two main types of older diesel-powered submarines, as well as more advanced nuclear-powered platforms, both classes capable of delivering nuclear-tipped missiles. Land-based Soviet missiles on the Cuban island were exchanged for Soviet missiles at sea. The two classes of Soviet subs were:

PLARK - nuclear-powered cruise missile submarines equipped with nuclear warheads and torpedoes: Soviet class Project 645-K27 (class November) and Project 675-K166 (NATO class Echo II).

PLARK with the missile launch lifted

And PLARB - nuclear-powered ballistic missile submarines equipped with nuclear warheads: Project 627 Russian class KIT, Hotel class, and nuclear stealth-designed K-137 *Leninets* of Project 667A, known in the West as *Navaga* (Yankee II class).

PLARB Pr. 667A, class Yankee II

The rest of our team continued working on

the design of commercial cargo terminals in the merchant port of Cienfuegos. To take advantage of the natural shape of the bay, the new port facilities would be widely spread along the coastline on both sides of Cienfuegos. My contribution was the design of an open terminal for general cargo such as gravel, sand, metals, wood, etc. Others in our group worked on designing different terminals for sugar, grain, chemicals, container cargo, general cargo, a deepwater oil terminal, an oil tank farm, an oil refinery, and some facilities for specialized cargo.

This strategy required total secrecy in order not to alarm Americans. With this in mind, a slow and inconspicuous start was decided upon. The Soviet strategy began with the deployment of the older diesel-powered submarines rather than the nuclear-powered submarines. Americans didn't know that those older diesel-powered subs (Foxtrot and Golf 1) had been modified and were now equipped with nuclear warhead ballistic missiles P-21 with a range of 1400 kilometers. It was planned to slowly escalate this fleet to the nuclear-powered submarines of the November class with nuclear warhead torpedoes, and later to nuclear-powered Echo II class submarines with nuclear warhead guided cruise missiles, which could be launched while they are submerged at a keel depth of around 50 meters. The next planned escalation was for Navaga-class Yankee II subs, which were fast and acoustically undetectable. We called them *Vanka Washington* (total 33 subs) and later

Murena Projects: 667B and 667BD (total 22 subs), in addition to Delfin project 667BDPM (total seven subs). These submarines were equipped with 16 P27 submarine-launched ballistic nuclear warhead missiles with a 3000-kilometer range, which could be launched from 50 meters under the surface of the water. Out of the preceding total, 34 were powerful ultra-quiet submarines for strategic and tactical nuclear weapons. These carried 544 nuclear warheads.

The first stage of naval infrastructure also provided for accommodations of Soviet administrative service personnel and marine crews. The residences, workshops, storage, and recreation facilities were built in Cayo Alcatraz, Punta Movida, and Jaruqua in the restricted military areas in the Bay of Jagua.

The airport at nearby St. Antonio de Los Baños was converted for the use of Soviet attack bombers MiG-23 and TU-95 and TU-142 fighter planes equipped with nuclear bombs, torpedoes, and ballistic nuclear warhead missiles against submarines.

Soviet MIGs in St. Antonio de Los Baños

Operationally, none of this would be possible without advanced global communication facilities. This function was fulfilled by 4 Soviet SIGINT (Signal Intelligence) collection facilities built in Cuba, the largest being at Lourdes (halfway between Havana and Cienfuegos) and operational since 1962.[88]

Ex-Soviet SIGINT Spy Center in Lurdes, Cuba

The Lurdes complex was capable of monitoring a wide array of commercial and government communications throughout the southeastern United States and between the United States and Europe. Lourdes intercepted transmissions from microwave towers in the United States, communication satellite downlinks, and a wide range of shortwave and high-frequency radio transmissions. It also served as a mission ground station and analytical facility supporting Russian SIGINT satellites that supplied the USSR with 75% of all global intelligence information over the next 20 years.

Abandoned Juragua nuclear plant and its special heavy cargo terminal

A special heavy cargo berth and deep-water buoys were also constructed for the future Juragua nuclear plant, built in the 1970s, which also required blasting of large volumes of ground rock for the water cooling channels.

The main objective of Soviet naval base facilities was to house and serve the Soviet submarine fleet (both diesel and nuclear-powered) in Jagua Bay (Cienfuegos Bay) to allow for refueling, repair, and supply. This base is intended to service Soviet subs, which patrol the American coast undetected. Their guided nuclear-armed missiles could be launched from 50 meters below the water and could hit American targets accurately in a matter of minutes, assuring the first-strike capability and significantly reducing the response capabilities of the US adversary.

Soviet military facilities in Cuba constituted the largest Soviet high-tech military and naval base outside of the Soviet Union. They were built in complete secrecy and in a relatively short period of time. According to Russian sources, published after the fall of the Soviet Union, these facilities operated successfully over the next 20 years, servicing Soviet nuclear submarines equipped with nuclear warhead missiles. There were 29 repair and supply service missions in Cienfuegos (each lasting from 40 to 90 days) from 1971 until 1991, the year the Soviet Union was dissolved.[89]

The American Government, surprisingly, showed little reaction to this blatant breach of the 1962 deal between Kennedy and Khrushchev to remove all nuclear missile capabilities from Cuba. Instead, there was some low-key, private, and inconsequential verbal diplomacy between Henry Kissinger and Andrei Gromyko.

In 1986, there was a fatal explosion near Bermuda of a K219 Navaga-Class nuclear-powered submarine cruiser with 16 ballistic missiles equipped with 34 nuclear warheads of 3000-kilometer range. Only when a Soviet Navy surface ship arrived to rescue the sub and tow it back to Cuba, did the incident call international attention to the heavily militarized Soviet naval presence in the area.

The theater stage was now set, and the show proceeded according to the playbill described in Appendix 1.

15. Crab on a Slow Boil

Back at the office, I met with Boris. He was already informed about the agreement reached in the Soviet embassy. However, he did not look pleased with this decision because it meant that I would disappear behind the walls of the Navy's office, and his assignments would become secondary. But after all, he was a foreign-assigned Soviet citizen, which means that he dutifully complied. It was well known in the Soviet Union that foreign assignments were awarded only after the accreditation in political maturity. I despised such behavior as demeaning conformism.

Cubans were learning these skills as well, but were still much behind us. Che Guevara only dreamed of creating a 'New Man'. We Soviet citizens living in the 1960s were the third generation of programmed 'Homo Sovieticos' known for self-censored cynicism and conformism, and who would reap the advantages at any cost and swing opinions in strict unison with the Party. To get where he was, Boris had to distinguish himself in this arena. I landed in a foreign assignment by accident, selected not according to my political credentials, but by being in the right time and the right place with a workable level of Spanish on account of my marriage to Eduardo.

After some bargaining with Boris, they agreed to a temporary change in priorities regarding sharing my time. This is how I was finally admitted into the walled cubicle of our naval team to tackle their mess of data and translate their paperwork. Working together on the same project with Alexey and Yuri helped us become friendlier towards one another, notwithstanding their formality and reserve. By now, I could better appreciate the reason for their aloof behavior after my briefings in the Soviet embassy. I understood that 'the security organs' would be keeping an eye on all of us.

When I was left alone with Boris, we continued to use our Odessan dialect in conversations because it relaxed us. I suspected that he was trying to ingratiate himself with me in an attempt to create an ambiance of intimacy and privacy between us, since the Russian-speaking outsiders could not understand us. In my longing for my father and Odessa, it was very welcome. I ignored his obvious patronizing attitude.

"What was all this '*tsuris*' (problem) about?" He looked at me, staring intensely into my eyes, and continued:

"Did you get a spanking from 'Pompa' (a reference to the KGB)? They asked for my opinion about you. Don't worry; I recommended you as a hard-working Soviet specialist with a family tradition in this field; except, you never told me that you are not even a member of Komsomol."

"You never asked," I responded, already feeling annoyed.

Now it was Boris who displayed anger:

"Pompa surprised me when he made clear that you were not mature, that you are not even a member of Komsomol, and that I was not thorough in my evaluation of you. Paulina, how could you avoid becoming a member of the Komsomol? This is stupid! How did that happen? You completely misled me about your political maturity. You let me down. Please enlighten me about the truth of how that could happen."

"I don't know Boris," I responded with my accustomed excuse, "It was just taken for granted that all students at the university are enrolled either with Komsomol or with the Communist Party. It was presumed that I was as well. When Komsomol asked me for my registration number, I confessed that I had none since I had missed the opportunity of joining when I was 15 years old. I explained that my construction company didn't have a Komsomol organization because our employees were older than the Komsomol age group. I promised to enroll as soon as possible, but was swept off my feet with the burden of work and my studies."

"*Taki da*! (for sure). Paulina doesn't make me laugh," Boris wasn't easily fooled. "You were not working full-time and studying at the same time during all five years at university, only the first two years!"

"This is true, but I became a married woman during my third year, and between the university, cooking, and looking after a baby, I felt too old and busy to join the crowd of 15-

year-olds in an enrollment ceremony at Komsomol. But at the same time, I was still too young to become a Party member, which I could do only at the age of 25."

"You are *brulliant chistoy vodi"* (Odessan irony for 'too smart')," he replied sarcastically. "But I was the one they requested to give you a recommendation, and I became implicated with an immature *'salaga'* (young and inexperienced) like you." He continued: "Remember this: if your big mouth spills a drop to anybody of what you are learning from the naval project, they will hang not only you but me as well since I recommended you."

"Boris, please don't make me feel guilty; I haven't done anything! You are angry at me, but I didn't ask for this new job! Please, Boris, help me understand why it is such a big deal?" I was pleading for his opinion in an attempt to learn more.

This project is so important that even I don't have sufficient clearance for it. I am angry that you might not appreciate how much I put myself at risk for you and had to put my head on the chopping block, which is not what I like doing, especially after this trouble with Nora. Why do I need this *'gembel'* (this complication), and where is my *'gesheft'*? (the gain)," he resentfully pointed out.

"Have you finally heard anything more about Nora? Where is she, and how is she?" I asked by way of changing the subject.

"No, I haven't. They don't want a Cuban translator anymore because the Soviet military projects will be in our sovereign control, operated exclusively under the command of our government, according to our operational plans. We will not have to share data and control with local *'tuzemtzami'* (aboriginals). Our security depends on it, and I hope you will finally behave responsibly, at least for our sake."- he finished lecturing me.

"Yes, the embassy made me sign a confidentiality agreement. But now tell me, how come we have all this missile technology and thousands of Soviet technical assessors in Cuba if we made a deal with the Americans to remove the missiles? Is it possible that we will make Americans angry again?"- I braved to ask him.

"Who gave you this information?"- he asked, surprised.

"Pompa, at the embassy! But isn't all this very dangerous if the Americans find out and start a war?"

"'*Chtobi da, tak net!'* (Odessan expression meaning 'not exactly'). It is *'chaloymis'* (meaning nonsense)! But generally, everything is possible, which is why it is such a big *'tsuris'* (problem). In the worst case, if Americans do find out about our naval base and commit the grave mistake of attacking Cuba, at least it will all happen very far from our homeland! Geographically, America is much closer to Cuba than to the Soviet Union. Look at the map:

only 90 nautical miles or 166 kilometers from the United States to Cuba. This fact alone should prevent American retaliation with nuclear missiles. Their reluctance to launch a nuclear attack against Cuba will give us time for diplomacy and an international media campaign to stop their aggression before retaliating on Soviet territory.

"American aggressors will always lose, even in this worst case. They know that, and they will not risk their reputation for a small island like Cuba. As soon as they confront us, they will lose politically at home and will be portrayed internationally as brutal villains, once again, against little Cuba. This will cost President Nixon his forthcoming election. His popularity at home will sink even deeper than it is now. And for what? For this small island with its antichrist for a leader? What a circus! No, Americans are not serious about Cuba; they are rich but not '*meshuga*' (crazy). This is why it is so important for you to keep your mouth shut, my dear. Remember, I am talking to you about this matter for the last time," concluded Boris.

"Where in all of this is the advantage for us?" I wondered out loud.

"We are defending Cuba and negotiating with Americans as a global player on our terms: from a position of power. If it becomes necessary to inflict the first strike, we can sneak up undetected and launch a missile attack from our submarine at close range and hit with precision multiple American targets in a matter of minutes."

"So, you don't think that this game is too dangerous?" I asked.

He answered with the Odessan skeptical expression: "No, it is not. *'Posmotri s Liuka na Diuka'* (reality is more complex than expectations). We don't believe that Americans will want to start the war. As a nation, they are flabby; they are too naive, spoiled, comfortable, superficial, well-fed, and internationally too inexperienced. They believe that the rest of the world is just like them. After Fidel's victory at the Bay of Pigs in 1961 and after Khrushchev's triumph during the Berlin Crisis of 1961, and, particularly, after the Americans took no action when their reconnaissance plane was shot down in 1962, our government became confident that *Amerikantsi* (Americans) are sloppy and unseasoned. Americans will not engage in a military conflict with the USSR, especially now, when their administration is busy dealing with Vietnam. After all, remember what Lenin said: 'The Capitalists will sell us the rope on which we will hang them.'"

"'Vsio v Azure!' (everything is taken care of)," he added, revealing that his claims of innocence regarding his knowledge of this very secret Navy project are false. I understood that the Soviet Government was betting on Americans being preoccupied with their forthcoming elections. They will overlook our tactics and fall asleep thanks to our clever incremental strategy described as 'Crab on a Slow Boil': rendering the crab drowsy in warm water while slowly raising the water temperature to the boiling point to have the

American crab fall asleep and get cooked without agitation.

For this game, we gambled on Cuban soil and not on ours. If this gamble fails, the Cubans will pay and not our homeland. A nuclear attack on Cuba was too close for Americans; so, whatever they did, they would lose. Americans will not dare to start the war, and when Americans get accustomed to the Soviet nuclear presence in Cuba, it will stop alarming them. This is how the Soviet nuclear Navy will establish its primacy in the region, and the "power game of détente" will be won by the Soviet Union.

Now, I can see how the pieces fit together. This essential Soviet strategy was needed to determine who was the top dog and who was fit to govern the world. Still, our government was only bullying; it did not have at the moment any intention to start a nuclear war. The Soviets were betting on the Americans blinking first in the game of nuclear chicken. The winner of this game would dictate terms during forthcoming detente negotiations. A Soviet win would mean world respect and new alliances. The only unpredictable, difficult, and hard-to-control factor in this equation was Cuba's Castro.

During 1968 and 1969, Cuban and Soviet media continued to be critical of each other. They conveyed the impression that both countries disagreed on basic ideological principles, both standing on the precipice of permanent discord. Still, when it mattered, Fidel Castro endorsed the policies of the Soviet

Union even at the cost of discrediting himself, as was the case with his public support for the Soviet invasion of Czechoslovakia in August of 1968 (even though, for many Cubans, it resembled the invasion of the Bay of Pigs). Like the chameleon, Fidel could change his colors to suit the camouflage conditions of any occasion.

During this period, the Soviet government invested massively (billions of American dollars) into their military build-up in Cuba and into the Cuban economy. Cuba was heavily subsidized by the USSR, but spent this assistance extravagantly, at least from the point of view of the Soviet government, by financing revolutionary military interventions in the Third World and successfully competing with their master on the ideological front. The Soviet government was faced with a *fait accompli*. On the one hand, they were extremely concerned with the partisan practices of Cuba, a country that was being run like the private estate of its patriarch, Fidel Castro and not collectively by the Cuban Communists loyal to the Soviet Communist Party. On the other hand, Cuba was of unique importance to the Soviet Union due to its strategic location at the doorstep of the Soviet's number one target, the USA.

The Soviet government was forced to mask its misgivings while providing brotherly economic and military support to Cuba. The Soviets did not and could not trust Castro, Cuba's delusional, unstable, melodramatic, and multi-faced leader. In reality, the price to pay for using Cuban territory as a permanent Soviet military nuclear base was hard to underestimate about five to six billion American dollars per year in economic subsidies alone. There was also a significant additional investment for a Soviet air force base in San Antonio de Los Baños (near Cienfuegos) for Soviet attack bombers. Finally, another major gain and expense without (the) support of which the Soviet Navy base would be dysfunctional was Lourdes - the largest Soviet SIGINT (intelligence gathering) outside the USSR, monitoring all satellite communications in the region.[90]

According to an agreement reached in the post-Cuban Missile Crisis settlement of 1962, the Soviet Union pledged to the US not to station offensive weapons or their components on the island; yet the newest Soviet ships and subs were just the carriers of such weapons. It was not known how Americans would react to their presence. After analyzing the errors of the first Cuban crisis, Moscow concluded that the overt act of deployment in US coastal areas would not work. Given the apparent superiority of the US Navy in its own waters and an understanding that aggressive steps will lead only to a new confrontation with the United States, it was decided to do things differently this time. The new line of conduct was the chosen policy of gradually and surreptitiously introducing Soviet nuclear weapons into the enemy region. The Soviet Union began to act slowly and in small steps, with each stage following seamlessly from the previous one.

The ultimate goal was to create a permanent Navy base in Cuba for subs equipped with nuclear warhead missiles supported by one of the world's largest signals intelligence centers in Lourdes and three other locations on the island.

This was the new secret plan which the Soviet Government launched in Cuba in 1968. I witnessed this process by helping Soviet naval designers with translations and by my participation in dual-purpose design functions. During this period of my career, I was absorbing new professional experiences like a sponge. The commercial port and naval base designers often shared technical data for the access channel and some of the berthing facilities. The channel had double usage, accommodating both submarines and the service fleet. Interesting work, field trips, and mentoring of my senior colleagues filled my life and made me feel useful and busy despite the frequent and often prolonged absence of Eduardo, who was now constantly traveling to Western and Eastern European countries on business for the Ministry of Transport.

16. Soviet Puppet or Caribbean Gaddafi

Our political officer at the embassy regularly briefed us on the political stance of the Soviet Union toward Cuba. This information was different from the public '*papilla*' (bland baby food) that the ordinary Soviet population was fed. The weekly *polithour* was directed at the narrow contingent of Soviet personnel directly involved in the military work of the Soviet government in Cuba. Attendance was obligatory. Its purpose was to inform the personnel about the latest tactical and strategic policies of the Soviet government.

Fidel continued to be an irritant to the Soviet political establishment. In their opinion, Fidel Castro ran his country like a theater director thanks to his use and complete control of television and the press, and his long, frequent, and impromptu rambling speeches, often delivered by him as if in a state of intoxication from steroids or pumped up with synthetic adrenaline. The effect of his extravagant theatrical deliveries in Cuba and around the world was to drive his home crowds into a frenzy and provoke Soviet resentment against his stealing ideological thunder at their expense. The Soviet leadership lacked such charismatic performers ever since Lenin ceased public speaking following his paralysis from an assassin's bullet. They were upset that Fidel's outstanding theatrical performance was unmanageable, driven as it was by his personal, fanatical ambition to become the world's savior. In their minds, this was the legitimate role of the Soviet Union and not for a new Caribbean actor whom they had sponsored and from whom, in exchange, they expected due obedience.

Ideologically, the Soviet leadership regarded Fidel's behavior as coming under the influence of Che Guevara's Trotskyism or Raúl Castro's Maoism - both ideologies considered vehement enemies of Soviet communism. In the opinion of the Soviets, Castro was not a team player; he was unreliable and unpredictable. He was a clever, highly intuitive opportunist and a chameleon of convenience to secure his absolute power. He could take opposite sides from one moment to the next, prompted only by his solipsistic neurosis.

Having never worked in his life, he was accustomed to obtaining financing by coercion or extortion. He dragged the Soviet Union, against its will, into covertly underwriting his global campaign to overthrow Latin American, African, and Asian governments while Fidel garnered all the credit. The Soviet leadership was very anxious as they watched him gaining world fame at their expense. Little Cuba was becoming a global military empire by exploiting its youthful and cheap soldiers abroad, diverting Soviet subsidies, and pumping up Fidel's charisma with deceptive revolutionary propaganda.

At the start, Fidel was convinced, with the persuasion of Raúl and Che, that he would solve all of his economic and military problems by joining the Soviet camp. However, just two years later, he discovered that he did not count for much in the eyes of the global powers when the Soviet Union and the US unilaterally made a deal to remove nuclear weapons from Cuba in 1962 without consulting him. Fidel was furious. His reaction was violent despite the detailed explanations and assurances from the Soviet Government's negotiator for Cuba, Anastas Mikoyan, and Khrushchev himself, **"that within the next five to six years, it will be possible to return Soviet nuclear weapons to Cuba."[91]**

An enraged Fidel Castro thought that he would become the most important leader in the nuclear world; instead, he now understood that this was not a Cuban decision. He created several provocations against Americans, despite orders from the Soviet Government to the contrary: such as shooting down an American surveillance aircraft. Finally, he bombarded Khrushchev with requests for a Soviet pre-emptive strike on Americans, a demand that scared the pants off Khrushchev, and he tried to block the removal of all Soviet nuclear missiles from their Cuban installations and their shipment back to the USSR.[92]

He organized massive demonstrations of Cuban mobs in front of the Soviet embassy in Havana, shouting angrily for hours, *"'Nikita, Nikita, mariquita, lo que se da, no se lo quita'* (Nikita, Nikita, you pansy, what you gave, you can't take away)." Regardless, the Soviets carted off all of the missiles, except for a nominal few left in Cuba for training.

It was important to understand the psychological traits of Fidel Castro when anticipating his reactions to those he might suspect of becoming his political adversaries. He has an innate talent for deceit, the good looks (from his mother Lina) of a dramatic hero, and an incorruptible belief in his special destiny thanks to his Jesuit education. Fidel was not a communist during his formative rebel years. After Fidel came to power, he skillfully began removing his adversaries through carefully orchestrated accidents and disappearances where his participation was hard to establish. Witnesses to those assassinations were liquidated as well. He did not spare even Soviet KGB operatives.

He and Raúl had ordered the assassination of the longest-serving and most valuable KGB asset in Latin America: Lieutenant General of the KGB Oswaldo Sánchez Cabrera, who established intelligence services and networks in Cuba's DGI together with his KGB team and hundreds of Soviet-Spanish KGB assessors. Ramiro Valdes, who was officially in charge of DGI, was untrained in security matters. Osvaldo Sanchez Cabrera and his lieutenants, Felix Fleet and Isidoro Malmierca, were shot down in flight by the Ejercito Rebelde anti-aircraft battery in 1961 before the attack at the Bay of Pigs.

This happened after Osvaldo Sanchez had already warned Cubans regarding the dates and place of the Bay of Pigs attack. The Soviet spies in Washington and Florida were well-informed, and they even published this information in a Pravda editorial four days before the start of the Bay of Pigs attack. The KGB believed that the real reason for the assassination of Osvaldo Sánchez and his lieutenants was that they knew too much and had become competitors to Fidel.

Soviet security has had an extensive file on Fidel since his early years. Some of Fidel's friends from the university belonged to the pro-Soviet original Cuban Communist Party and reported his assassination attempts of student movement opposition leaders at the university; for example, the attempt to kill Lionel Goméz, a strong competitor in federal student elections. Fidel sprayed him with bullets late at night on Rionda Street and thought that Lionel was dead, but Lionel survived despite having a bullet shot through his lung. After several months in the hospital, Lionel reported to UIR (Insurrectional Revolutionary Movement) the names of the assassins. These names were Fidel Castro and Chino Esquivel. Fidel never attempted to apologize to his victim; instead, he recruited Lionel's gang members.

Another valuable KGB operative, Alfredo Gamonal, was killed in a staged car accident in Santiago de Cuba in 1962. This was followed by the expulsion of Anibal Escalante, the old PCP (Cuban Communist Party) leader, who had the strongest ties with Moscow and had to take refuge in Czechoslovakia for three years. Afterward, in May of 1961, the Moscow-backed PCP was dissolved and replaced by Fidel's own

Communist Fidelista Party, PCC. Then, thirty-five original communist leaders of PCP, all with close ties to Moscow, were arrested on charges of conspiracy and propaganda against the party line. They were imprisoned for fifteen years as a "micro-faction" (the "old-guard" Cuban communists identified in the past with pro-Soviet positions).[93] Rudolf Petrovich Shlyapnikov, the chief KGB adviser with the Cuban Ministry of the Interior, was alleged to have conspired with the micro-faction and was sent back to Moscow.

"In Cuba," he claimed, "conditions are present for a new Hungary (i.e., a revolt against Moscow). Internal dissension is great. The existing Cuban security apparatus contained too many petit bourgeois to deal with a revolt."[94]

Moscow accused the Soviet ambassador Shitov (Alexseev) of letting his friend Castro get out of control and replaced him with Alexander Soldatov. The Soviet press kept quiet about the whole affair, merely reporting the purge of the micro-faction without comment or mention of the details.[95] Moscow understood that they could expect Fidel Castro to behave with the Soviet Union as he had with his father, Angel. He would beg for economic and military support from the Soviet Union, but he would scorn and despise the benefactor as soon as it was guaranteed. After the Soviet invasion of Czechoslovakia, Czech technical advisers and Cuban sympathizers paraded through Havana with banners 'Russians Go Home from Czechoslovakia'.

In response, Shlyapnikov had to caution the leader of the macro-faction (the Cuban Communist Party, controlled exclusively by Fidel Castro) that the Soviet oil supplies to Cuba would be cut. This and a warning from Raúl awoke Fidel to the realization that the Cuban industry could come to a halt and its economy collapse. But Fidel Castro got the message and smartened up by endorsing on radio and television Moscow's invasion of Czechoslovakia, declaring: "The socialist camp has a right to prevent counter-revolution." In any event, the Soviet force and violence were closer to Fidel's methods. In return for his declaration of loyalty, the Soviet Union once again bailed out the Cuban economy.

Moscow was cautious: Fidel depended economically on the USSR, but he was a 'wild card' and a 'petit bourgeois (a generic communist term to describe enemies of the Revolution) with totally unrealistic global ambitions of world conquest at the cost of his Soviet benefactors. He was a gangster, a very crafty and vindictive megalomaniac, hard to control. Under the influence of his younger brother Raúl and the dead martyr, Che Guevara, Cuba was constantly sliding into Trotskyism[96] - the worst ideological enemy of Soviet doctrine since the early 1920s. The Soviets saw a dangerous parallel with Cuba, whose political system was popularly recognized as Fidelismo. The cult of the *caudillo* or *cacique* is a habit very particular to Latin America, where this concept took its historical roots from conquistadors and later from the Spanish agrarian landowners. They ruled despotically over their slaves and the local Indian population. But with the support of the church and military, they were considered patriarchs of the nation. This caudillo concept allows the patriarchs to make mistakes; still, the nation will follow him blindly, and if necessary, into the abyss because their ultimate trust is in him.[97] Now, Fidel was playing the role of Communist Caudillo, pretending to offer protection to a poor and insecure Cuban population.[98]

In countries less strategically important than Cuba, other leaders of the Communist alliance already would have been removed and severely punished by Moscow, as happened to Hungary and Czechoslovakia for lesser misdeeds. However, in the case of Cuba, the Soviets had to be more careful since Cuba was close to the USA but far from the USSR. Soviet tanks could not simply roll in by crossing the border. What Fidel had done - arresting pro-Moscow communists and badmouthing his Soviet benefactors - would cause immediate suppressions in any other Soviet satellite. But Cuba represented a strategic military platform for the Soviet Union against their first enemy, the USA. The Soviet government found itself obliged to resort to alternative means of persuasion.

In 1970, the DGI (Cuban intelligence) was purged of officers considered anti-Soviet by the KGB, and a team of KGB advisers headed by General Viktor Semyonov was installed next to the office of Redbeard (ManuelPiñiero), the head of the DGI. With the assistance of KGB subsidies, the DGI began a rapid expansion of its operations. At this time, the economy of Cuba was under the gross mismanagement of revolutionary dreamers and was in a state of permanent disaster. Nevertheless, Cuba was shamelessly exporting violent revolutions in Africa and Latin America.

Unable to provide any financial return on the Soviet Union's multi-billion-dollar investment (more than 100 billion American dollars was invested by the USSR over 30 years), Cuba helped substantially bankrupt the USSR. This investment, from an economic point of view, was a disaster; but from a strategic standpoint, it was a costly but geopolitically paramount opportunity in the power struggle with the United States. At the same time, the presence of Soviet nuclear weapons was the best assurance for Fidel with his pretensions to global power. This was the true reason for the mutual dependence of the USSR and Cuba: their corresponding imperialistic ambitions and not fanatical ideological posturing, to which the leaders of both countries were publicly affecting their uneasy relationship.

Even today, the current leaders of these two countries, Russia and Cuba, hope that all roads will lead them to global influence. Their communist ideology was simply replaced by extreme nationalism. Ultimately, what counts is omnipotence; masks and verbal expressions could be changed. Traditional victims are the populations of these countries who are not allowed to complain about their lives wasted in misery. Historically, however, they were accustomed to such lives and became cynical and docile in response.

At the time, however, I did not share the feelings of mocking superiority over Cubans, which my compatriots displayed in private. That is because, in comparison with our Soviet leaders, Fidel Castro and his government were only a baby Caribbean version of the cannibalistic state despotism of the Soviet Union. In this field, nobody, not even Hitler, could compete with our Soviet history, which witnessed unimaginable savagery and depravity over the previous fifty-five years by murdering more of our citizens than ten times the entire population of Cuba. Accordingly, nobody could compete with Soviet cynicism forged like steel in high heat and freezing cold.

A Caribbean Island with a population of seven million in 1960, Cuba was not in the same league as the Soviets. Fidel, Raúl, Che, and Ramiro Valdes managed to eliminate thousands of their often-innocent citizens, so-called 'enemies of the revolution'. Still, those were relatively very small numbers (due to the island's small population) in comparison with the victims of Soviet oppression. Cuba is only an island, while the Soviet Union spanned two continents.

As it appeared to me, Cuba's biggest drama was a continuous assault on the economy due to chaotic and arbitrary policies based on the whims and moods of individuals in the Cuban leadership. Despite the Cuban economic mess and the economic abuses by Cuban '*nomenklatura*' (privileged senior officials), I sympathized with the Cuban people. I felt sorry for their naiveté about all the ideological posturing of our respective leaders in pursuit of their objectives. All the while, my Soviet colleagues also knew the truth, but instead of sympathizing with the Cuban people, they acted arrogantly like a superior colonizing race.

I was squeezed between Soviet chauvinism and the nationalistic, tribal pride of Cubans. Though welcomed by both groups, I felt resentful when my compatriots privately referred to Cubans as '*tuzemtzi*' (aboriginals) and when Cubans privately called Russians '*boles*' (round heads), alluding to the Slavic head shape, clumsy dress, and absence of deodorant. Large Soviet divisions stationed on the island were traditionally recruited in the USSR from poor peasant agricultural collectives or kolkhozes. Even the poorest Cuban peasant was clean and dignified in comparison with such Russians. When Che Guevara, the fanatical admirer of the Soviet Union, returned from his first visit to his Soviet Wonderland, he bragged that the Soviet Union, with all its industrial and military might, did not have the quality of life that Cubans enjoyed in Havana.

My husband's attitude was different than mine. The Cuban Revolutionary leadership only recently announced an official twist towards so-called 'Caribbean socialism', which, in the opinion of many Cubans, represented temporary political maneuvering necessary to stabilize the Cuban economy. Eduardo wanted with all his heart to believe in a better future for Cuba. He was still optimistic that the current political alliance of the Cuban government with the USSR was necessary, but not for long, and that Cuba would evolve into Fidel's promised functioning democracy after the military and economic crises were solved. He was patriotic, hopeful, and enthusiastic.

Eduardo's work related to new Cuban commercial projects dealing with requirements for ocean service vessels, their engineering evaluation, and recommendations about specific vessels for Cuban purchase abroad. His purchasing responsibilities required frequent international travel, and according to him, he managed to comply with these responsibilities without becoming corrupted. Cuban personnel working abroad were permitted very modest daily expenses, which led Eduardo to economize on his small food allowance to purchase gifts for me, our children, and his family.

These sacrifices were considered normal and standard for Cuban and Soviet technical personnel on foreign assignments. I would not vouch for the same among the diplomatic, political, or security staff in Soviet or Cuban embassies. As I learned, later on, they participated in all kinds of black markets and currency trading for personal profit. But Eduardo was not involved in any of that. His status was junior, and he was an enthusiastic apologist for his country's direction. He often martyred himself to prove his compliance above and beyond the rules and expectations.

Like everybody else in my country, I was terrified by the KGB and kept my written promise not to disclose classified work. This was not difficult for me; on the contrary, it came naturally. In the Soviet Union, we were accustomed to the idea that everything was a state secret. We knew that punishments for blabbing could be very serious. However, I was not acting so seriously about the request from Pompa to inform him monthly of any wrongdoing by my colleagues. Traditionally, for the last 40 years, all Soviet citizens working abroad, and often even at home, were subjected to such requirements, but I hated the idea of snitching even in school. To me, this practice was despicable and absurd for anyone, anywhere, at any time, especially outside the Soviet Union, where we felt relatively free. Being raised under these draconian Soviet rules, we Soviet citizens had to be very careful with each other in our personal comments about our country. We got into this habit from the day we were born, not trusting each other, not criticizing or joking about our political system. However, in the case of foreign countries, we were awarded a patriotic break. It was okay and even considered patriotic to criticize a foreign state in favor of the Soviet Union. Accordingly, maligning Cuba had become a safe outlet for jokes among my Soviet compatriots.

17. You Can Be a Very Rich Girl

Edik's famous British leather jacket and boots, Havana 1971

It was a fantastic life for a young, healthy Soviet family in Cuba in the late 1960s. We were privileged in so many ways compared to our life back home, especially now when Eduardo brought us from his foreign business trips gorgeous Western clothes and shoes. I can't forget how much wonder and admiration were aroused by those bright colors and stretch materials unknown to my compatriots. I can't forget the marvel of tall leather boots for Edik. He was so proud of them that he refused to take them off even at night in bed. Any attempt to remove his new leather jacket and new leather boots in the hot tropical climate produced an unstoppable crying.

Edik began speaking fluent Spanish, and I insisted that both boys learn Spanish because it was a unique opportunity; everybody around us, including in their daycare, spoke Spanish. In comparison with my situation as a young Soviet woman in Odessa, I felt miraculously transformed in Cuba into a privileged '*apparatchik*' (a full-time functionary in a position of bureaucratic or political responsibility). A metamorphosis from an Odessan '*Koziavka*' into a member of the elite. Anywhere we traveled, the Cuban people would turn their heads to look at us. The men would express their admiration by whistling, and the women by smiling and trying to gain my confidence. I loved this attention and the Cuban people for their positive disposition towards me.

The children were traveling with me every day to and from work. At the daycare, they were fed and well looked after. Since we moved from Maria's apartment into the Hotel National and later into Hotel Capri, the boys stopped catching flu and colds and were healthy, alert, and energetic. They enjoyed running in the park and swimming in the pool of the Hotel National after we returned from work and on weekends. It was a good life, a comfortable life. I was allowed to shop at a special warehouse store for foreign technical and military personnel, where many different products were sold in unlimited quantities, none of which ordinary Cubans could purchase in their stores. There were many varieties of imported goods to purchase, including cheese, which disappeared in Cuba after the Revolution. Young Cubans had already forgotten what it was and how it tasted. My only limitation in purchasing enough food for all my friends and family was our modest salaries. I believed it was important to use this privilege to help our Cuban relatives and friends, despite the resistance from Eduardo, who was simply afraid that it would compromise his reputation as a pure revolutionary. I never accepted payment from anyone for the food I purchased for them in that store for foreign techs; they, too, had to live on even smaller incomes than ours. My objective was to help the relatives and not to create a resale business.

Our residence in hotels and my work status as a Soviet assessor prohibited us from receiving Cuban rations. Only Cuban citizens residing at a Cuban-registered address and approved by the state neighborhood committees were given food rations and the right to purchase ration products. Those who were not officially registered as residents at approved addresses got no rations at all. This way, nobody could migrate internally within the island unless the government sponsored their move. This enabled the Cuban government to exercise total control over its population, which now became dependent upon the government for their very basics of survival. This system was identical to how food rations were used to control population movements in the USSR.

Because Eduardo felt embarrassed by this privilege, he never accompanied me to this special store for foreign technicians. Eduardo's silly embarrassment at my shopping privileges created plenty of friction between us. He would say that the children and I, being Soviet citizens, had every right to shop in the store for foreigners, but he was Cuban, and it was ideologically wrong for him to take advantage of this privilege intended only for foreign techs. He insisted that he should eat and survive in the same conditions as other ordinary Cubans. Often, when angry, he would take off to his mother's Cuban apartment, where she kept our bedroom vacant for our use.

Maria disagreed with her son over his embarrassment about our shopping privileges. His mother was more practical and supportive of my shopping. She always managed to convince Eduardo to return to the hotel to be with the children and me, despite his naive ideological torment. She was my main Cuban mentor, teaching me that Eduardo and I are valuable to the Cuban state and deserve to have appropriate housing and provisions, no less than other important individuals in Cuba.

Eduardo always told me that he would be happier if we lived in Maria's apartment, conveniently ignoring that Maria was the one who hardly enjoyed and protested the overcrowding of her apartment with all her children and grandchildren in the barbaric conditions of the near absence of municipal services. Eduardo's brother, who had a Ph.D. degree in science from Germany, was moving out of Maria's apartment because he was awarded a small house near his work on the periphery of Havana. Eduardo's mother was a strong believer that if Eduardo couldn't provide for our residence, then it was me who should do so, given an opportunity.

Eduardo and I argued about whether it was appropriate to purchase food for others, for Cuban families and friends, given that this practice was against state rules. Eduardo considered my generosity dangerous, especially for his reputation. However, I always won support from his mother and from others in the family, who all benefited from my shopping. I had to admit that I was risking my privileges as a foreigner, but I could not act differently, seeing the suffering of Cubans.

Actually, this kind of shopping was hard work. Because of my disagreement with Eduardo, I went shopping at the store for foreign techs while he was away, but it also meant that I had to look after both our babies while shopping. In those times, it was not simple for a parent with two small toddlers. There were no shopping carts in Cuba in which I could drive small children around the store. Also, there were no price tags on food items, so I would often load myself with products for which I lacked sufficient money to pay and was forced to leave some goods at the cash register. Then, I needed a car that would help me distribute the purchased food among Cuban family members.

The only car available was often an old American car without brakes, belonging to Angelito, the entrepreneurial uncle of Eduardo. He drove his huge 15-year-old American car around Havana without ever being able to repair its brakes. This was a real circus because we drove around Havana very slowly to be able to stop the car by gravity alone or by friction when he would open his door and push the sole of his well-worn left shoe hard against the pavement. We risked being discovered by the police and being accused of food trafficking because this food was intended solely for foreign consumption and not for Cubans. If I had lied that this food was intended for me, the Cuban police would inquire why, if the store was just a few blocks away from my hotel, all this food had found its way to Havana's suburbs, far away from the store and the hotel.

My only excuse then would be that I paid for it and had a right to make gifts to whom I pleased, but we all knew this excuse wouldn't fly with the authorities. My well-intended actions were circumventing the unequal food and goods supply system implemented by the Cuban government. Eduardo feared that he would be punished if I was caught. Still, I continued this practice, all the while provoking his constant anxiety. I felt compelled to continue helping his family and our friends because they were, in my opinion, wonderful people suffering unjustly. If I could help, I would do it even at the expense of frequent disagreements with my obstinate husband, who preferred to fight for the right to be purer than anyone else in Cuba. Our persistent arguments over his fanatical idealism caused the first ruptures to take place in our marriage.

Perhaps my shopping habits were risky, but

a more dangerous encounter was waiting for me. In the spring of 1969, I experienced one frightening episode with a visiting Swiss businessman who traveled to Cuba often and stayed in our hotel for a couple of weeks during his visits. He had been coming to Cuba for the past six years on the business of a large Swiss chemical company for which he was working. We met when he asked my permission to sit at our table in the restaurant of our hotel one day. Nothing unusual happened. However, he returned to our hotel on his next trip and now considered himself to be an old friend, frequently sitting at our table again. He was in his early 30s, tall and good-looking, a Nordic athletic type. His manner was amicable, relaxed, easy-going, and disarming.

In the beginning, he would talk about himself. He impressed me by speaking in perfect Spanish and claiming complete fluency in at least five other languages. He spoke mostly about himself and proudly showed me a photo of his new BMW car at home. To a married woman, he probably could be regarded as dangerously attractive, but he sounded very sincere when, from the start, he informed me of his recent marriage and that he could not wait to return home. He said that he didn't enjoy staying in Cuba because of the hot climate and the weeks wasted securing meetings with officials in the Cuban government. He missed his young wife, friends, and his country and couldn't wait to take off. His open, unaffected, and decent behavior was disarming.

In the beginning, he did not ask many

personal questions, except about where my husband was and what he was doing. I told him that my husband was a naval architect and an engineer traveling on Cuban business on foreign assignments. To his question about why the children and I didn't travel with my husband, I had to explain that my Soviet citizenship made that impossible. He never asked me if I was working, but one day, he alarmed me, out of the blue, when he said that his Cuban friend mentioned meeting me at the Ministry of Transport.

"Possibly," I replied, "that is where I work in the design of a sugar terminal for Cuba."

Nothing special was said again during our brief encounters in the hotel. On the following weekend, early on Sunday morning, I took the children to the local small rocky shoreline on the Malecon, not far from our hotel. Strangely enough, he came to the same shoreline and sat beside me, not to swim but to talk.

I can't remember all of our small talks during the next couple of hours while bathing my children in the warm, shallow water. However, I do remember clearly how he scared me when he disclosed that he knew who I was and with whom I was working in the Ministry of Transport. To that effect, he was about to make a startling proposition.

"I am not an important person in the Ministry of Transport, only a junior engineer. How is it that being so unimportant, I became so famous that your friends notice me and talk about me socially?" I asked, surprised.

To that effect, he was about to make a startling proposition: "You are working with the Soviet team on a Soviet Navy project in Cienfuegos. This was what my friend told me. I will offer you a lot of money if you tell me about it and take photographs of documents or drawings of this project. You can become a very rich girl."

It was shocking. I could never imagine myself being confronted with an invitation to treason, like in a spy movie. Still, this bait was wrong. He missed the point that I was raised in the USSR, where the possession of money did not translate into purchasing power and only served as a negative and even criminal connotation. No, I wasn't prepared to risk my life and the lives of my family for monetary gains.

He reached into his pocket and discreetly showed me a tiny photo camera, about the size of a dime. He suggested that I could attach it inside the collar of my shirt and take pictures by simply lifting the collar of the shirt and pressing the edge of the collar; the camera will take pictures of the documents. Truly, I was impressed by the sophistication of this camera. Until that moment, I never in my life seen such a miniaturized and remarkable camera. I also felt indignant, frozen with fear, and chilled despite the heat of the Cuban sun. It seemed like it took me a long while to recover from such an insulting and unpleasant surprise. This spying was a terrifying and spooky business. I had to regain my composure to formulate a refusal as firmly as possible.

"You are insane," I rebuked him. "I am working on the project for a sugar terminal in Cienfuegos, and we are not permitted to bring photo cameras into our offices. I was taught in my country from very early childhood that what you suggested is treason. I would never attempt this kind of crime, even if I had access to documents. I don't want to talk to you again or be seen near you because I am insulted by your suggestion. I would never do anything of the kind, and if you don't leave my children and me immediately, I will call the police."

I felt disappointed, afraid of him, and worried about what would happen if he became angry at me for my refusal. But he was not. He seemed to be puzzled and annoyed.

"No intention to offend. You are a smart girl, and I am willing to pay a lot of money," he persisted. "I will pay for your risk. If you take just a few photos for me, you will become rich. Nobody will suspect you. You could bring your children to the daycare center of the Ministry at seven o'clock in the morning when it opens, before your colleagues arrive at eight. After leaving the children in daycare, you could take the fire-escape staircase to your office and shoot a few photographs of the plans of the naval base; then you would return to the daycare by the same fire-escape staircase as if you had forgotten to leave instructions to the nurses of your children. At that point, you will remove the camera from your collar and give it to the person waiting for you on my behalf near the daycare entrance. After talking to the nurse in the daycare center, you will take an elevator to return to your office. You are known in the Ministry for running up this fire escape staircase to the fourteenth floor every day, as I was told, for pure exercise. It will look completely innocent and natural, no? I repeat my willingness to pay you a lot of money for this favor."

"You know everything about my running up and down the staircase every day, and you have somebody reporting to you about the daycare of my children, but you are grossly mistaken in offering money to me!" I said, feeling deeply insulted. "If you are trying to find girls to commit the crime for money, you should look for prostitutes. I am not interested in this kind of money because I could wind up paying not just with my freedom but also with my life and with the lives of my family. Apart from that, I despise traitors and would never become one for the money. How could you dare talk like this to me? You must leave me alone immediately, or I will call the police."

We were lucky that there were no other people who could overhear me because I was very angry and probably spoke too loudly; even the children looked at me, startled. Understanding that I had become dangerously emotional, he left looking quite discouraged. I never saw him again, but felt terrorized by this incident for a long time. Who knows from where the wind blows! It could have been a provocation set up by the KGB.

I lost sleep thinking about what I must do to protect myself and my family. I knew too well that, even though I did not agree to his proposal and had not breached the confidentiality agreement, my legal obligation when approached by a spy was to report this incident immediately to my Pompa (a security officer at the Soviet embassy). If I was accused of not reporting such a criminal proposition, I could be punished with lengthy incarceration. But if I do report, it could also be interpreted as my fault to some degree. Even if it was not construed as my fault, I would still become the object of attention from the KGB for the rest of my life.

Honestly, I was hesitant to report this incident for numerous reasons, the biggest being my unwillingness to cause the arrest of this man, even though he could have been a spy provocateur. He could have been an agent of the KGB or DGI sent specially to test me. I overheard our Pompa while partying with my Soviet colleagues during a Soviet national celebration, bragging that all CIA agents in Cuba are KGB and DGI triple agents and provocateurs. I agonized with doubts about what I could do. If he was an agent provocateur and I failed to report him immediately, despite my refusal to collaborate with him, I still would be arrested and accused of protecting a spy. They would ship me back to a Soviet prison.

On the other hand, if the Swiss man was a true foreign spy and not a spy provocateur working for the Soviet KGB or Cuban DGI, then my reporting about his offer could mean his arrest, torture, and death. I would feel terrible guilt for his suffering. Also, I would be dragged into lengthy and probably horrible interrogations by security. I felt that I was not capable of inflicting this harm on another human being. I never saw him again at our hotel or anywhere else, and I was afraid even to ask about him at the hotel desk. Finally, after spending several days aggravating myself with these anxious thoughts, I decided against reporting this incident to Pompa, our KGB coordinator in the Soviet embassy; nor did I ever share this experience with anyone, not even with Eduardo, because this kind of episode would scare the daylights out of him, and he would blame me. It was better not to implicate him.

When Eduardo returned from his trip abroad, I didn't mention anything to him because, in my mind, it could be a dangerous time bomb, and I was not yet completely sure if the incident would have any further consequences. I felt better over time. Nobody ever questioned me about the Swiss hotel guest who used to join us at our hotel dinner table, and I started thinking that the Swiss guy was a real spy from a foreign agency, and felt truly glad that I didn't report him. At least, my conscience was free of guilt. But for the first time in my life, I understood that the feeling of fear was a wrenching game of Russian roulette. I never knew which chamber was loaded. Anyway, at that point, I decided that my involvement with the naval project was too dangerous, and I needed to remove myself from such a hot-button security project.

Luis, the new translator with the security

clearance who recently arrived from Leningrad, was sent to Cienfuegos full-time because they have already started construction. However, he was anxious to spend more time in Havana. A single, middle-aged but unattractive Spaniard, he loved the nightlife in Havana and grouched about the small and old provincial town of Cienfuegos where he was based. He was happy to support me because replacing me in Havana would justify his transfer from Cienfuegos to Havana.

I began pushing Boris to request my full-time work to complete the design of the bulk and general cargo terminals. I hoped that by complaining about the heavy burden of work with Alexey and Yuri, I was short to learn more from Boris about best design and construction practices. I probably touched the right key because, in this case, he stood up for me (normally, no Soviet functionary could be expected to speak up about anything). He argued with our navy colleagues that they should bring Luis from Cienfuegos to allow me more time to work on the design of the commercial project. He justified his intervention on my behalf by arguing that he needs my help in the design work of industrial oil and sugar terminals, adding that he has responsibility for my technical evaluation, which will depend on our timely commissioning of the Cienfuegos cargo terminals.

Top photos: deepwater bulk and sugar terminals
Bottom photos: oil tank farm and terminal

A few months later, my navy colleagues informed me that Luis was now ready to undertake most of the translations in Havana, and I was allowed to work full-time with Boris; except, from that moment on, I got into new, unexpected, and very serious trouble. This time with Boris, for a reason not entirely related to rockets.

18. Boris Becomes a Beast

I wanted to be like the Soviet astronaut Valentina Tereshkova.

There was a vast difference in sexual temperaments between Cuba and the Soviet Union. Our moral attitudes and behavior in the Soviet Union were distinct on account of many factors. The Soviet Revolution took place 50 years earlier, much before the sexual revolution. After the Bolshevik Revolution, the Soviet Union was isolated from the rest of the world. During the 1920s, sexual freedoms in the USSR were promoted by Leon Trotsky and later qualified by Stalin as an anti-revolutionary crime following the expulsion of Trotsky from the country. The renewed restrictions on sexual freedoms were set in concrete after Trotsky was murdered during his Mexican exile for opposing Stalin's pact with Hitler in 1939. A strict puritanical approach to sex became Stalin's answer to Trotskyism. Due to poverty and lack of housing, the nation adopted the traditional, austere rules about sex, now buried beneath shyness and ignorance. There was no literature or film to address the subject. Parents, teachers, and even friends never spoke about this forbidden and secret matter. The education of girls and young women in schools and families was based on female models of the most productive workers, professionals, and even astronauts. None of them could be characterized as sexy. Despite my understanding that I could never reach the heights of astronaut Valentina Tereshkova (given my ethnic and non-political status), she was my idol and role model.

Meanwhile, despite their Catholic upbringing (especially among whites), Cubans seemed unabashed about the public display of their amorous and lustful inclinations. Men on the street, neighbors, males at work, or in stores would turn around to follow with their carnal gaze a passing female, especially a young one. Some would even whistle. When I became the subject of this ostentatious voyeurism, I reacted at first with a mixture of shyness and annoyance. However, with time, I became accustomed to these vulgar courtesies and began to take pleasure in such exhibitions of attention. Though I never fully understood or appreciated the erotic aspect of Cuban society until I read, years afterward, the following frank travel guide observations:

"The liberation of women achieved by the Revolution has also made Cuba one of the most sexually liberated countries in the world. However, Cubans have always been sensual and seductive in a colonial society that largely meant the young women casting smoldering looks from behind the safety of wrought-iron grilles. It was not until the student activity during Machado's years, in the early 1930s, that women in Havana began to share any public space with men. Nowadays, Cuba is an avowedly promiscuous society. Men and women alike slip in and out of bed with uninhibited ease. The sexual activity starts young, helped by '*escuela del campo*' (field school - an obligatory for all secondary school children), which is notorious as sexual experimental grounds."[99]

I can't say for certain how much of this is accurate. Thirty years earlier, it was only partly true for Eduardo's family, where Maria watched over the chastity of Eduardo's sister like a hawk and where only males were sexually unbridled. In my experience, the parents of teenage girls in Cuba went to extraordinary trouble, including chaperones, to secure the virtuous behavior of their daughters. But truly, my knowledge of the Cuban people was too limited to talk about this subject in general terms. There is also the influence of tropical temperament and a racially mixed population.

Cuba is a tropical island with American culture; the Soviet Union is a northern country that was isolated from the rest of the world for 50 years. Neither do I have the authority to speak too generally about the sexuality of Russians because I left my country while still quite young. Nevertheless, Cubans considered the Soviets "anti-sexual," probably because Soviet mariners, while in Cuban ports, were closely watched by KGB agents and did not venture out in the company of Cuban prostitutes with the same frequency as the mariners of other nationalities. There was also less sexual provocation in a Soviet popular culture where films and literature were devoid of erotic content.

Eduardo and I, due to our cultural differences, had very different perceptions about promiscuous sex. This is possibly why Eduardo so often displayed suspicion and jealousy in our relationship. At the time, I could not figure it out and could not understand him. I felt as if I was undergoing a transformation, trying, not without success, to fit into this Americanized Cuban culture and modify my values. Instead of being praised for my efforts, I was insulted by my husband. I was angry at Eduardo for what I perceived as his lack of understanding and basic trust in me. After all, I came from a different culture and with different experiences. My parents were always discreet on the subject of sex, and so was my entire society. There were no psychologists or family advisers available to help us with these issues.

In retrospect, Eduardo was a product of a sexually promiscuous society and perhaps assumed this quality in others, as the French say: *Honi soit qui mal y pense* (Evil to him who evil thinks). The differences between Cuban and Russian sexual cultures revolved around the element of repression. The suppression of sexuality in Russia no doubt resulted in many cases of hidden sexual brutality. It was not common for a man in Russia to whistle at women on the streets, but men could secretly abuse, brutally attack, and rape women. This was precisely what happened to me with Boris.

This shocking and sinister incident took place on the same day that Nina, the wife of Boris, urgently left Cuba for Odessa due to an emergency with their daughter. Boris used this opportunity to lure me into his house, where he attempted to rape me. For Boris, it was an event of sexual opportunism. For me, it was much more: it was my shattered nostalgia for my parents and for the city where I was raised and which I adored. It was a knife in my heart, treachery against my trust in a family friend, something that I would never expect, especially so distant from my home and my family. I was traumatized, and I panicked.

I knew such treason would be equally emotionally shocking to Eduardo. It was treason not just against the trust between Boris and me, but even more, the trust of my father, who asked Boris, as his friend, to look after his only daughter in a faraway foreign country. This incident forever altered my relationships with Boris, with my colleagues, and with the Soviet embassy. I couldn't find the courage to share this traumatic event with Eduardo or with anybody else in Cuba because I was so embarrassed, not for myself, but for my compatriot, my boss, and a good friend of my father.

I could never suspect such behavior or anticipate this problem, especially after more than two years of working with Boris, whom I admired as a talented and knowledgeable design engineer and my first real-life professional teacher. I looked up to him and learned from him. Boris was my mentor and a substitute for my father in Cuba. His wife, Nina, was a large, middle-aged, typical Russian homemaker: warm, hospitable, and attentive to her husband and daughter's smallest wishes. I respected him and Nina, his wife, often feeling like their adopted daughter. My parents carried on, separately from me, correspondence with Nina and Boris to inquire about me independently. They told me about it only later. I could never believe that such betrayal might happen; neither could Eduardo nor my parents. It was beyond the scope of our worst imagination.

But it happened on the same Sunday that Boris took Nina to the airport early that morning. His attack was premeditated because he misled me about the day of her departure. On Friday, before we finished work, Boris told me that they had not yet succeeded in purchasing Nina's return flight home, but they hoped to be able to do so over the next week. He will let me know for which date the ticket was purchased because I planned to give Nina some small Cuban souvenirs for my parents. Nina also wanted to meet with me before her departure to leave me some cooking utensils and other household items that Boris, being left alone, would not need. When he called me on Saturday to say that Nina would be expecting me to come over on Sunday afternoon, I took for granted that Nina would succeed in purchasing her flight for early next week, as they were planning.

Still, something instinctively worried me that I could not identify. I asked Eduardo to come with me despite our suspicion that Eduardo would encounter difficulties entering the Soviet compound. It was a guarded Soviet compound, and Cuban visitors were not allowed without a written permit from the head of the compound. I was hoping that on Sunday, it would be less formal and easier to convince the head of the compound to issue such a permit for Eduardo. In the worst case, if we have entrance problems, we could ask Boris to intervene on behalf of Eduardo. To be safe, I called Boris and asked him to get Eduardo's permit to enter beforehand, if possible. Eduardo was flexible and said that, as a last resort, if for some reason we don't get him a permit, he will be glad to go to the coast of Cojimar and have a swim before his return home.

Early Sunday morning, we came with the children for a traditional visit to Eduardo's mother and sister in the center of Havana. We left our two boys with them since we thought of sparing them the long wait and rough ride in an overcrowded Cuban bus bursting with the beach crowd en route to Cojimar for Sunday swimming. This trip by car is normally about 30 minutes, but we did not have a car and were forced to take public transportation to Cojimar in a densely packed and overheated bus. Service was infrequent, and it was possible to have to wait several hours to catch the bus. When we finally arrived after a long walk from the bus stop to the Soviet compound in Cojimar, Soviet guards refused to let Eduardo through. Boris was called on the intercom. He answered and explained that, unfortunately, he tried but could not obtain a permit for Eduardo because he failed to locate the manager of the Soviet compound. However, he offered to borrow a car from a Soviet colleague to drive me home safely after our visit.

I was disappointed but told Eduardo to go for a swim and then wait for me at his mother's apartment, where I would return by car with the things Nina would give me after my visit with her and Boris. Eduardo left the gates of the compound while I entered and walked its length until I reached the house of Boris and Nina at the far end. When I knocked at their door, Boris opened it straight away. I was astonished and disturbed to see him dressed only in standard Russian-style black boxer underwear shorts made of thin, revealing material. Staring at his bare hairy chest and overhanging belly, I was revolted by his appearance. Without clothes, he was ugly, physically large, fat, smelly, and reddish from the sun. It was perverse to meet me dressed like this. He invited me in and locked the door, greeting me in the Odessan manner in an attempt to trivialize his appearance in a joking way, "*S privetom, diko izveniaus za costume* (Hi, my wild excuses for my dress). Please come inside and wait in the living room."

I thought that he was embarrassed to receive me in his underwear - but after all, we were in a tropical climate, and for a Russian, it could have been unbearably hot. I thought that he would change and put on something more decent while Nina joined me. I entered and sat at the dining table in their living room. The music on the living room radio was too loud. I shouted over the music: "Nina, I am here." But instead of her, it was Boris who emerged, again in his black underwear. He continued to play down the awkward situation with his light-hearted Odessan manner, "*Shaaa!* (quiet!) Why are you making such a noise? She already left this morning."

At this moment, I understood that something terribly wrong was happening.

"Why didn't you tell me on the phone, Boris? This is not funny." I said, perplexed.

"I will give you what she left for you, and you will like it," he answered and moved very close to me.

"Nina left this morning. She is already on her way to Moscow. We are alone, and I wanted you to come over to have all these things she left for you," said Boris.

Now I was frightened. I had not yet recovered from the initial shock and was not so sure what to do. I got up from the table to leave for the exit door.

"Eduardo is waiting for me in the hot sun outside of the compound; I must go immediately to him, or he will come to get me."

"Why such *shucher*? (rush in Odessan)

Please stay with me longer," Boris suddenly grabbed me from behind and pressed me tightly against him. He was hot and disgustingly sweaty and smelly. I was struggling desperately, trying to dislodge his lecherous hands.

"Let me alone, let me go, you are acting like a fucking beast, a bandit! How can you do this to me? I will tell your wife!" I shouted, feeling the futility of my physical efforts. He was much stronger than me, and all I could do was produce as much noise as possible or shout for help, hoping that his neighbors would hear. But his house was the last in the Soviet compound, removed from the others, and the music in his living room was playing at an uncomfortably high volume.

"Shut up. We don't want a scandal, do we? Why don't you want me?" he said and slapped me hard on the face. Recovering from his heavy slap and struggling to shout again, I did not answer. This scene was inconceivable. For me, here in Cuba, Boris had been like a personification of my father, my only family, and protector far away in a foreign land.

The nightmare continued. He covered my mouth tightly with his hand and began dragging me towards the bedroom. I resisted with all my strength. Now, I was fighting, biting, and screaming despite his attempts to cover my mouth, but the damn music blanketed my shrieks. Finally, his dragging allowed me to distance my leg to kick him hard in the groin with my high heels, using all my strength.

It was the only reliable method my father taught me to stop a male attacker: by inflicting on him the greatest possible pain in the most sensitive area of his anatomy. When I was still a child, I told my father about the attempt of abuse by someone else, and my father taught me how to kick an adult man to immobilize him temporarily. He warned me that this kind of blow should be landed with maximum power since a weak kick might be ineffective and could only provoke severe reprisals from the assailant. The attacker could be badly hurt and even damaged by such a blow, and I should do it only as a last resort.

Boris was wearing flimsy underpants and, as such, was poorly protected against my then-fashionable, metal pointed-toe high heels. I gave him the strongest, violent kick with my metal-reinforced, pointed toe. Boris was suddenly immobilized with pain and bent down onto the floor in anguish. Everything became surreal; I felt a lightness as if I was removed from my body and a strange buzzing in my head. In a dream-like state, my soul was desperate to fly away.

The front door was locked. Somehow, I managed to find the keys on the table beside the door to open it and ran outside in the same state of surrealistic stupor without even closing the door, afraid to look back. In a panic, terrorized, and deeply embarrassed by the attempted rape by my friend and mentor, I was traumatized and frightened at the force of my wild blow, which could have wounded him badly and even killed him. I took off my high heels and was running in bare feet while holding the high heels in my hand. This is how I reached the guardhouse.

I put my shoes back on and allowed myself a backward glance, a last look at the crime scene. Nobody followed me. Boris was probably still in serious pain and hadn't yet called for help. I slowed down and only then realized that I had forgotten everything lying on his dining room table: my purse with all my documents and money, as well as the large bag to carry home Nina's gifts. But this could not be helped. I would not return to pick up my documents and money. So, I continued walking toward the highway, hoping that Eduardo might still be around, maybe at the bus stop. The guards let me through without question; they remembered me entering only recently.

Eduardo was nowhere on the road, and I was afraid to go to look for him at the beach, where Soviet guards could easily detect me. All I wanted to do was to hide at home under the protection of Eduardo and his mother. I began walking to the bus stop, which was quite far away from the Soviet compound, in the desperate hope that Eduardo might still be at the bus stop. But he wasn't there. The sun was really strong, and all I could do was wait there for the bus. Still in shock and confusion, I realized that I might have killed Boris and that eventually, the police would pick me up.

Now, while waiting for the bus on the open highway, I was exposed to the blistering midday sun and possibly to the police who would be searching for the assailant of Boris. My situation appeared to be completely insane. Despite some sore spots and minor pains from the blows exchanged in the struggle with Boris, I still could not believe that this terrifying incident actually happened. After a long wait for the bus (over an hour or more), I regained my ability to speak to ask the bus driver for a free ride because I lied that somebody had stolen my purse on the Cojimar beach. The driver looked at my dress (I was relatively clean and decent), and he took pity on me, permitting me a free ride.

On my arrival at Maria's home without my purse or explanation for its absence, I found the door locked and no sound inside. She soon returned from the local playground where she had taken the children. Nobody questioned me because Eduardo hadn't yet returned from Cojimar. He was still swimming. I would probably have searched the coastline instead of waiting for him at the bus stop if I had known that. But after all, it was a Sunday, and the coastline of Cojimar was crowded. He would be difficult to locate. I was embarrassed and afraid to bring myself to confess to anyone of attempted rape and that I may have killed Boris and left all my documents on his table. I was too ashamed, not for myself, but for my tribe. It was like incest, being sexually assaulted by a man so familiar, so close to my family and me.

I could not possibly tell this story to Eduardo because it was just too bizarre and too dramatic. It was crazy and seemed unreal. Eduardo would not possibly believe this story;

nobody will. I wouldn't believe this nightmarish tale if someone told it to me. Still, it would be a greater disaster if Eduardo believed me, and Boris survived my counterattack. Eduardo will kill Boris and maybe me as well. Eduardo had a very explosive Latin temperament and, when jealous, could completely lose his rational mind in the realm of romantic relations. What happened to me on Sunday was outside the normal spheres of sanity. How could I tell him? Would he trust me? Would he help me in any way by calming me down? Or would he lose his mind the way he did when he unjustly suspected me of coquettish behavior on another occasion and acted like a total imbecile?

On that occasion, four years earlier, we were walking together from our university towards my home along Deribasovskaya Street, Odessa's busy main avenue. We were married, and I was eight months pregnant with Edik, proudly carrying my large belly in front of me. Walking towards us was Ibrahim, a North African student from our university. Ibrahim was a personal friend of Eduardo, and they saw each other quite often at our university and even in our room at the university residence. Ibrahim is as dark as the night and very tall. His features are European, but his skin is black; he is elegant and rich, and he lives permanently in Paris.

One of my old friends, Natasha, started dating him. Eduardo and I saluted Ibrahim and exchanged a few phrases, then continued walking down the street. Suddenly, Eduardo stopped me and slapped me hard across my face. I was completely taken by surprise when I lost the ability to react. Seconds later, still in shock, I could only ask: “Why?”

“Because of the way you looked at him; you were seducing him,” answered Eduardo.

“I don’t want you ever again to come to see me. You are an imbecile,” I murmured, turned around, and went fast towards the home of my parents, which was only a block away. He followed me, but I refused to talk to him. I was furious at the injustice of Eduardo’s insult to my proud, pregnant self. I hid from him for a week at home and explained to my parents that I decided to divorce him for slapping my face, not trusting me, and acting in a despotic and ridiculous fashion.

“How could you think that I was flirting with somebody else when I am walking beside you, so proud of my big tummy? How could you lift your hand against me, and for what? Don’t you understand, you stupid idiot, that I am eight months pregnant and that you could have damaged not just me but also our child?” I said that when under his and my parents' pressure, I agreed to talk with him.

“Why were you seducing him? My apologies, and I beg your pardon, but I don’t remember slapping you at all. Let's go back to the student residence where we can talk about it,” he begged.

“No, I will not come with you. I will stay with

my parents. What do you mean you don't remember slapping me? I almost lost my teeth. What do you mean that I was seducing him? How? By the way, Ibrahim is your friend, not mine, and he started dating Natasha, who is my friend. You know that, don't you? This doesn't mean anything to you? I did not look at him to seduce him. I would not seduce even Don Juan himself in my advanced state of pregnancy. It was daylight outside, and maybe I looked with curiosity at his face in daylight. So what?"

"Please forgive my slapping you because I don't remember doing that," he continued, repeating. Still, I stayed home with my parents all week until I relented after his inane apologetic torrents.

Later, I understood that he might have the ability to forget things that are not convenient to remember. It might be true that he could physically strike someone, and then his mind would erase the experience he found inconvenient to recall. I watched him act like this on other occasions. Eduardo was not a male chauvinist; his violent outbursts could not have been family-influenced. His family and mine never expressed themselves violently. However, it could have been the cultural influence of Latin machismo. In the mental health field, a rage of jealousy, loss of control, and violent attack resulting from what is called appropriately "Othello's syndrome" or delusional jealousy.

I knew his temperament, and I understood that his nature could not be contained; once he starts suspecting someone of any infidelity, he would react with fury, displaying the rage capable of harming himself and my family. I could not share with him my pain about the incident with Boris. If I didn't kill Boris, he would kill Boris and me as well - without remorse. This is what they call in Cuba, *macho* (a real man) or *Caballo* (stallion).

I decided to swallow my tears and hide the incident with Boris from Eduardo. There has been just too much shame, revulsion, and fear for sharing the incident with anyone. I was not at fault, but there were no other witnesses. Even if there were witnesses and my innocence was proven, this would not help any of us get over the trauma. Trust is fragile like a rare and valuable vase; you can't glue it back together once it is fractured. As well, there is the general perception in any rape attempt that the female is guilty of provocation, of bringing it on herself. Both Soviet and Latin societies exhibited extreme male chauvinism.

So, I didn't tell Eduardo the truth. I only said that I missed Nina because she left, and this is why I returned home without gifts. Nor could I bring myself to go to work the next morning, where, if Boris was still alive, I would meet him face to face in the office. He is probably alive since the police have not yet turned up looking for me. Afraid even to discover the outcome of my violence with Boris, I called in sick. Instead of taking the children to their daycare and going to my office, I spent the whole day with them in the hotel park, hiding in our de-luxe cave. The truth was that I needed to recover, regain my composure, and think about the situation without Eduardo observing my mood. Neither did I know about the condition of Boris, how he had survived my blow, nor if security had already found my purse with documents on his living room table. Even if Boris recovered and was well, I could not face him yet, nor did I know what to do next. I preferred to wait for news in the safety of the hotel, pretending that nothing had happened.

APPENDIX 1: Rockets Around The Clock

One summer day in 1961, Khrushchev was sitting in his dacha in Sochi, thinking about the American nuclear missiles based in Turkey and aimed at the USSR. At that moment, he began to develop a strategy to get the Americans to remove those missiles. There were two stages to this strategy: the first was to create a war dance on the island of Cuba to intimidate the Americans. If this military theater failed to produce the desired results, the second stage was to establish a first-strike nuclear capability with nuclear weapons based in Cuba and aimed at the United States.

In 1962, Soviet leaders, lulled by a belief in the weakness of President Kennedy, were pushed by the quixotic Fidel Castro into a fabricated conflict with the Americans. However, the Soviets were not prepared for a proper conflict in 1962 because their Navy lagged too far behind the Americans technologically. They did not even bother to keep the missile batteries in Cuba camouflaged as part of their war dance strategy, and this was how the United States was able to catch them with their pants down; but after all, the dangerous debacle served the advantage of Cuba because Kennedy was forced to promise not to invade the island in the aftermath of the Cuban Missile Crisis.

By 1968, Soviet leaders learned from the master of deception, Fidel Castro himself, how to train Americans with bold theatrical demonstrations intended simply to get the United States accustomed to the strong presence of the Soviet Navy cruising near an American coastline.

In July of 1969, a large Black Sea Fleet Squadron, under the command of Admiral Stepan Stepanovich Sokolanu, was formed especially for this mission. The fleet carried ballistic and cruise missiles with nuclear warheads into the Atlantic Ocean close to the American coastline. This fleet made an impressive showing:

- Ballistic Missile Battleship *Grozniy*,
- ASW Battleship *Soobraznitelniy*,
- Ballistic Missile Warship *Bedoviy*,
- Two specialized fuel tankers, *Karl Marx* and *Lena*,
- Modernized Floating Naval Base *Tobol* - a tender for conventional and nuclear submarines,
- Two PLARK diesel-powered submarines with cruise missiles, Project 641, class Foxtrot,
- PLARK diesel-powered submarines with cruise missiles, Project 670, class Charlie-I,
- Nuclear-powered submarine APL project 627A, November class, with torpedo missiles converted to carry nuclear warheads,
- Diesel-powered submarine B611 with ballistic missiles adapted to carry nuclear warheads.

Their demonstration parade was held in the Atlantic along the American coastline, north to Canada, and back to Cuba. After arriving in the Gulf of Mexico via the Florida Straits, Soviet submarines proceeded in secret: one under the tender (floating base) and the second under a battleship. They were not detected by the US until they surfaced. The surface ships had anchored in the middle of the Gulf of Mexico, where they were surrounded by helicopters with American television reporters who were speculating about the combat capabilities of the Soviet ships. But when the submarines surfaced the next day on orders from Moscow, the American TV reporters almost lost their minds, nearly jumping on the decks of the subs, in the vivid description of my colleagues. This reaction led the Soviets to the conclusion that the Americans were caught by surprise, and the secret passage of submarines went unnoticed. The mission had been successful. The squadron then proceeded to the main objective of their assignment - a visit to Cuba.

Soviet Navy squadron entering Havana with the submarine B611 in the forefront.

On July 20, 1969, the flag was raised, and the entire Soviet fleet (except for the nuclear-powered submarine, which stayed back in neutral waters) entered Havana Port. A huge cohort of the Cuban population of Havana came to greet the Soviet fleet. Fidel Castro, Raúl Castro, Osvaldo Dorticos, Aldo Santa-Maria, and other Cuban dignitaries visited the vessels and conducted joint exercises with the Cuban fleet outside Havana's bay in the Atlantic Ocean. Why such a publicized theatrical demonstration? Because there was no way that Americans could object to such a harmlessly friendly event carried out so openly. Little by little, our Soviet leaders predicted, the US would get used to the presence of a powerful Soviet Navy at its shores. The Americans did not know that the onboard missiles were adapted for and provided with nuclear warheads.

A Soviet submarine with cruise missiles, classed Foxtrot

The Soviet press claimed that the overpowering Soviet visit in July frightened the Americans, and this is why the US administration was compelled to begin the SALT I negotiations in November of 1969.[100] This is how the Soviet military's backstage maneuvering (the naval demonstration parade) played its part to pressure Nixon into ongoing détente negotiations with the Soviets. This method to assure an advantage is called in Russian *'jhod koniom'* (in English, "a move by the knight" – a popular chess expression, meaning a cunning move, an unexpected turn of events, a workaround in a confrontation).

One of the factors (not mentioned in the Soviet press) motivating the Soviets to negotiate détente was the Soviet border conflict with China involving a series of armed clashes, one of which was known as the Zhenbao Island Incident in March of 1969. Moscow approached Washington to ask about their reaction if the USSR destroyed China's nuclear weapons facilities. The Americans, fearful of large Chinese casualties, refused to give their blessing. The Sino-Soviet conflict was one reason why the Soviet Union felt compelled to negotiate détente with the USA.

Still, the presence of large Soviet battleships and attack submarines equipped with nuclear warheads, ballistic and cruise missiles, as well as the submarine tender in the Caribbean Sea, was the first step in re-animating Soviet nuclear confrontation for arms parity (a condition of détente) with the USA: this time, in the American backyard.

It turned out that Fidel was right when, in 1963, he suggested that there would be no protest from the American side and that the Soviets would be given the green light for reviving Soviet military ambitions from a position of strength. The task of establishing a

Soviet nuclear naval presence in the American region was accomplished, and the Soviet squadron departed from Havana on July 27, 1969. The engineering design of the first stage of Cienfuegos naval base facilities was now completed, and in the autumn of 1969, the Soviet Government gave final approval for the construction of a naval base, including repair and service facilities for submarines.

Cuba became the objective of the first Soviet global naval exercise under the code name Ocean.[101] The Cuban role was to allocate the appropriate airports for Soviet bombers Tu-95, which were used for surveillance, naval air support, and attack. They were equipped with nuclear bombs and missiles.

Six Tu-95 bombers landed at San Antonio de Los Baños Soviet military airport. This created an additional precedent for the Soviet government: the stationing of Tu-95 bombers in Cuba violated the 1962 agreement with the Americans since they represented, once again, an imminent military threat to the United States. Still, there was no protest from the American side.

The Soviet government concluded that Americans were asleep or afraid to rock the boat. Another Soviet naval squadron, part of the naval exercises Ocean under the command of Admiral Kudelkin, entered Havana port for refueling and service from May 14 to May 27, 1970. This new Soviet naval squadron consisted of 7 attack platforms:

- The ASW (large anti-submarine cruiser*) Vice-Admiral Drozd,*
- The destroyer class Gremyashchiy,
- A submarine tender *Tobol,*
- A specialized fuel tanker, and
- Four diesel-powered submarines: project 629 (class Golf I) and project 641 (class Foxtrot)[102],
- Two nuclear-powered submarines, PLARK project 675, K-166, (class Echo-II).

ASW "VA Drozd" and submarine tender "Tobol" in Cuba

After the Americans had noticed the Soviet nuclear-powered submarines, the American battleship Wainwright III (DIG-28) was instructed to wait at sea for the approaching Soviet squadron and escort them until they entered Cienfuegos port on May 14, 1970. As the American press described later, the United States was worried about two Soviet nuclear subs and four diesel-electric subs, each equipped with four cruise missiles (with a range that could cover the entire territory of the USA), parading in their backyard. What they did not know was that these missiles were adapted and fitted for the deployment of nuclear warheads. Apart from providing an escort, the American government once again did not formally protest. Meanwhile, Soviet submarines (November and Echo class), equipped with nuclear warhead torpedoes and cruise missiles, were serviced in

Cuba.

Wondering about the reasons for the absence of American reaction, the Soviet government was puzzled by Washington's apparent lack of concern in the context of their 1962 understanding. Soviet concern became so acute that Urey Vorontsov (the temporary Soviet envoy to Washington) was instructed, despite the serious risk of attracting undue attention to the issue, to meet with Henry Kissinger to ask him to confirm the intention of the American Government regarding their current commitments to the 1962 understanding with the Soviet Government.[103] Now that Kennedy was dead and Khrushchev had been removed in a Kremlin power coup, Moscow wanted confirmation that the deal still stands. The surprised Kissinger had to confirm to Vorontsov the continuing commitment of the American government that Soviet missiles were removed from Cuba, and the US would refrain from any aggression against the island.

Meanwhile, the Soviet Navy was using Cuban territory to station nuclear weapons, another breach of the 1962 accord, but there was no protest from the American side, which encouraged the subsequent steps of Soviet escalation. The next Soviet naval squadron, under the command of Admiral Soloviov, entered Cienfuegos Bay on September 9, 1970. It consisted of 7 battleships and a submarine tender for nuclear-powered subs:

- Ballistic missile cruiser,
- Destroyer,

- Submarine tender for nuclear submarines,
- A large amphibious landing ship of Project 1171 (Alligator-class LST),
- An ocean-going submarine rescue tug,
- Two special-purpose barges for servicing nuclear submarines,
- A specialized rescue submarine,
- The Cienfuegos entrance channel was protected by a chain-link anti-submarine gate. The submarine tender was anchored in the bay.

PLARK – nuclear-powered submarine with guided nuclear warhead cruise missiles, Project 675 (Class ECHO-II)

Then, the Soviets became alarmed when the Americans commenced frequent U-2 air surveillance flights over Cienfuegos. Possibly, this increased surveillance was their reaction to the surprise inquiry from the Soviet envoy to Henry Kissinger seeking to confirm the American commitment to the 1962 deal. On September 9, 1970, an American U-2 spotted the construction of a Soviet submarine base in Cienfuegos. It made photographs of the site, including the small island Cayo Alcatraz, where the Soviet submarine crews had their repair shops, administrative buildings, and residences. President Nixon was then informed by

Kissinger that the Soviets were building a permanent naval base in Cienfuegos.

Kissinger proposed to Nixon that if this submarine naval base was intended to provide service to the Soviet submarine project K-137 *Leninets* (known in the West as 667A Navaga, class YANKEE-I), which was equipped with nuclear warhead ballistic missiles, it would create a very serious threat to American security. Soviet submarines, Project 667A Navaga, recently began patrolling in the North Atlantic. Henry Kissinger suggested that they could endanger the existing strategic missile balance. However, Nixon did not want to hear him. Instead, Nixon suggested employing discreet diplomacy rather than making a formal protest. He did not want to spook the Soviets before his European visit from September 27 to October 5 to discuss SALT. Nixon needed this political payoff internationally because America was mired in the disastrous Vietnam War and rising domestic protests. He had already lost much of his presidential popularity at home and abroad. This was when Kissinger rebelled, according to an interview with Kissinger reported by Raymond Garthoff and published in the *New York Times* (September 25, 1970).[104]

The New York Times story revealed the photographic data shot by U-2 surveillance cameras over Cuba. This information was leaked intentionally by Kissinger, who warned the Soviet government that the USA would regard the presence of a Soviet submarine base in Cienfuegos as a serious breach of the 1962 agreement. He demanded that the

Soviets remove all the attack weapons and their components from the territory of Cuba.

Neither Soviet nor Cuban citizens had access in those years to the *New York Times,* but we learned about the answer of Anatoly Dobrynin (the permanent Soviet ambassador to Washington) on September 27. Dobrynin disavowed any breach of the 1962 agreement and firmly denied any presence of Soviet attack weapons in Cienfuegos. During the next meeting with Henry Kissinger on October 5, 1970, Anatoly Dobrynin again confirmed his nation's commitment to the 1962 agreement. He declared that in the name of the Soviet government, he is confirming officially that the Soviet submarines equipped with ballistic missiles will never use Cuba as a base. Kissinger responded that if the Soviet Union removes its submarine tender from Cienfuegos, America will be willing to consider the Soviet presence there as simply a naval training exercise.

On October 9, Kissinger presented Dobrynin with a declaration from President Richard Nixon, who characterized it as an update of the 1962 agreement since the weapons technology had evolved during the past eight years. Nixon welcomed Soviet guarantees and responded with his revised American version of the 1962 agreement. According to this declaration, the American side wanted official confirmation that the Soviet Union would not use Cuba as a base for attack weapons installed on the surface or submarine naval vessels. Also, according to this proposed version, the Soviet Union could not keep a naval base for the repair and service of Navy vessels (both surface and submarine) equipped with ballistic missiles carrying nuclear warheads. In the appendix to the proposed declaration was a list of five concrete actions that the American government would consider a breach of the 1962 agreement.

Anatoly Dobrynin protested immediately against this proposed extension to the agreement, which, in his opinion, was detrimental to the interests of the Soviet Union. "Such an extension would negatively reflect on Soviet capabilities," he said.

On October 10, 1970, the submarine tender and the submarine rescue tug departed once again from Cienfuegos Bay. On October 13, 1970, the Soviet Press Agency TASS officially denied Western publications regarding the construction of a permanent Soviet base for nuclear submarines in Cuba. American sources confirmed that the Soviet submarine tender departed from Cienfuegos. The American government concluded that all problems with the Soviets were solved. During this period, the US administration had its hands full. The government was the target of intense student uprising across the country over the Vietnam War. Washington was also dealing with the issue of Soviet support for Salvador Allende, Chile's leftist presidential candidate. Additionally, the escalation of the Arab Israeli crisis in the Middle East continued to worsen. The popularity of President Richard Nixon was disappointingly low. The President needed to communicate good news.

The Soviets concluded that Americans were too preoccupied to react seriously and reconfirmed their decision to secretly build and complete the naval submarine base with nuclear weapons in Cuba, including the development of a new ocean floor-based service facility for nuclear-powered submarines.

On October 22nd, Soviet Foreign Minister Gromyko met with Nixon to confirm their joint commitment to the 1962 agreement once again. New photographs made by U-2 on that date showed the cessation of construction. On October 23rd, the American administration officially responded that the issue of submarines in Cuba was resolved. The United Nations was not involved in this matter at all. The American solution to the crisis needed to be seen as as propitious as possible for domestic political purposes.

"The mini-crisis of 1970 rose in August and September, and was resolved by October," concludes Raymond L. Garthoff in his analysis of the situation reported in *Handling Cienfuegos Crisis* (*International Security*, Vol.8 #1, 1983, MIT Press).

Of course, nothing at all was resolved in October of 1970. The Soviets never had any intention of honoring their accords with the USA in the post-1962 era. Henry Kissinger understood that; however, his hands were tied. Nixon did not want another international scandal at this juncture and permitted a complete cover-up of the Soviet strategic nuclear arms expansion just 90 miles away from American soil.

At the same time, Soviet subs changed their dance tune from the FOXTROT class, which is referred to as diesel-powered subs, to a spicier class of modern submarine nuclear arms platforms, starting with nuclear-powered submarines of Project 627A (with torpedoes and cruise missiles carrying nuclear warheads), classed November. The next escalation was PLARB (Nuclear-Powered Ballistic Missile Submarine) pertaining to strategic nuclear weapons, namely Project 667A Navaga K-137 *Leninets* (Yankee I Class), precisely the type of Kissinger protested about.

On November 7, 1970, the submarine tender and submarine tug were back, entering Cienfuegos again after finalizing their voyage around the island. Then, at the start of December 1970, the Soviet press announced a new visit to Cuba by a large naval squadron, including submarines.

There was an American reaction this time. The US informed Dobrynin once again that the continual presence of Soviet submarines in Cuba would endanger the relationship between the Soviets and the American people. To allay American concerns, the Soviet submarine tender departed from Cienfuegos in January 1971; except that it was replaced immediately by a similar Soviet submarine tender that entered Cienfuegos Bay on February 14, 1971. Additionally, just a week before that, there was a new visit by a Soviet naval squadron, which berthed in Cienfuegos Bay (from February 9 to February 25, 1971):

- Large ASW *Vice Admiral Drozd* (minesweeper cruiser),
- APL Project 627A (Nuclear-powered submarine with nuclear warhead cruise missiles of Project 627 A, class November),
- Ocean submarine tender classed UGRA,
- Oil tankers for submarines and
- Nuclear submarine service ships.

Henry Kissinger sent a new message to Dobrynin on February 22, 1971: "The presence of the Soviet submarine tender for 125 days out of the last 160-day period does not correspond to our 1962 agreement."

The submarine tender and submarines again departed from Cienfuegos on February 25, just to return a month later. Soviet personnel were now being entertained by this never-ending game of 'hide and seek'. Moscow learned how to take advantage of the internal politics of the United States. They were waiting until Nixon signed the SALT Agreement in Moscow in May 1971 before embarking on the next hide-and-seek maneuver.

After signing the SALT Agreement in Moscow, the Soviet Navy sent to Cuba a naval squadron with the Large ASW *Sevastopol*, with the destroyer *Skromniy* as well as the nuclear-powered PLARK (nuclear-powered submarine with guided nuclear warhead cruise missiles) Project 675 (class ECHO-II) and the older diesel submarine of Project 629A class GOLF-II equipped with three ballistic nuclear warhead missiles launched from under the water with a range of 1400km.

Again, in this case, the American government did not protest, but its Navy squadron followed the Soviet submarine with ballistic missiles within the Gulf of Mexico. This was an indication to Moscow that it had become necessary to switch to Plan B concerning the ocean bottom servicing. According to internally published Soviet Navy sources, these ocean bottom service facilities became known as Nuclear Deepwater Stations. Their main function was to supply and service the nuclear submarines underwater. At the time, the autonomy of Soviet nuclear submarines was limited to 50 days, the main reason for the requirement for service stations.

In retrospect, it could be said that the lack of response from the American side reassured the Soviet Union and allowed them to develop the deployment of Soviet nuclear weapons in the Caribbean, such as opening the possibility for a pre-emptive strike (decapitation). Delighted with the American faith in diplomacy, the Soviet government ordered the acceleration of the construction of the naval base in Cienfuegos.

According to Russian sources[105], an additional 29 Soviet naval squadrons were serviced (each lasting from 40 to 90 days) in Cienfuegos over the subsequent 20 years, following my defection in May of 1971.

The silence surrounding these Soviet missions to Cuba was interrupted in 1986 when a fatal explosion took place near

Bermuda of a K219 Navaga-Class nuclear-powered submarine cruiser. The sub carried 16 ballistic missiles equipped with 34 nuclear warheads of a 3000-kilometer range. The accident attracted international attention when a Soviet surface naval rescue ship attempted to tow it back to Cuba. The story is told in the 1997 BBC film *Hostile Waters.*

Both classes of Soviet submarines: PLARK and PLARB, were serviced in 1971

End Notes

---

1 *"To a drunk, the sea is only knee deep."* is an old Russian proverb used by my father to rebuke me when I acted dangerously, meaning that I am underestimating the depth of the sea if I imagine it could be walked across - a sentiment reflected in a Soviet navy song we loved to sing.

2 The Law "Especially Dangerous State Crimes", prior to 1960, addressed treason and defection under the dreaded Article 58-1a "Special Part of the Criminal Code of the Russian Federation". It was introduced by Decree of the USSR Central Committee on 8th of June, 1934:

Treason - acts committed by citizens of the USSR to the detriment of the military power of the USSR, its state independence or integrity of its territory, such as espionage, issuing military or state secrets to the enemy, and flight or flight abroad, shall be punished in the highest measure of criminal punishment: shooting with confiscation of all property, and if mitigating circumstances, imprisonment for a term of 10 years with confiscation of property.

Then in 1960, Article 58 became superseded by Article 64 of The Criminal Code of the Russian Federation and by Article 54 of The Ukrainian Criminal Code. These new Articles were in force and applied vigorously until the dissolution of the Soviet Union in 1991. They stated the same punishment for defectors:

Treason, that is an act intentionally committed by a civilian citizen of the USSR to the detriment of the sovereignty, territorial integrity or public safety and defense of the USSR: for the benefit of the enemy, spying, issuing state or military secrets to a foreign state, flight abroad or failure to return from abroad to the Soviet Union, the provision of assistance to a foreign state in hostile activities against the Soviet Union, as well as conspiracy to seize power - shall be punished by imprisonment for a term of ten to fifteen years with confiscation of property.

Their relatives living together with him or as his dependents at the moment of the perpetration of the crime who failed to report these criminal intentions to authorities are to be punished with a term of two to five years.

Usually, after years of investigations and interrogations in prisons, the remainder of the punishment was served in forced labor camps.

3 Cubana's flights CU-T668 Havana-Prague-Moscow were using four Bristol Britannia turboprops purchased in Britain. These aircrafts had to be leased in 1962 to CSA Czechoslovakian Airlines to allow this route to be operated by CSA instead of Cubana. The main reason for the transfer was the problem with Cuban pilots who were defecting during the refueling stop in Gander. The East European transatlantic routes were very important for the Cuban Government because the majority of foreign recruits from Latin and North American countries, enrolled in Cuban international terrorist training, came to Cuba via Prague. Bristol Britannia turboprops did not have the fuel capacity to cover the Havana-Prague distance nonstop and had to be refueled in Gander, Newfoundland, Canada. On their way back from Prague to Havana these flights had an additional refueling stop in Shannon, Ireland about which I found out only later.

4 MVD is the "Soviet Ministry of Internal Affairs" which replaced NKVD - "People's Commissariat for Internal Affairs". MVD was in charge of exit visas and travel permits for Soviet citizens.

5 Gulag derives from the acronym GULag for its Russian name translated as "Chief Administration of Corrective Labor Camps and Colonies", which refers to the vast Soviet network of prisons, forced labor camps, psychiatric hospitals and special laboratories for deadly experiments on humans that collectively housed millions of prisoners. The Gulag system was identical to the German Nazi forced labor camp system, both of which were used as a slave labor contribution to the national economies. The Soviet version of these camps came into existence in 1920.

6 Kildin is a small Russian island in the Barents Sea, off the Russian coast and about 120 kilometers from Norway. Kildin accommodated the Soviet Nuclear Missile Base under the code name "The Arrow" as well as anti-aircraft batteries. Kildin missile base included a nuclear warheads manufacturing plant. According to the Norwegian Organization for the Protection of the Environment, the island today is a depository of expended reactors from Soviet nuclear submarines.

7 There was no information in print or otherwise available to the public about the Special Nuclear Missile Base on Kildin Island until late in

2006 when Victor Potapov and Uriy Shiluk, both veterans of this base (named BRAV 616), published 400 copies of their book *Beregoviki Zapoliaria* in Sevastpol, Russia.

8 http://vmnews.ru/uncategorized/2009/07/25/zapretnyiy-ostrov **and** http://www.youtube.com/watch?v=U9UDZmLIF0Q

9 'To a drunk, the sea is only knee deep' is an old Russian proverb used by my father to rebuke me when I acted dangerously, meaning that I am underestimating the depth of the sea if I imagine it could be walked across - a sentiment reflected in a Soviet navy song we loved to sing.

10 These foreign friends were brought to Cuba at Cuba's expense since 1959 by Che Guevara as the volunteer members of "International Solidarity Brigades" and "Venceremos Brigades" organized, financed and directed by DGI (Cuban Intelligence Services).

11 *Direción General de Inteligencia* (DGI) - Cuban Intelligence Services headed by "the Redbeard" (Manuel Piñiero Lozado) and supervised by the large Cuban-based Soviet KGB contingent of intelligence officers and trainers headed by Victor Semionov, a KGB General.

12 Carlos Marighella. *Mini Manual of the Urban Guerilla*. The manual contains instructions in urban terror tactics, kidnappings, etc. The manual was translated and distributed worldwide in many languages by Cuba.

13
http://en.wikipedia.org/wiki/List_of_Cuba_%E2%80%93_United_States_aircraft_hijackings

14 http://cuban-exile.com/doc_226-250/doc0230.html

15 Georgie Anne Geyer. *Guerrilla Prince: The Untold Story of Fidel Castro.* Kansas City: Andrews and McMeel, 1993: p. 302.

16 Carlos Franqui, a renowned Cuban writer and journalist, head of the underground revolutionary newspaper, a former ally of Fidel Castro and ex-Chief Editor of "*Revolución* - the first official newspaper of the Cuban Revolutionary Government. Carlos Franqui, *Cuba, La Revolución: Mito o realidad? Memorias de un Fantasma Socialista.* Peninsular, 2006: pp. 226-275.

17 The Weathermen group was an American splinter organization from Students for a Democratic Society formed in the 1960s. They declared

war against the United States with the goal to "lead white kids into armed revolution". In the view of the group, "revolutionary violence" was necessary to combat what they perceived as a war against African-Americans and military actions overseas, such as the Vietnam War and the invasion of Cambodia.

18 International Brigades were organized in 1969 by the Weathermen for the disaffected to become trained in Cuba in guerrilla warfare, insurrection tactics, and explosives.

19 *Macheteros*: a Puerto Rican terrorist group that provided aid and training to the Black Panthers and the Black Liberation Army, as well as a safe haven in Cuba for black revolutionary leaders. Castro continuously promoted the independence of Puerto Rico and supported the *Macheteros* who committed terrorist acts and bank robberies in the United States.

20 Cuba trained and gave sanctuary for the *ETA*, where it established its headquarters. *ETA* is the military wing of the Basque National Liberation Movement and classified as a terrorist organization by Spanish Governments.

21 Salvador Allende had publicly condemned the Soviet invasions of Hungary in 1956 and of Czechoslovakia in 1968.

22 Ostensibly, because Chile recognized Communist China diplomatically in 1971 even though, to continue the irony, the United States began its official courtship of Communist China the following year.

23 *Homo Sovieticus*, pseudo-Latin for "Soviet Man" (or Che Guevara's "*Hombre Nuevo*") is the term created by Alexander Zinoviev (ex-Soviet sociologist) for the average citizen living in a communist system. It represents a sarcastic and critical reference to a category of robotically trained humans with obliterated personality and alcohol controlled intelligence. They live like zombies, manipulated by the state in all aspects of their lives. Inside the Soviet Union their slang name was *Sovki.*

24 *Sovok,* translated from the Russian means "dustpan", but in Soviet slang, refers to the mass of typical Soviet citizens characterized by ideological bias, lack of freedom, spiritual indecisiveness, social

dependency, anti-democratic tendencies, intolerance of other people's opinions and other people's individuality. This name originated in the Gulag or Soviet forced labor camps. Its popularization is illustrative of prisoners' mentality broadly spread across the country.

25 *Spy vs. Spy* was a long-running Mad Magazine cartoon feature, the brainchild of Antonio Prohías, a popular Cuban political cartoonist. His political parodies of the newly installed Fidel Castro drew foreboding criticism from the Revolutionary regime. He left abruptly for the United States in 1960, just days before Castro nationalized the press and countered press criticism with arrest, prison, or execution. http://en.wikipedia.org/wiki/Spy_vs._Spy

26 Favio Grobart, Polish-born communist who immigrated to Cuba in the early 1920s on orders of the Comintern (Communist International) and became a founding member of the Cuban Communist Party in 1925. Grobart's blunders were at least partially responsible for the outlawing of the Cuban Communist Party (CCP) in 1948, and resulted in his deportation. In the 1960s, he directed *Cuba Socialista* (Journal of the Central Committee of the Communist Party of Cuba) and was a top planner guiding orthodox ideology. As he grew older, he was considered the Party's historian. He died in Cuba on October 22, 1994.

27 Oswaldo Sanchez Cabrera, alias *bestia* (the beast), was a Cuban who volunteered during the Civil War in Spain and was brought to the USSR after the war for specialized training in the KGB Academy. Upon graduation, he was awarded the rank of General of KGB and was sent as a 'resident' (head of intelligence) to Mexico and later on to Cuba. He became second in command for army intelligence in Cuba (G2) which was designed and organized under his management. He was the intelligence contact with the USSR. He was assassinated jointly with his close associates in a very strange 'accident' in 1961 engineered by the Cuban Revolutionary army in Varadero.

28 Christopher Andrew and Oleg Gordievsky. *KGB - The Inside Story*. New York: Harper Collins, 1990: pp. 466-468.

29 PSP - *Partido Socialista Popular*, formerly PCC (Partido Communista de Cuba), the original Cuban Communist Party formalized in 1926 and which enjoyed traditional trust and support by the Soviet Union.

30 Christopher Andrew and Oleg Gordievsky. *KGB - The Inside Story. Op. cit.*, p. 563.

31 Nikolai Sergeevich Leonov became a Deputy of the Russian State Duma (Russian Parliament) on behalf of Putin's ultra conservative Nationalist movement *Rodina* (The Motherland) currently named United Russia. He is closely identified with the current Kremlin administration and is a long-time friend and mentor of his former KGB subordinate and possibly life-time President of Russia, Vladimir Putin.

32 http://tvtorrent.ru/forum/all_1/thematic_19_1/topic_934/

33 Christopher Andrew and Oleg Gordievsky. *KGB - The Inside Story*. Op. cit., p. 468.

34 Comandante Ramiro Valdés, a communist revolutionary and member of the Politburo of the Communist Party of Cuba, was appointed to head the Department of Intelligence of the Cuban Army (Departamento de Inteligencia del Ejercito Rebelde, or DIER), known in the West as "Cuban G2".

35 *Spetsnaz* were the special action forces under GRU - Soviet Military Intelligence.

36 Comandante Manuel Piñeiro (called by Cubans *Barbarroja* - red beard), member of the Politburo of the Communist Party of Cuba and deputy of Ramiro Valdés, was appointed to lead the Cuban external security intelligence, namely DGI (General Intelligence Directorate) who were trained not only by Soviets but also by Stasi - East German Ministry for State Security. As a result, DGI became the most prolific and successful intelligence organization in the communist bloc; although, according to Soviet security analysts, they were party boys with money to throw around (infamous for womanizing and drinking) and single-mindedly obsessed with their hatred of America. Consequently, in the eyes of the more austere and sophisticated KGB, they cared less about other important objectives of intelligence gathering.

37 SIGINT - intelligence derived from intercepting, analyzing and decrypting signals.

38 'aboriginals' is the disparaging term given to Cubans by Soviet personnel working in Cuba.

39 Nikita Khrushchev. *Khrushchev Remembers: The Glasnost Tapes*. Boston: Little Brown, 1990, pp 177-183.

40 Lev Davidovich Bronstein, alias Leon Trotsky, was initially a supporter of the Menshevik Internationalists faction of the Russian Social Democratic Labour Party. He joined the Bolsheviks immediately prior to the 1917 October Revolution and eventually became a leader within the Party. Stalin was afraid of Trotsky because Trotsky was more popular than him. Stalin solved the problem by isolating Lenin who favored Trotsky and expelling Trotsky from the Soviet Union. While in exile in Mexico, Trotsky was murdered by the Soviet agent Ramon Mercader whom I met in Cuba twenty years later - at the Hotel National, of course.

41 '*Swallow'* is the KGB tradecraft term for women and 'raven' the term for men, both trained to seduce intelligence targets. In the west, the term the intelligence services employ when sexual entrapment is used as a tool to obtain confidential information or recruit a foreign official, is "Honey Pot" or "Honey Trap".

42 Evgenia Albats, *The Mine of Slow Action.* Russian Publishing House Ruslit (in Russian), 1992: p. 163.

43 Great Patriotic War is how the Second World War was called in the Soviet Union.

44 The *Haskalah* or Jewish Enlightenment, was an intellectual movement in Europe that was inspired by the European Enlightenment but had a Jewish character. The *maskilim* (followers of the *Haskalah*) tried to assimilate into European society in dress and language. The *Haskalah* eventually influenced the creation of the Jewish Reform movement.

45 *Pogrom* is a name of Russian origin which was used to describe the violent massacres of Jewish populations in Russia, Ukraine and Poland. In modern times, this term could be used to describe outbreaks of ethnic cleansing in other geographical areas and among other ethnic groups.

46 On February 23, 1922, a decree was published by the Soviet Central Committee regarding expropriation of all religious properties by the state. On May 15, 1932, a Soviet Government decree, signed by Stalin, announced the immediate implementation of 'anti-religious measures' designed to completely eliminate the name of God from the minds of people on the territory of the Soviet Union and the closure of all remaining religious institutions in the USSR.

47

http://www.missiontoseafarers.org/ports/odessa/our-port

48 The revolutionary fathers of our Soviet State - Lenin, Trotsky, Stalin and others - subjected the whole country, and in particular Ukraine (because it was the bread basket for the USSR), to three major famines to teach the peasants and the nationalists a lesson in loyalty to the Soviet State. The first famine (1921-1922) was caused by state grain requisition and export sales, not by drought or poor harvest. Most of the victims were Ukrainians though national minorities like Germans, Jews and Russians also suffered. Between the fall of 1921 and the spring of 1923, as many as two million people died from starvation in Ukraine while grain was shipped by the Soviet state to Europe for hard currency. The second famine ravaged Ukraine in 1932-1933 and caused the deaths of seven to ten million people. This one too was caused by "our dear leaders" as a result of industrial collectivization of all farm land.

The third famine in 1946-1947 was intentionally forged by Stalin in order to punish 'Ukrainian bourgeois nationalism' and categorically forbade any assistance to those starving in Ukraine. During this period, grain was exported from Odessa to Europe. While people in Ukraine were dying of famine, Poland, Czechoslovakia, Hungary, France and Italy received millions of tons of Ukrainian grain as a tool for Soviet propaganda and foreign currency income for the USSR.

49 According to The Ukrainian Memorial Society: "various branches of the Registry of Births and Deaths in Ukraine alone registered nearly one million deaths by starvation only in 1947." http://memorial.kiev.ua/expo/eng/1947_2.html

50 In the days when Stalin was Commissar of Munitions, a meeting was held of the highest ranking Commissars, and the principal matter for discussion was the famine then prevalent in the Ukraine. One official arose and made a speech about this tragedy - the tragedy of having millions of people dying of hunger. He began to enumerate death figures. Stalin interrupted him to say, "If only one man dies of hunger, that's a tragedy. If millions die, that's only statistics." *Washington Post*, January 30, 1947: p. 9.

51 Black Sea Institute is an abbreviated title from the Russian *CHERNOMORNIIPROEKT* (Black Sea Scientific Research and Design Institute), http://www.paco.net/~blasdari/index.html - a Black Sea R&D division of *SOUZMORNIIPROEKT* (All Union Scientific Research and Design Marine

Institute) of the Ministry of Transport of the USSR in Moscow.

52 Food rations were very small: 600 grams of bread (about half a loaf) per day per working person; 250-150 grams of bread for adult dependant. Artificial ingredients (more than 40%) were mixed into that bread, including sawdust and celluloid.

53 http://memorial.kiev.ua/expo/eng/1947_2.html

I.M. Volkov. “Drought and Starvation: 1946-1947”, *Magazine Science*, 1991. № 4, Page: 3 - 19. or www.fedy-diary.ru/?page_id=5751

54 Black Sea Institute: Marine Design and Research Institute for The Black Sea region of The Ministry of Transportof the USSR.

55 *Mannaya kasha* means “food from heaven”. It is a creamed porridge made from wheat semolina, lard and salt or sugar.

56 Zima, V. F., The Famine of 1946-1947 in the USSR: Its Origins and Consequences. Ceredigion, UK: Mellen Press, 1999.

57 Pushkin had been exiled to Odessa during 1823-1825 by Czar Alexander I - a rather salubrious punishment considering how the Bolsheviks treated their exiles in Siberia. In that period, Russian intellectuals were typically exiled to Odessa.

58 Kulak - a member of the class of peasants who became proprietors of their own farms. After the October Revolution, the kulaks opposed collectivization of land. Since 1929, they were all arrested with their entire families and sent to forced labor camps in Siberia with all of their possessions confiscated by the state.

59 Yuriy Druzhnikov, a onetime Soviet dissident and vice-president of International PEN for writers in exile. In his book, *Informer 001: the Myth of Pavlik*

Morozov (Transaction Publishers, 1997), he demonstrated that Pavlik and his brother were killed, not by their own family, but by OGPU agents (predecessor of the KGB). To buy her silence, the KGB gave Pavlik's mother a large new house in Crimea and a big monthly pension for the rest of her life. What emerges from these details is a complicated tale of a nasty teenager who wants to punish his father for leaving his mother. Discovering he enjoys his new found power, Pavlik continues to inform on villagers until security agents kill him to stop his continuing attempts to extort pay-offs from state security for keeping his mouth shut.

60 The Doctors' Plot in 1952, at the pinnacle of the aged Stalin's paranoid schizophrenia, ignited a national wave of barbaric anti-Jewish hysteria in the Soviet Union, involving mass false accusations of Jewish doctors and intellectuals in order to unmask the group of prominent Jews purported to be the conspiratorial assassins of Soviet leaders.

It started with the newly born State of Israel allying itself with the West in 1948. Stalin, who was counting on Israel becoming a Soviet ally in the Middle East, reacted with obsessive vengeance against all Jews. His initial retaliation was the elimination of the Jewish Anti-Fascist Committee in 1948 and launching of a campaign against so-called 'rootless cosmopolitans'. After show trials of 13 internationally prominent members of the Jewish Anti-Fascist Committee, they were secretly executed on Stalin's orders. The episode became known as The Night of the Murdered Poets. This event was followed by show trials of other Jewish intellectuals and anti-Semitic propaganda in state-run mass media. Many Soviet Jews were promptly dismissed from their jobs, arrested, sent to the Gulag, or executed.

Stalin's dread of his own death, aggravated by his advanced state of delusional paranoia, resulted in constant suspicions and fears towards medical doctors. In his later years, he refused to be treated by physicians, and would only consult about his health with veterinarians. At this time, 37 of the most prestigious and prominent Kremlin doctors in the USSR were accused of taking part in a vast plot to poison members of the top Soviet political and military leadership. *Pravda*, the official newspaper of the CPSU, beneath the headline *Vicious Spies and Killers under the Mask of Academic Physicians* reported the following accusations:*The bigwigs of the USA and their English junior partners know that to achieve domination over other nations by peaceful means is impossible. Feverishly preparing for a new world war, they energetically send spies inside the USSR and the people's democratic countries: they attempt to accomplish what the Hitlerites could not do - to create in the USSR their own subversive fifth column.*

The accusations began with 37 doctors, but the number quickly grew into the hundreds. Outside of Moscow, similar denunciations quickly appeared. For example, Ukraine discovered a local 'doctors' plot' allegedly headed by the famous endocrinologist Victor Kogan-Yasny (the first in the USSR to treat diabetes with insulin and save thousands of lives). Thirty-six plotters were arrested there.

61 That is because Leonid Moyseevich (doctor of my father in Moscow) and his wife were practicing in Moscow. I overheard my father commenting how dangerous it was for Leonid Moyseevich to work in Moscow. However, my father said that at the time he didn't know that Leonid Moyseevich and his wife were already transferred somewhere in the North.

62 The employees in all public services, including schools and universities, mail and rail services, plants and theaters (more than half the country's adult population) were required to denounce anyone they hear about or notice committing an offense. The reported offenders (often innocent people) could be arrested and sent to labour camps or shot. The habit was so widespread in Soviet mentality that nobody was surprised or shamed when named a *stukach* (informers). Some people denounced their wives, husbands, neighbors, professors, colleagues and superiors not only to settle a personal vendetta, but more often for pragmatic reasons such as getting a promotion, better grades, to claim the property of the accused, or simply to obtain a credit with internal security.

63 This epoch which we called *Vegetarian* was confusing and controversial. For the first time in the history of our country, the government apologized for a wrongdoing. On February 14, 1956, Khrushchev presented his internal report *Cult of Personallty* (the euphemistic phrase he gave to the policy of genocide of innocent Soviet citizens), while noting the effectiveness of Stalin's secret services for crushing the enemies of the people. Then, on June 30, 1956, the Central Committee of the Communist Party publicly adopted a resolution where, amidst congratulations for the victory of socialism assured by Stalin, for the first time mention was made of some extreme abuses of power that resulted from Stalin's personal defects. When Soviet citizens learned the news, the information only confirmed what they already knew partially and unofficially. The principal difference was that before 1956, it was largely believed that those arrested had to be guilty to some degree for something; otherwise, it would seem too monstrous and irrational to arrest innocent citizens and punish them with sentences from 10 to 25 years in labor camps. But now we were witnessing the Party's admission that those arrested and enslaved were indeed the innocent victims.

Regardless of the news revealing the enormity of the evil perpetrated, we were still expected to remain happy and obedient within the same ideological framework and were prohibited from saying, reading or listening to anything outside of approved and published Communist Party literature and other media. Approximately one million military and Party prisoners were freed nationwide from the Gulag camps. They were exonerated and returned to their homes and to their families (if, indeed, there were still any survivors among their families). Only those, so-called, political prisoners were not exonerated and remained in the Gulag.

The process of exoneration or amnesty (what the Soviets called Rehabilitation) could drag on for years; for example, Isaak, the younger brother of my father, was arrested in 1943 and was posthumously exonerated only in 1986 when another million former prisoners were also exonerated.

Apart from those who died in the camps, the ones who were repatriated to civilian life could not even attempt to seek the return of their stolen apartments and possessions or even basic compensation or assistance. All of them had lost their jobs and could not return to their institutions of work. If they managed to get hired at all for any work, the pay would be miserable. Most were very ill after years of brutal, inhuman abuse in labor camps and did not live long after their release. Because of gross mismanagement of the economy, the Soviet Government still required free slave labor on a large scale; therefore, it continued to make arrests but on a scale less gigantic than during the Stalinist era. Other employed workers were compensated with absurdly low pay, with the exception of high Party or government elites and those who stole and were corrupt. Any criticism of this system would still result in long, forced labor camp sentences. Compared to the victims of this system, my family and I were very fortunate. Through a subtle process of passive resistance, the three of us managed to stay clear of political affiliation and political controversy. My parents always said, "It is better to sleep at night with a peaceful conscience than with guilt for the price of more comfort during the day."

64 Alexander Zinoviev. *Homo Sovieticus*, London, Paladin Grafton book, Collins Publishing Group, 1986.

65 Under the new educational reform of 1958, university entrance required, at minimum, 6 years: 4 years of high school and 2 years of proletarian work. In our scheme, we substituted those 6 years with 3 years of proletarian work and night school.

66 As a child, I loved Lego toy-building bricks and the Meccano model construction kits. They shaped my inclination to want to construct things. This early experience led me as a teenager to select bricklaying as a skill to learn and, later, to a life-long career in coastal and offshore engineering.

67 Mikhail Voslenski. *Nomenklatura*, London: Overseas Publications Interchange Ltd., 1990, p.4.

68 The principal and early part of our obligatory university curriculum consisted of such subjects as: History of KPSS (Communist Party), Marxist-Leninist Philosophy, Marxist-Leninist Ethics, Basis for Scientific Communism, Basis of Marxist-Leninist Esthetics, and Basis of Scientific Atheism. Clearly none of the students who were pursuing technical careers were enthusiastic about these subjects. Still, everyone managed a public display of interest while pretending to digest nearly 600 academic hours dedicated to irrelevant courses because their attendance was obligatory.

69 Due to state expropriation of all private property, agriculture and industry in the Soviet Union were completely destroyed by 1920. This is why Lenin introduced, temporarily, the NEP in 1921 which he called state capitalism. Allowing some private ventures, the NEP permitted small animal businesses or smoke shops, for instance, to re-open for private profit while the state continued to control banks, foreign trade, and large industries. By 1927, when the agricultural and industrial sectors had recovered, Lenin shut down the NEP and arrested, shot or sentenced to forced labor camps the new private owners. Music written in the period of the NEP in Odessa was cosmopolitan and personal in character rather than political or patriotic.

70 Slavs - members of the most numerous ethnic and linguistic body of peoples in Europe, residing chiefly in eastern and southeastern Europe but extending also across northern Asia to the Pacific Ocean.

71 Unfortunately, the contemporary quality of hospitals in Cuba is adequate only for senior Cuban officials and foreigners who have to pay for these services with a lot of hard currency. Otherwise, for ordinary Cubans, the hospitals are atrocious - dirty and lacking medicines, similar (or worse) to what I experienced in Odessa's maternity hospital.

72 Unfortunately, the contemporary quality of hospitals in Cuba is adequate only for senior Cuban officials and foreigners who have to pay for these services with a lot of hard currency. Otherwise, for ordinary Cubans, the hospitals are atrocious - dirty and lacking medicines, similar (or worse) to what I experienced in Odessa's maternity hospital.

73 INRA - National Agrarium Reform Institute headed by Che Guevarra, which later became the Ministry of Industries in charge of all developments in the country, including road-building and tourism.

74 Carlos Franqui. Cuba, La Revolución: Mito o Realidad? Memorias de un Fantasma Socialista. Op. cit., pp. 261-265.

75 Mikhail Heller and Aleksandr Nekrich. *Utopia in Power: The History of the Soviet Union from 1917 to the Present.* English Edition published by Summit Books, New York, 1986: pp. 15-50.

76 Cathy Frierson and Simyon Vilensky, *Children of the Gulag.* London: Yale University Press, 2010.

77 The Popular Socialist Party (Partido Socialista Popular) was a Communist Party in Cuba. Originally called the Communist Party of Cuba (Partido Comunista de Cuba), it was formed in 1925 by a group includingBlas Roca, Anibal, Fabio Grobar and Julio Antonio Mella. The latter acted as its leader until his assassination in Mexico in 1929. It was later renamed the Popular Socialist Party. In 1961, the Party merged into the Integrated Revolutionary Organizations (ORI), the precursor of the current Communist Party of Cuba.

78 'Niños' is how Soviets called the thousands of children evacuated without their parents during the Spanish Civil War. These children belonged mainly to parents who were active in Spain's anti-Franco resistance (Spanish "communists"). These Spanish children where brought, on Stalin's orders, to the Soviet Union and placed in their own special and very privileged Spanish schools where they were educated and indoctrinated in Soviet communist ideology. As they came of age, they were trained in KGB schools before being sent, as the first Soviet emissaries to Cuba, to prepare for appropriate indoctrination or training of Cubans and the creation of a Soviet-Cuban intelligence network.

79 Soviet identification documents, including internal and external passports, have a so-called 'fifth graph' where the ethnicity of the citizen is defined by the ethnicity of both parents. Individuals with full "bad" ethnicity (Jewish in my case) were not allowed to enroll in prestigious universities; neither, could they expect prestigious careers or job promotions. The "half-breeds" were given a little more leeway: they could choose the nationality of their father (by cultural tradition) and take advantage of the special quotas permitting them to enter in limited numbers into some less prestigious universities. None of this was a part of Soviet law, but all Soviet institutions and organizations were obliged to follow Party instructions requesting "no Jews admitted or Jewish quota".

80 I did not understand this argument. In my mind, Judaism meant the Jewish religion. Almost all religious institutions in the Soviet Union were closed and forgotten long ago; so, why would government officials make a reference to religion? Certainly, in the case of a non-religious population, this made no sense; and why should half-Jews be blamed for cosmopolitism? My generation of Soviet youth knew nothing about religion or the international community. Nor, were we interested in 'the outdated ancient folklore designed to subdue the uneducated peasants' as religion was described to us in our schools. We accepted the current rational scientific explanations of nature; as well, we were fully assimilated into our society. Still, we felt utterly confused as to how and why it was possible to unleash this vile and absurd discrimination against ethnic groups in communist states when such behavior was absolutely contrary to the actual principles of Marxism-Leninism and international communist theory.

Many years later, it was revealed, (though not accepted officially by the Soviet Government), that Stalin was paranoid from early childhood. His irrational fear of persecution was joined with a character capable of savage cruelty and reinforced by an ancient tribal tradition of revenge practiced in the Caucasion mountains of Georgia where he grew up. All his life, he engaged in merciless retribution against anyone, including friends, offenders and their families and relatives and entire ethnic groups, members of whom he suspected of questioning, insulting or challenging him. For example, in December of 1927, the renowned psychiatrist and neurologist Vladimir Bechterev was to attend, as sitting President, the First Congress of Neurologists and Psychiatrists of Soviet Russia, held in Moscow. Unexpectedly, he received a telegram from the medical department at the Kremlin summoning him urgently to the capital. He had been called to diagnose an ailment of Stalin. Afterwards, Bechterev arrived late at an important Congress session. When asked about the reason for his delay, he answered only that he had just examined a “paranoid man with a withered hand”. Within a few days, on Christmas Eve, Dr. Bechterev was found dead of unknown causes at the age of 70. He was known for his good health and his colleagues suspected he was poisoned by the secret police after his remark about Stalin was reported. Shortly after, his institute in Leningrad was closed down, his scientific papers discarded and his reputation buried until after the death of Stalin. Members of his family were arrested and imprisoned. (*Annals of the National Academy of Medicine Journal*, 2010, 180/1, pp. 33-36).

Among professionals in the field of psychopathology, it is generally agreed that Stalin’s warped personality and character centered around two pathological states: megalomania and a persecution complex (which mirror one another in interesting but deadly ways). Bechterev’s untimely demise was only one tragic consequence of a slip of the tongue in the Stalinist era.

It is impossible to account for all victims under the paranoid and delusional leadership of Stalin. Many forms of persecution and elimination of citizens were often conducted in secret and intentionally were not documented. In the estimation of some ex-Soviet historians, approximately 66,700,000 innocent Soviet citizens from many different ethnic origins became victims of repressions and terrorism from October of 1917 to 1959; and about 75 million by 1980 according to Alexander Solzhenitsyn (these numbers are not officially confirmed). More formally, between 36 and 50 million victims in the Russian Federation alone were reported by the *State Commission for Rehabilitation of Victims of Soviet Repression* led by Alexander Yakovlev in a report officially commissioned by the Russian Government. Yakovlev who earned a doctorate from Colombia University and was the Soviet ambassador to Canada, was also the intellectual and moral influence behind "*Glasnost and Perestroika*".

81 Many thousands of Soviet military were permanently based in Cuba. All travel documents of Soviet military identified them as "agricultural technical assessors" to ensure the secrecy of their true mission in Cuba. We often joked about this because the climate and agriculture in Cuba and in the Soviet Union could not be more dissimilar.

82 Article 58-10 of the Soviet Criminal code and the Article 62 of Ukrainian Criminal Code of 1960:

The propaganda or agitation containing an appeal to overthrow, undermine or weaken the Soviet regime or to commit some counter-revolutionary crimes as well as the distribution, manufacture or possession of literature with the same content will result in imprisonment for seven years.

83 Letter of Fidel Castro to Nikita Chruschevo of October 25, 1962

84 Carlos Franqui, a Cuban writer, journalist and poet was a revolutionary guerilla closely allied with the brothers Castro in the Sierra Maestra. He ran the Revolution's radio station (*Radio Rebelde*) and was the chief editor of the newspaper Revolución and its cultural supplement Lunes which was highly acclaimed in Cuba. Despite the fact that Carlos Franqui saved the life of Fidel during a bombardment of Sierra Maestra by Batista's army, the editorial staff of Revolución and Franqui himself were persecuted in 1967. Revolución was shut down and is known today as Granma, the official newspaper of the Cuban Government. Franqui and his family were allowed to go into exile in Europe in 1968 from where Franqui protested against the Soviet invasion of Czechoslovakia. His latest books *Family Portrait With Fidel* and *Diary of the Cuban Revolution* are particularly important references for the Cuban Revolutionary period. Franqui died in Puerto Rico in 2010.

85 http://www.marxists.org/espanol/khrushchev/1962/oct/30.htm 30/01/2013

86 http://digitalarchive.wilsoncenter.org/document/110773

87 The only version of the 1962 Cuban Missile crisis that was available to me and to all ordinary citizens of the USSR and Cuba was that in 1962 Fidel Castro asked for Soviet protection from the USA which was about to invade the island. When Soviet missiles were delivered, Fidel sent an ultimatum to President Kennedy consisting of five conditions (including removal of the Guantanamo American base) on fulfillment of which Cuba promised to remove all Soviet missiles from its territory. But Kennedy "cheated" Cuba and the Soviets by agreeing to the ultimatum but not fulfilling his promises. Once again, our embassy's political officer justified current Soviet policy by the fact that Americans failed to keep their promises.

88 SIGINT is the acronym for Signals Intelligence and refers to data gathered by interception of signals from satellites, microwave transmissions and radio. Lourdes allowed the Soviets to monitor all U.S. military and civilian geosynchronous communications satellites. Currently, the facilities in Lourdes house *la Universidad de Ciencias Informáticas* (UCI), used for training in electronics, programming and cyber warfare for Cuban electronics and software students. The intelligence gathering was moved into three other facilities: Bejucal in Santiago de Cuba, Wajay, and Paseo (La Calle 11y13) in Vedado, Havana.

The Bejucal center is a modern electronic espionage base currently used by Cuban and Chinese intelligence to intercept and process international communications passing via communications satellites and to provide this information to their traditional clients in Venezuela, Iran, Ecuador, Bolivia and Nicaragua. Other divisions of SIGINT intercept messages from the Internet, from undersea cables, from radio transmissions, and from secret equipment installed inside embassies.

89 Russian sources:

- Yury Apalkov. Submarines of Soviet Fleet of 1945-1991, Morkniga, 2011.
- Vadim Truchachev. "Russia will restore its foreign navy bases" published in the newspaper *Pravda*, January 24, 2009. http://www.pravda.ru/world/asia/middleeast/24-01-2009/299641-navy-0/
- Sergey Telegin. "Cuba which we are losing" published in the newspaper *Soviet Rossia* of 27.12.2001. **http://cubafriend.narod.ru/bibleo/telegin.htm**
- Newspaper *Krasnaya Zvezda* of: 20.07.1969, 14.05.1970, 11.09.1970, 06.02.1971, 23.05.1971, 21.10.71.

- Newspaper *Izvestia* of: 28.05.1970, 15.09.1970, 08.12.1970.
- Newspaper *Morskaya Gazeta*, attachment to Fleet of 01.07.1999, page 1.
- Newspaper *Na Strazhe Zapoliaria* of 18.03.2000, page 2.
- Alexander Rozin. "Second Cuban Crisis", *Autonomka* http://www.avtonomka.org/vospominaniya/istorik-rozin-aleksandr-vladimirovich/412-vtoroy-kubinskiy-krizis.html
- S.S. Berezhnoy. "Nuclear submarines of BMF and Rossia", *Special Review* 2001.
- Sergey Brilev. "How many Caribbean crises were there?" newspaper *Komsomolskaya Pravda*, 1998.
- Capitanets. "BMF in After the War Period" published in magazine *Navy Collection* #2, 1994.
- Vladimir Chozikov. "Assembly line for Submarine cruisers", *Shipbuilding* #6 of 1997. http://www.cnw.mk.ua/weapons/navy/submarin/667.htm

90 According to the Intelligence Resource Program of the Federation of American Scientists Report of 2001:

"The SIGINT facility at Lourdes is among the most significant intelligence collection capabilities targeting the United States. This facility, less than 100 miles from Key West, is one of the largest and most sophisticated SIGINT collection facilities in the world. It was jointly operated by Soviet military intelligence (GRU), Soviet Federal Agency of Government Communications and Information (FAPSI - a KGB's SIGINT service), and Cuba's intelligence services. According to Russian press sources, the Russian Foreign Intelligence Service (SVR) also has a communications center at the facility for its agent network in North and South America.

The complex is capable of monitoring a wide array of commercial and government communications throughout the southeastern United States, and between the United States and Europe. Lourdes intercepts transmissions from microwave towers in the United States, communication satellite downlinks, and a wide range of shortwave and high-frequency radio transmissions. It also serves as a mission ground station and analytical facility supporting Russian SIGINT satellites.

The facility at Lourdes, together with a sister facility in Russia, allows the Russians to monitor all U. S. military and civilian geosynchronous communications satellites. It has been alleged that the Lourdes facility monitors all White House communications activities, launch control communications and telemetry from NASA and Air Force facilities at Cape Canaveral, financial and commodity wire services, and military communications links. According to one source, Lourdes has a special collection and analysis facility that is responsible for targeting financial and political information. This activity is manned by specially selected personnel and appears to be highly successful in providing Russian leaders with political and economic intelligence.

From this key facility, first the Soviet Union and now Russia have historically monitored US commercial satellites, and sensitive communications dealing with US military, merchant shipping, and Florida-based NASA space programs. According to a 1993 statement by Cuban Defense Minister Raúl Castro, Russia is said to obtain 75 percent of its military strategic information from Lourdes.

The Lourdes facility enables Russia to eavesdrop on US telephone communications. US voice and data telephone transmissions relayed by satellites visible to the facility are vulnerable to Russian intercept. Although sensitive US government communications are encrypted to prevent this intercept, most other unprotected telephone communications in the United States are systematically intercepted."

91 http://digitalarchive.wilsoncenter.org/document/110773

92 Letter of Fidel Castro to Nikita Khruschev

93 These terms: 'micro-faction' and 'macro-faction' were introduced by Fidel Castro in order to separate the Communist Party in Cuba into two groups: the small one with old communists he named micro-faction and the large one with the communists loyal to him he named macro-faction.

94 William Corson and Robert Crowley. *The New KGB: Engine of Soviet Power*. Hartwell, 1986, pp. 258-262.

95 Newspaper *Pravda*, January 30, 1968.

96 Trotskyism, a Marxist ideology based on the theory of permanent revolution first expounded by Leon Trotsky, one of the leading theoreticians of the Russian Bolshevik Party. Initially, as a Menshevick, Trotsky was forced to join the Bolsheviks prior to the start of the Revolution. Despite that, Stalin expelled Trotsky from the Soviet Union and had him murdered in Mexico. Millions were arrested, tortured, and shot by Soviet security on suspicion of having any contacts with Trotskyism.

97 Volker Skierka. *Fidel*. Roca, Spain: Publishing House Ediciónes Martinez, 2004, p. 241.

98 *Caudillo* in Spanish refers to a political-military leader at the head of an authoritarian power structure. Traditionally, it meant chieftain, a name used in Latin American countries where all properties were in possession of a few authoritarian Spanish landlords who managed them in an extremely autocratic fashion but with

support of church and army. The Caudillo was revered as a patriarch.

99 *Time Out Guide: Havana & the best of Cuba*. New York: Penguin Group, 2001, p. 31.

100 SALT I, the first series of Strategic Arms Limitation Talks, extended from November 1969 to May 1972. During that period the United States and the Soviet Union negotiated the first agreements to place limits and restraints on some of their central and most important nuclear armaments.

101 'Ocean-70' or simply 'Ocean' was the code name for large-scale naval exercises of the Soviet Navy, held from April 14 to May 5th of 1970, in honor of the centenary of the birth of Lenin. Under the leadership of the Chief of the Navy Sergei Gorshkov, the full forces of the Soviet Navy fleets participated in the maneuvers. Included were hundreds of combat units - surface ships, nuclear and diesel submarines, missile and torpedo boats, landing ships and dozens of support vessels, as well as coastal missile forces, long-range aircraft and air defense. For the first time in the history of the Soviet navy, there were a large number of nuclear submarines armed with ballistic and cruise missiles and self-guiding torpedoes.

102 Project 629 (Golf class) and Project 641 (Foxtrot class), were the modernized Soviet diesel-electric submarines equipped with ballistic missiles adapted for nuclear warheads.

103 It was not a formal inter-governmental agreement but the exchange of correspondence between Kennedy and Khrushchev, which took place in 1962. Neither of them wanted to publicize the deal at the time because it could provoke criticism and have a negative effect on their own domestic politics. The real deal was that the US will remove its missiles (Jupiters) from Turkey and promise not to invade Cuba, in exchange for which the Soviet Union will remove its missiles from Cuba and will promise not to employ Cuban territory for any type of armed threat against America. It was a direct deal between the USSR and the USA and Fidel Castro was not even informed of it, which infuriated both him and Che Guevara. In their zeal, they would have preferred a military confrontation, later confirmed by former Secretary of Defense Robert McNamara. Neither Cuban nor Soviet citizens were informed of the true events.

104 Raymond L. Garthoff in his analysis of *Handling Cienfuegos*, *International Security,* Vol.8, No1 (summer 1983), MIT Press, p. 66:

"The outcome of the Cuban missile crisis had been a rankling defeat in the Cold War (for USA). Hence in 1970, as the Soviet Union was acquiring strategic parity, the Soviet leaders sought to circumscribe the limitations imposed in 1962 on their military presence in Cuba, to erase that legacy from a time of American superiority and Cold War, an imposed constraint not in keeping with 'parity' with the United States as a global power, to which they now aspired. The 'mini-crisis' of 1970 rose in August and September, and was resolved by October."

105 For the Russian sources see endnote **87**

www.ingramcontent.com/pod-product-compliance
Lightning Source LLC
Chambersburg PA
CBHW051411090426
42737CB00014B/2619

* 9 7 8 0 9 9 1 8 5 3 8 3 0 *